The Best of
Clean Eating

Improving your life one meal at a time.

The Best of
Clean Eating

Improving your life one meal at a time.

FROM THE EDITORS OF **Clean Eating** MAGAZINE

RKP ROBERT KENNEDY PUBLISHING

Published by Robert Kennedy Publishing
400 Matheson Blvd. West
Mississauga, ON
L5R 3M1 Canada
Visit us at www.rkpubs.com
and www.cleaneatingmag.com

Managing Senior Production Editor: Wendy Morley
Online and Associate Editor: Vinita Persaud
Production Editor: Cali Hoffman
Assistant Editor/Marketing Coordinator: Stephanie Maus
Assistant Editor: Rachel Corradetti
Online Editor: Kiersten Corradetti
Editorial Assistants: Meredith Barrett, Chelsea Kennedy and Sharlene Liladhar
Art Director: Gabriella Caruso Marques
Assistant Art Director: Jessica Pensabene
Editorial Designers: Ellie Jeon and Brian Ross
Art Assistant: Kelsey-Lynn Corradetti
Indexing: Karen Petty and Meredith Barrett
Proofreading: Karen Petty and Meredith Barrett

Library and Archives Canada Cataloguing in Publication

The Best of Clean Eating / from the editors of Clean Eating Magazine

Includes index.
ISBN 978-1-55210-085-1

1. Cooking (Natural foods). 2. Cookery. 3. Reducing diets--Recipes.

TX741.B48 2010   641.5'63   C2010-904870-9

10 9 8 7 6 5 4 3

Distributed in Canada by
NBN (National Book Network)
67 Mowat Avenue, Suite 241
Toronto, ON
M6K 3E3

Distributed in USA by
NBN (National Book Network)
15200 NBN Way
Blue Ridge Summit, PA
17214

Printed in Canada

Dear readers,

In our three years we have continued to evolve and will always strive to give you the most up-to-date information. Some of these recipes may contain ingredients we have decided to no longer use, such as agave nectar, canola oil and canned goods. We do not state that these food items are bad, but simply have chosen not to use them because of questions regarding their safety or the practices involved in their processing. Please use the following substitutions, but keep in mind the recipes were not tested using the replacement ingredients.

Agave nectar – raw honey

Canned products – dried or jarred or BPA-free cans
    (such as Eden organic products), or foil pouches

Canola oil – olive oil or grapeseed oil

Table of Contents

Chapter 3: Five-Ingredient Meals 92
the exquisite taste of simplicity

Chapter 4: Seasonal Foods 116
the freshest ingredients for the freshest flavor

Chapter 5: Healthy Snacks 142
for kids and adults alike

Chapter 6: Recipes for One or Two People . . 166
because we're not all cooking for four

Each comforting, delectable and satisfying meal in this book was included with you in mind.

Introduction

The Secret Ingredient

When we launched *Clean Eating* three years ago, we knew we wanted a wide and colorful array of recipes inspired from all over – some crisp, fresh and obviously healthy, some completely counterintuitive with a sinful appearance but a nutritional profile that tells a different story. Above all, we knew we wanted our recipes to be straightforward and doable, each and every one bursting with protective nutrients.

Today, with nearly 20 issues and 1,000 recipes published, we have a pretty good idea of what our readers crave. Each comforting, delectable and satisfying meal in this book was included with you in mind. If there's one thing I can say about *Clean Eating* readers, it's that you're not afraid to speak up. We've had our share of critique but we've also had an astounding and encouraging amount of praise for our recipes.

A few dishes that brought in rave reviews and prompted us to publish this book are the Windy City Pie Deep-Dish Pizza (p. 76), Portobello Mushroom Ragout (p. 102), Asparagus Primavera with Couscous (p. 50), Thai Coconut Shrimp with Brown Rice Pasta (p. 53), Apple Grilled Cheese with Grainy Mustard (p. 177), Coconut Cardamom Sweet Potatoes (p. 204) and, of course, our biggest hit of all time – a decadent dessert with just 110 calories, three grams of sugar and one-and-a-half grams of saturated fat – our famed Almond Butter Chocolate Chip Cookies (p. 224).

Inside you'll find 10 helpful chapters built around the things you've told us you want most: quick and easy family dinners, 20-minute meals, budget-friendly suppers, five-ingredient creations, seasonal recipes, low-fat snacks, recipes for one or two, holiday menus, family BBQ fare and desserts. And our recipes have something unique that other recipes don't. You'll notice *Clean Eating*'s Nutritional Bonuses peppered throughout the book. Designed to help you understand the health benefits of each recipe in layperson's terms, these bonus bits of information will tell you which vitamins, minerals, antioxidants and phytonutrients you're getting and how they will benefit your body.

But that's not all you'll find in the 10 well-thought-out chapters of this book. Inside, you'll enjoy mouthwatering food photography that practically leaps off the page. (Skip the temptation to lick the pages!) And you'll uncover the secret ingredient to a lifetime of happiness and love: the food. The star ingredient in life should always be the nourishing, soothing and soul-feeding power of food.

Think of the food in this cookbook as glue. It's the social glue that brings your family running to your table. It's the glue that forms bonds and memories of special occasions, shared meals, meaningful conversation and bouts of laughter. It's the glue that pulls your family away from the TV, the BlackBerry, the computer or the Xbox and brings them to the hub of your home – the kitchen. It's the glue that keeps your family's health strong, their minds sharp and their values intact. And it's the glue that brings good friends together and perpetually coming back.

To great food and even better health,

Alicia

Alicia Rewega
Editor in Chief

Quick & Easy Meals for the Family

Balsamic-Marinated Pork
Chops & Grilled Peaches, p. 23

Time is tighter than ever, but that doesn't mean you have to sacrifice taste and flavor when your family sits down to eat together. We've put together our quickest, easiest and most delightful meals for those days when dinner has to be on the table five minutes ago. Try our Windy City Pie Deep-Dish Pizza or our Pasta Roll-Ups with Turkey & Spinach, both guaranteed to be a big hit with kids and adults alike. And many of our recipes can be on the table – from start to finish – in 20 minutes or less. Healthy, flavorful and fast – just the way you like it!

Clean Eggs Benedict

Serves 4 to 6. ***Hands-on time:*** 15 minutes. ***Total time:*** 30 minutes.

Instead of the traditional ham or bacon topping, portobello mushrooms are called upon to provide a meaty texture and a rich, woodsy flavor.

INGREDIENTS:

- 2 Tbsp whole-wheat flour
- 1 cup skim milk
- ¾ cup shredded low-fat sharp cheddar cheese
- ¼ tsp sea salt
- ½ tsp fresh ground black pepper, divided
- 2 tsp extra-virgin olive oil
- 6 packed cups fresh baby spinach
- 3 cups chopped portobello mushrooms
- Olive oil cooking spray
- 10 egg whites
- 4 whole-grain English muffins, split and toasted

INSTRUCTIONS:

ONE: Place flour in a heavy saucepan over medium heat. Gradually add milk, stirring with a whisk until blended. Cook for about six to eight minutes or until thickened. Remove from heat, add cheese, salt and a quarter-teaspoon pepper, stirring until melted.

TWO: Heat oil in a large nonstick skillet over medium heat. Add spinach, mushrooms and remaining quarter-teaspoon pepper and sauté until spinach is wilted and mushrooms are tender, about five minutes.

THREE: In a separate skillet coated with cooking spray, scramble egg whites over medium heat for three to five minutes. Top English muffin halves evenly with scrambled egg whites and spinach-mushroom mixture, then drizzle with cheese sauce. Serve immediately.

Nutrients per serving (1½ English muffin halves, ¼ cup egg whites, ¼ cup spinach mixture, 2 Tbsp cheese sauce): *Calories: 270, Total Fat: 4.5 g, Sat. Fat 1 g, Carbs: 36 g, Fiber: 7 g, Sugars: 10 g, Protein: 22 g, Sodium: 580 mg, Cholesterol: 5 mg*

Grilled Flank Steak
WITH TOMATO-JICAMA RELISH

Serves 4 with leftovers. *Hands-on time:* 20 minutes. *Total time:* 30 minutes.

Sometimes called the "Mexican potato," jicama is the crunchy, sweet root of a legume and adds a zippy and exotic touch to these grilled steaks. Best of all, it provides great flavor without adding many calories.

INGREDIENTS:

- Olive oil cooking spray
- 2 lbs flank steak
- Sea salt and fresh ground black pepper, to taste
- 1 cup diced ripe tomatoes (beefsteak or Roma)
- 1 small green bell pepper, seeded and diced
- ½ cup finely diced jicama
- ¼ cup finely diced white onion
- 2 Tbsp chopped fresh chives
- 2 Tbsp red wine vinegar
- 1 Tbsp honey

INSTRUCTIONS:

ONE: Coat a stovetop grill pan or griddle with cooking spray and preheat to medium-high. Season both sides of steak with salt and black pepper, to taste. Place steak on hot pan and cook five minutes per side for medium doneness. Remove steak from pan and let stand five to ten minutes before slicing.

TWO: Meanwhile, in a medium bowl, combine tomatoes, green pepper, jicama, onion, chives, vinegar and honey; then toss to combine. Season, to taste, with salt and black pepper.

THREE: Slice steak, across the grain, into thin strips. Serve half of steak (save rest for leftovers). Spoon all of the tomato-jicama mixture over top.

Nutrients per serving (9 oz steak and 2 oz relish): *Calories: 260, Total Fat: 9 g, Sat. Fat: 4 g, Carbs: 10 g, Fiber: 2 g, Sugars: 6 g, Protein: 33 g, Sodium: 220 mg, Cholesterol: 50 mg*

TIP:
As you're assembling the Spanakopita, keep phyllo strips not in use covered with a clean damp dishtowel so they do not dry out.

Spanakopita Casserole

Spanakopita Casserole

*Serves 6. **Hands-on time:** 15 minutes. **Total time:** 1 hour.*

Spanakopita, or spinach pie, is a classic fixture in Greek cuisine and is most often sold as individual triangular pastries. But you can easily turn this Mediterranean tradition into an American comfort food favorite – the casserole.

INGREDIENTS:

- 1 tsp olive oil
- 1 Tbsp finely chopped sweet red pepper
- ¼ cup finely chopped sweet onion
- 3 large bags fresh spinach (9 oz each) or 36 cups loosely packed spinach
- 1 Tbsp finely chopped fresh dill
- 1 tsp finely chopped fresh mint
- 1 large egg white
- ½ cup feta, crumbled
- 4 sheets whole-wheat phyllo dough (13 x 18 inches each; Try: The Fillo Factory)
- Olive oil cooking spray

INSTRUCTIONS:

ONE: Preheat oven to 375°F. Heat oil in a large sauté pan over medium-high heat. Add pepper and onion and sauté for about two minutes. Add spinach in batches, waiting two to three minutes between intervals; cover tightly and cook, tossing frequently, for about 15 minutes.

TWO: Drain spinach mixture in a colander, removing any excess liquid, before placing it in a large bowl; set aside. When spinach mixture is cool, mix in dill, mint and egg white. Then fold in feta until well blended. Set aside.

THREE: Working quickly, roll phyllo out onto a clean work surface. Carefully cut each sheet lengthwise into four pieces, approximately three inches wide. (TIP: Or cut each sheet in half lengthwise, then halve each of the two sections again to create four equal pieces.) Place three or four strips across the center of a 9 x 9-inch casserole dish misted with cooking spray, leaving about three to four inches of excess hanging over on both ends. The strips should overlap slightly. Mist strips with cooking spray. Turn the casserole dish clockwise and place three or four strips across the original layer, at a 90-degree angle. Mist strips with cooking spray. Continue turning and layering until all strips have been used, about four layers in total, misting with cooking spray after each layer.

FOUR: Spoon spinach mixture into center of phyllo-covered dish. Fold phyllo hanging over edges into the center of spinach mixture, covering the top (no spinach should be visible). Mist with cooking spray.

FIVE: Bake in preheated oven for 30 to 35 minutes or until lightly brown and crispy. Let casserole sit for 10 to 15 minutes before slicing. Cut into six pieces and serve.

TIP: Phyllo can be cut with a knife, kitchen scissors or a pizza cutter.

Nutrients per slice: Calories: 140, Total Fat: 3 g, Sat. Fat: 1.5 g, Carbs: 24 g, Fiber: 8 g, Sugars: 1 g, Protein: 7 g, Sodium: 450 mg, Cholesterol: 5 mg

Roasted Pork Tenderloin
WITH CREAMY POLENTA

*Serves 4. **Hands-on time:** 15 minutes. **Total time:** 45 minutes.*

Doctoring store-bought tomato sauce by adding roasted vegetables such as mushrooms increases the sauce's nutritional offering.

INGREDIENTS:

- 2 (1 lb) pork tenderloins, trimmed of any visible fat
- Olive oil cooking spray
- 1½ tsp dried oregano
- ¾ tsp sea salt, divided
- Fresh ground black pepper, to taste
- 1 lb white mushrooms, sliced
- 1 (24 oz) jar all-natural tomato-basil pasta sauce
- 2 cups instant polenta
- 3 Tbsp chopped fresh basil leaves (optional)

INSTRUCTIONS:

ONE: Preheat oven to 450°F. Cover two rimmed baking sheets with aluminum foil. Place tenderloins on one sheet. Mist with cooking spray and season with oregano, half of salt, and pepper. Roast for 25 to 27 minutes or until internal temperature registers 155°F on an instant read thermometer. Let pork rest for 10 minutes (temperature will rise to 160°F during resting time).

TWO: Meanwhile, spread mushrooms out in a single layer on remaining baking sheet and season with pepper. Transfer to oven and roast for 20 minutes (simultaneously with pork) or until tender and lightly browned, stirring once halfway through.

THREE: Pour pasta sauce into a medium saucepan and turn heat to medium-low. Cover and cook, stirring occasionally, until sauce is hot, about five minutes. When mushrooms finish cooking, add to sauce and cook until heated through.

FOUR: Bring eight cups of water to a boil in a large pot over high heat. Season with remaining salt. Reduce heat to medium and slowly add polenta, stirring with a large, long-handled spoon. Reduce heat to low and continue stirring until liquid is absorbed and polenta is thick and creamy, two to three minutes.

FIVE: To serve, cut one tenderloin on the diagonal into slices one-third-inch thick. Put three-quarters of a cup polenta on each of four plates. Top each with a quarter of the sliced pork, half-cup tomato-mushroom sauce and half-tablespoon basil, if desired.

SIX: Place remaining tenderloin in a heavy-duty zip-top bag and refrigerate. Put remaining tomato-mushroom sauce in an airtight container and refrigerate. Spoon remaining polenta into an 8 x 8-inch baking dish, smooth into an even layer, cover and refrigerate. These ingredients may be kept, refrigerated, for up to three days.

Nutrients per serving (4 oz pork, ¾ cup polenta, ½ cup sauce): Calories: 320, Total Fat: 3 g, Sat. Fat: 1 g, Carbs: 42 g, Fiber: 6 g, Sugars: 5 g, Protein: 30 g, Sodium: 585 mg, Cholesterol: 73 mg

Balsamic Roast Chicken
WITH POTATOES & GREEN BEANS

*Serves 4. **Hands-on time:** 25 minutes. **Total time:** 2 hours.*

French-style green beans taste similar but are thinner (translating to faster cooking!) than the standard green bean variety. If you have only the thick, regular kind on hand for this recipe, don't fret: simply add two to three minutes to the steaming time.

INGREDIENTS:

- 1 (5 to 6 lb) whole chicken
- 1¼ tsp sea salt, divided
- 1½ tsp dried thyme, divided
- 1½ tsp dried rosemary, divided
- Fresh ground black pepper, to taste
- 4 tsp olive oil, divided
- 3 Tbsp balsamic vinegar
- 1½ lbs baby red potatoes, halved
- 2 tsp chopped fresh rosemary
- 1 lb French-style green beans
- Juice of ½ lemon

INSTRUCTIONS:

ONE: Preheat oven to 400°F and line a roasting pan with foil. Set chicken on a rack inside the roasting pan with breast facing up (if your roasting pan does not have a rack, set chicken directly on foil). In a small bowl, combine one teaspoon each salt, thyme and dried rosemary, plus several grinds of pepper. Rub half the oil over chicken. Loosen the skin covering the breasts and rub about half of herb mixture directly onto meat. Rub remaining herb mixture over outside of skin and inside cavity. Drizzle vinegar all over chicken and rub to coat evenly.

TWO: In a large bowl, mix potatoes with remaining two teaspoons oil, quarter-teaspoon salt and half-teaspoon thyme and dried rosemary. Season with pepper. Spread potatoes around chicken on rack. Place roasting pan in center of oven and cook for 45 minutes. Open oven and loosely cover chicken with foil to prevent over-browning. Cook for 45 more minutes, until juices run clear when chicken is pierced in the deepest part of the breast or the internal temperature of breast meat reaches 160°F on an instant read thermometer (thigh meat should reach 170°F). Remove roasting pan from oven. Transfer chicken to a cutting board and let rest for 10 minutes (temperature of breast meat will rise to 165°F while resting). Transfer two cups of potatoes to a serving bowl and sprinkle with fresh rosemary. Store remaining one cup potatoes in an airtight container and refrigerate for up to three days.

THREE: Add one inch of water to a large saucepan. Place a steaming basket in saucepan, cover and bring water to a boil over high heat. Put beans in steamer and reduce heat to low. Cook, covered, until beans are tender, about six minutes. Transfer two cups of beans to a serving bowl and drizzle with lemon juice. Store remaining beans in an airtight container and refrigerate for up to three days.

FOUR: To serve chicken, remove legs, thigh and wings, discard their skin and pull meat from the bones. With a large chef's knife, cut along both sides of breast bone, following ribs down as a guide. Remove skin and cut breast meat into slices up to half an inch thick. Shred a third of the meat (mix of light and dark) into bite-size pieces to yield two cups; refrigerate in an airtight container for up to three days. Serve remaining chicken with potatoes and green beans.

TIP: To cut down on weeknight cooking time, roast your chicken and potatoes up to three days ahead; keep covered and refrigerated. You can also freeze the roasted chicken meat (remove meat from the bones to facilitate even thawing) for one month. But don't pop the potatoes in your freezer – the texture won't hold up well.

Nutrients per serving (¾ cup chicken, ½ cup potatoes [about 6 pieces], ½ cup green beans): *Calories: 319, Total Fat: 10 g, Sat. Fat: 3 g, Carbs: 23 g, Fiber: 4 g, Sugars: 2 g, Protein: 34 g, Sodium: 537 mg, Cholesterol: 93 mg*

Chicken Souvlaki
WITH VEGETABLES

*Serves 4. **Hands-on time:** 15 minutes. **Total time:** 1 hour, 15 minutes (includes marinating).*

Souvlaki, which means "little swords" in Greek, is characterized by skewered chicken or pork and typically served with a pita or slice of bread. We decided to replace the bread with a fresh vegetable salad.

INGREDIENTS:

- ½ cup finely chopped fresh oregano (about 1 cup packed fresh oregano leaves)
- 2 tsp finely chopped fresh dill
- 3 cloves garlic, crushed
- 1 Tbsp lemon zest
- 3 Tbsp fresh lemon juice
- 4 tsp olive oil, divided
- ½ tsp crushed red pepper flakes
- ¼ tsp sea salt
- 16 oz boneless, skinless chicken tenderloins, cut into 7 or 8 pieces
- 4 medium Yukon gold potatoes, washed and left unpeeled
- ½ lb fresh or thawed-from-frozen green beans (about 4 cups)
- Olive oil cooking spray (optional)
- 2 Tbsp finely chopped green onions
- 1 large tomato, coarsely chopped
- 8 Kalamata olives, pitted and chopped

EQUIPMENT:

- Metal or wooden skewers (soak wooden skewers in water for at least 20 minutes prior to use)

Continued ▸

INSTRUCTIONS:

ONE: In a small bowl, blend together oregano, dill, garlic, lemon zest and juice, one teaspoon oil, pepper flakes and salt. Rub two tablespoons of this mixture over chicken and let marinate in refrigerator for at least one hour or overnight in a bowl covered in plastic wrap. Reserve remaining marinade in refrigerator.

TWO: Preheat broiler to high. Bring about one cup water to boil over high heat in a large pot. Cut potatoes in quarters and add to a metal steamer basket placed in pot; cover and steam for 15 to 20 minutes or until tender. Carefully remove potatoes and set aside to cool; when cool cut each piece in half again.

THREE: Cut green beans in half, then add to steamer basket, place in pot (you may need to add more water) and steam, covered, for five to seven minutes. Remove from steamer basket and set aside to cool.

FOUR: Thread chicken onto skewers, about two or three pieces per skewer, and place on a foil-lined baking sheet misted with cooking spray, or stoneware. Broil for seven to ten minutes; set aside.

FIVE: While chicken rests, carefully mix potatoes, green beans, onions, tomato and olives in a large bowl. Whisk remaining three teaspoons of oil into remaining reserved marinade and pour over vegetables; gently toss. To serve, place two cups vegetable mixture on a plate and top with two skewers of chicken (about four ounces in total).

Nutrients per serving (4 oz chicken and 2 cups vegetable mixture): *Calories: 430, Total Fat: 11 g, Sat. Fat: 2 g, Carbs: 52 g, Fiber: 12 g, Sugars: 3 g, Protein: 33 g, Sodium: 320 mg, Cholesterol: 65 mg*

Nutritional Bonus:

A single small potato is a good source of fiber, potassium, and vitamins C and B6 – all in a neat 110-calorie package. It's also loaded with antioxidants such as lutein, which promotes eye health and sharp vision by scavenging damaging free radicals and providing natural sun protection for your eyes.

Chicken Parmesan with Pasta

Serves 4. **Hands-on time:** 15 minutes.
Total time: 45 minutes.

We've lightened up this traditional dish by using whole-wheat breadcrumbs and making them stick with Dijon mustard instead of eggs. Healthy and delicious!

INGREDIENTS:

- Olive oil cooking spray
- 2 tsp olive oil
- ½ cup diced white onion
- 1 green bell pepper, seeded and diced
- 2 to 3 cloves garlic, minced
- 2 tsp dried oregano, divided
- 1 (28-oz) jar crushed organic tomatoes
- 1 Tbsp sun-dried tomato paste or organic tomato paste
- ½ cup whole-wheat panko bread crumbs
- 1 Tbsp grated reduced-fat Parmesan cheese
- ½ tsp dried thyme
- ¼ tsp sea salt
- ¼ tsp ground black pepper
- 4 (4-oz) boneless, skinless chicken breasts, pounded to 1-inch thickness
- 1 Tbsp Dijon mustard
- ½ cup shredded part-skim mozzarella cheese
- 8 oz cooked whole-wheat penne (or your favorite pasta)
- ¼ cup chopped fresh basil

INSTRUCTIONS:

ONE: Preheat oven to 400°F. Coat a large baking sheet with cooking spray.

TWO: Heat oil in a large saucepan over medium heat. Add onion, bell pepper and garlic and sauté three to five minutes, until vegetables are soft. Add one teaspoon oregano and stir to coat. Cook 30 seconds, until oregano is fragrant. Add tomatoes and tomato paste and bring to a simmer. Reduce heat to low, partially cover and simmer 20 to 30 minutes.

THREE: Meanwhile, in a shallow dish, combine panko, Parmesan, remaining teaspoon of oregano, thyme, salt and black pepper. Mix with a fork to combine. Brush both sides of each chicken breast with mustard. Transfer each breast to panko mixture and turn to coat both sides. Arrange chicken on prepared baking sheet. Coat surface of chicken with cooking spray. Bake for 20 minutes.

FOUR: Top each chicken breast with two to three tablespoons of tomato sauce and two tablespoons of mozzarella. Return chicken to oven and bake 10 minutes more, until crust is golden brown and cheese is melted and bubbly.

FIVE: Arrange pasta on a serving plate and top with remaining tomato sauce. Serve chicken with pasta on the side, garnishing both with basil.

TIP: Make your chicken Parm more golden in color by toasting the panko in a skillet over medium heat before making this dish.

Nutrients per serving (4 oz chicken, 2 oz pasta):
Calories: 439, Total Fat: 12 g, Sat. Fat: 2.5 g, Carbs: 43 g, Fiber: 5.5 g, Sugars: 3 g, Protein: 34.5 g, Sodium: 585 mg, Cholesterol: 70 mg

Veal Scaloppine & Roasted Vegetable Sandwiches

Serves 4 to 6. **Hands-on time:** 25 minutes. **Total time:** 1 hour.

Scaloppine-style cooking is an extremely flavorful Italian method of preparing meat, which requires very little fat for the initial sear and incorporates plenty of flavor and moisture from the accompanying sauce.

INGREDIENTS:

- 2 medium green bell peppers, stemmed, seeded and cut into ½-inch strips
- 2 portobello mushroom caps, sliced into ½-inch strips
- 1 small eggplant, quartered and sliced into ½-inch pieces
- 1 medium red onion, thinly sliced
- 1 Tbsp plus 2 tsp extra-virgin olive oil, divided
- 2 Tbsp balsamic vinegar
- ¼ tsp kosher salt
- ¼ tsp fresh ground black pepper
- ¼ cup whole-wheat flour
- 2 lbs boneless veal cutlet (often called leg round), sliced and pounded very thin
- 1 (28-oz) jar no-salt-added whole Roma tomatoes (or no-salt-added diced tomatoes)
- 3 cloves garlic, thinly sliced
- 5 large basil leaves, chopped
- 2 sprigs fresh oregano, leaves chopped
- ½ cup loosely packed parsley, chopped
- 4 to 6 soft whole-wheat ciabatta rolls or a whole-wheat baguette, sliced
- 2 oz part-skim mozzarella cheese, grated

INSTRUCTIONS:

ONE: Preheat oven to 375°F.

TWO: Combine peppers, mushrooms, eggplant and onion in a 13 x 9-inch baking dish. In a small bowl, whisk together one tablespoon oil, vinegar, one tablespoon water, salt and black pepper. Pour oil-vinegar mixture over vegetables and toss to combine. Cover baking dish loosely with foil or a glass lid, and transfer to oven. Roast vegetables for 30 to 45 minutes, until they are tender.

THREE: While vegetables roast, prepare veal and sauce: Put flour in a shallow baking dish and dredge each piece of veal in it, shaking off excess.

FOUR: Brush the bottom of a large sauté pan over medium-high heat with remaining two teaspoons oil. When pan is hot, add veal and cook each side for two minutes. You may have to cook veal in batches to avoid crowding the pan. Transfer first cooked batch to a plate and add a little water to the hot pan to deglaze it, scraping bits up from the bottom as water sizzles. Pour the liquid on top of the cooked veal and start again with the next batch. Divide oil accordingly for batch cooking.

FIVE: Once all veal is cooked and removed from pan, pour juice from canned tomatoes into pan and scrape bits from the bottom as juice sizzles. Add garlic and sauté just until fragrant, about 30 seconds. Pour tomatoes into pan and crush with a fork or potato masher. Stir in a quarter-cup water and herbs. Return veal to pan, tucking it in the sauce. Cover pan and lower heat to simmer until vegetables are done.

SIX: Slice rolls in half. Put a piece of veal on bottom half of each roll and top with a pile of roasted vegetables. Spoon sauce on vegetables, sprinkle with cheese, top with other half of roll and serve. If desired, return sandwiches to the hot oven for a minute or two to melt cheese.

Nutrients per sandwich: Calories: 470, Total Fat: 12 g, Sat. Fat: 3.5 g, Carbs: 43 g, Fiber: 10 g, Sugars: 11 g, Protein: 46 g, Sodium: 560 mg, Cholesterol: 120 mg

Shrimp, Spinach & Mushroom Barley

Serves 4. **Hands-on time:** 20 minutes. **Total time:** 1 hour.

Barley is a versatile grain with a chewy, pasta-like consistency and rich nutty flavor. To mix up your menus, try it in any dish that calls for rice.

INGREDIENTS:

- 1 cup dry pearl barley
- 3½ cups low-sodium vegetable broth
- 3 shallots, chopped
- 2 cups chopped mushrooms of your choice
- 1 Tbsp extra-virgin olive oil
- 4 cups baby spinach
- ½ lb cooked shrimp, peeled and chopped
- ¼ tsp ground black pepper
- ¼ cup fresh sage, torn
- Kosher or sea salt, to taste

INSTRUCTIONS:

ONE: In a medium pot on high heat, bring both barley and broth to a boil. Cover and let simmer on low to medium heat, so liquid doesn't boil over. Set timer and cook for 50 minutes.

TWO: In a nonstick skillet, sauté shallots and mushrooms in oil for five minutes over medium-high heat. Add spinach and lightly sauté for about three minutes, until bright green.

THREE: At 50 minutes check on barley. When there is no more remaining broth, add shrimp and pepper to barley; turn to medium heat if not already. Cook for five minutes.

FOUR: Add shallot-mushroom mixture, sage and salt to barley. Stir and cook five to ten minutes. Best if enjoyed within four or five days in fridge, or store for up to six months in freezer.

NOTE: Barley can take up to 60 to 75 minutes to soak up broth. Be certain to not add remaining ingredients if there is a lot of broth left, or it will never evaporate.

Nutrients per 1½-cup serving: Calories: 320, Total Fat: 5 g, Sat. Fat: 1 g, Carbs: 50 g, Fiber: 10 g, Sugars: 3 g, Protein: 19 g, Sodium: 310 mg, Cholesterol: 85 mg

Pearl Barley Risotto with Scallions, Asparagus & Peas

*Serves 6. **Hands-on time:** 15 minutes. **Total time:** 35 minutes.*

Scallions are strongly flavored green onions that no well-stocked kitchen should be without. They give a pleasant punch to this risotto dish.

INGREDIENTS:

- 2 Tbsp olive oil, divided
- 6 medium scallions, white and pale green parts, thinly sliced
- 2 medium shallots, minced
- 4 cups low-sodium chicken broth
- 1½ cups pearl barley
- 12 oz asparagus, trimmed and sliced ½-inch thick on the bias
- 1½ cups frozen peas
- ¼ cup thinly sliced fresh basil
- ¼ cup finely chopped fresh Italian parsley
- 1 tsp lemon zest
- Kosher salt and fresh ground black pepper, to taste

INSTRUCTIONS:

ONE: Heat one tablespoon oil in a medium pot over medium heat. When it shimmers, add scallions and shallots and cook until translucent, about two minutes.

TWO: Add broth, one cup water and barley and bring to a simmer. Reduce heat to medium-low and simmer, stirring occasionally, until liquid is almost completely absorbed and barley is just tender, about 25 minutes.

THREE: Add a half-cup water, asparagus and peas; cook, stirring, until barley is tender, about five more minutes.

FOUR: Stir in herbs, zest and remaining tablespoon of oil. Season with salt and pepper, to taste, and serve immediately.

Nutrients per 1½-cup serving: Calories: 290, Total Fat: 7 g, Sat. Fat: 1 g, Carbs: 50 g, Fiber: 11 g, Sugars: 2 g, Protein: 7 g, Sodium: 95 mg, Cholesterol: 0 mg

Smothered Cheeseburgers

*Serves 4. **Hands-on time:** 25 minutes. **Total time:** 35 minutes.*

Fresh homemade burgers topped with cheese, mushrooms, onions and peppers? Enough said. Try it on the BBQ for a summer treat.

INGREDIENTS:

- 1 lb 96% lean ground beef
- 2 Tbsp finely minced white onion, plus 1 cup, thinly sliced, divided
- 3 Tbsp Italian parsley, finely chopped
- 1 tsp chile powder
- ½ tsp sea salt, plus additional to taste
- Fresh ground black pepper, to taste
- 2 tsp olive oil, divided
- 1 cup pre-sliced button mushrooms
- 1 small red bell pepper, cut into strips (about 1 cup)
- 4 thin slices reduced-fat deli Swiss cheese (¾ oz each)
- 4 standard-size whole-wheat hamburger buns
- 4 romaine lettuce leaves, thick stems removed
- 4 tomato slices (¼-inch thick each)

INSTRUCTIONS:

ONE: Place beef, minced onion, parsley, chile powder, salt and black pepper in a large bowl. Hand mix until just combined. Gently form beef mixture into four equal patties, about one-half to three-quarters-of-an-inch thick. Transfer to a broiler pan or rimmed baking sheet. Cover and refrigerate.

TWO: Add one teaspoon oil to a medium nonstick skillet and set over medium heat. When oil is hot, add mushrooms and cook until golden brown and soft, stirring frequently, about eight minutes. Transfer to a small bowl. Add remaining oil to skillet and return to medium heat. Add red pepper and cook for four minutes, stirring occasionally. Add sliced onion and continue cooking for six more minutes or until vegetables are tender and lightly browned. Add to bowl with mushrooms. Season vegetables with salt and black pepper and stir to combine.

THREE: When ready, preheat broiler to high or a grill to medium-high.

FOUR: Place patties under broiler about 10 inches from heat source, or on a grill. Cook four to five minutes per side, until meat is no longer pink in center or the internal temperature registers 160°F on an instant-read thermometer. Immediately place one slice cheese on each hot burger. (If you want cheese very melted, place on the burgers 30 to 60 seconds before end of cooking time.) To serve, layer each bun with one lettuce leaf, one slice tomato, one cheeseburger patty and one-third of a cup of vegetable mixture.

Nutrients per cheeseburger: Calories: 320, Total Fat: 10 g, Sat. Fat: 3 g, Carbs: 25 g, Fiber: 4 g, Sugars: 5 g, Protein: 33 g, Sodium: 570 mg, Cholesterol: 78 mg.

Smothered
Cheese-
burgers

TIP:
You can save even more time during your busy weeknight routine by removing your prepared quesadillas from the freezer in advance and defrosting them in the fridge. It will reduce your meal time to a mere 16 to 18 minutes!

Chicken, Spinach & Ricotta Quesadillas

Chicken, Spinach & Ricotta Quesadillas

Serves 8. **Hands-on time:** *20 minutes.* **Total time:** *35 minutes.*

The zip in these hearty whole-grain quesadillas will fill you with health and goodness, while the protein and fiber content will satisfy and keep you hunger-pang free for hours. Now that's a meal.

INGREDIENTS:

• 8 oz boneless, skinless chicken breasts
• 2½ tsp extra-virgin olive oil, divided
• Sea salt and fresh ground black pepper, to taste
• 1 medium white onion, finely diced
• 1 medium red bell pepper, diced
• 1 bag spinach (6 to 8 oz), stems removed
• ¾ cup low-fat ricotta cheese
• ½ cup navy beans, drained and rinsed under cold water
• ¾ cup shredded low-fat mozzarella cheese
• ¼ cup chopped fresh herbs (flat-leaf parsley and rosemary)
• Juice of ½ lemon
• Pinch freshly grated nutmeg
• 8 small herb and whole-grain tortillas (6-inch diameter each)

INSTRUCTIONS (PREP & FREEZE):

ONE: Preheat oven to 350˚F.

TWO: Lightly coat chicken with a half-teaspoon oil. Season with salt and black pepper. Place chicken on a parchment-lined baking sheet and roast for 14 to 16 minutes, or until fully cooked. Remove from oven and let cool.

THREE: Meanwhile, heat one teaspoon oil in a large nonstick sauté pan over medium-high heat. When oil is hot, add onion and red pepper, stirring frequently until softened, about two to three minutes. Add spinach to pan and stir to combine, until spinach is slightly wilted, about one minute. Remove mixture from pan and pour into a paper-towel-lined bowl. Set aside and allow to cool.

FOUR: In a large mixing bowl, combine ricotta cheese and beans, mashing beans slightly. Add mozzarella cheese, herbs, lemon juice and nutmeg. Season with salt and black pepper, and stir well to combine. Set aside. When chicken is cool enough to handle, dice into half-inch pieces and add to cheese mixture.

FIVE: Working in small batches, squeeze excess moisture from spinach mixture with your hands. Discard any liquid, and then add spinach mixture to chicken-cheese mixture. Mix until thoroughly combined. Taste and adjust seasoning if needed.

SIX: On a flat surface, lay out tortillas and scoop about one-third cup mixture into center of each tortilla. Fold each tortilla in half, pressing gently to flatten filling evenly, until filling is about a quarter-inch from edge (you want to prevent the filling from leaking out during cooking). Lightly brush both sides of quesadilla with oil and season with salt and black pepper. Wrap quesadillas in plastic wrap or resealable plastic bags in packs of two and lay flat in freezer if not cooking immediately. Quesadillas may be kept frozen for two to three months.

WHEN IT'S TIME TO EAT:

Preheat oven to 350˚F. Remove quesadillas from freezer and allow to defrost just enough that the quesadillas may be pulled apart from each other. Place frozen quesadillas on a parchment-lined baking sheet and bake in oven for 24 to 26 minutes, or until filling is hot throughout and tortillas are golden brown and crisp. Allow filling to set for three minutes before cutting. Cut in half and serve immediately.

Nutrients per ½ quesadilla: *Calories: 290, Total Fat: 7 g, Sat. Fat: 2.5 g, Carbs: 36 g, Fiber: 6 g, Sugars: 4 g, Protein: 20 g, Sodium: 590 mg, Cholesterol: 25 mg*

Balsamic-Marinated Pork Chops & Grilled Peaches

Serves 4. **Hands-on time:** *10 minutes.*
Total time: *1 hour, 20 minutes (includes 1 hour marinating).*

Marinating these lean pork chops infuses them with flavor, but you won't be paying a fatty price for the greater taste.

INGREDIENTS:

• ⅓ cup balsamic vinegar
• ⅓ cup extra-virgin olive oil
• 3 Tbsp honey
• 1 Tbsp chopped fresh rosemary
• 4 (5-oz) lean boneless pork chops, trimmed of visible fat
• Olive oil cooking spray (optional)
• Sea salt and fresh ground black pepper, to taste
• 4 peaches, halved and pitted
• Fresh thyme leaves for garnish

INSTRUCTIONS:

ONE: In a small bowl, whisk together vinegar, oil, honey and rosemary. Reserve two tablespoons and add the rest to a one-gallon zip-top bag. Add pork to bag and refrigerate for one hour, turning occasionally.

TWO: Preheat broiler to high or coat a grill pan with cooking spray and heat to medium-high over stove. Remove pork from fridge, discard marinating liquid and season with salt and pepper. Broil or cook in grill pan until pork is opaque throughout and feels firm to the touch, or until internal temperature reaches 160°F on an instant-read thermometer, about five to six minutes per side.

THREE: Meanwhile, cook peaches under broiler or in a grill pan over medium heat until tender and juicy, three to five minutes. Transfer to a plate, season with pepper and brush with reserved two tablespoons marinade. To serve, place a pork chop on each of four plates and top with two peach halves. Garnish with thyme leaves.

Nutrients per serving (5 oz pork chop, 1 peach, 2 Tbsp marinade): *Calories: 310, Total Fat: 10 g, Sat. Fat: 3 g, Carbs: 23 g, Fiber: 1 g, Sugars: 21 g, Protein: 31 g, Sodium: 125 mg, Cholesterol: 95 mg*

For a photo of this recipe, see p. 10.

Lemony Almond Spinach Pesto Pasta
WITH TUNA

*Serves 4. **Hands-on time:** 20 minutes. **Total time:** 30 minutes.*

Classic pesto recipes call for basil, garlic, pine nuts, cheese and olive oil, but we've modified this uncooked sauce made from herbs and leafy greens for taste and function.

INGREDIENTS:

- ½ lb whole-wheat pasta, any shape
- 3 cups tightly-packed baby spinach (3 oz)
- ½ cup packed fresh mint
- 1 clove garlic, minced
- 1 Tbsp grated Pecorino Romano cheese
- Zest and juice of 1 large lemon (2 tsp zest, ⅓ cup juice), divided
- 1 Tbsp olive oil
- ¼ cup unsalted toasted almond slivers
- 1 (6-oz) can solid white tuna packed in water, no salt added
- 1 yellow bell pepper, cored, seeded and diced small
- 1 small zucchini, diced small
- 1½ cups cooked white beans (or one 15-oz can low-sodium white beans, drained and rinsed)
- Sea salt and fresh ground black pepper, to taste

INSTRUCTIONS:

ONE: Cook pasta according to package directions. Drain pasta and rinse with cold water to stop it from cooking further. Set aside.

TWO: Put spinach, mint, garlic, cheese and lemon zest in a food processor and pulse to form a chunky paste. Combine lemon juice and oil in a liquid measuring cup. With food processor running (on but not pulsing), add juice-oil mixture through the food chute in a slow drizzle until a thick, smooth pesto forms. Combine pesto with cooked pasta in a large bowl.

THREE: Put almonds in processor and pulse about 10 times, until finely chopped. Stir almonds into pasta.

FOUR: Drain tuna and flake it with a fork. Add it to pasta, along with yellow pepper, zucchini and beans. Toss to combine and season with salt and black pepper.

Nutrients per 2-cup serving: Calories: 450, Total Fat: 11 g, Sat. Fat: 1.5 g, Carbs: 66 g, Fiber: 14 g, Sugars: 6 g, Protein: 28 g, Sodium: 190 mg, Cholesterol: 15 mg

Caponata Sandwiches
WITH GOAT CHEESE & BASIL

*Serves 4. **Hands-on time:** 20 minutes. **Total time:** 35 minutes.*

Caponata is a Sicilian relish made from eggplant and other chopped vegetables, often used as a pasta sauce or as part of an antipasto platter. You'll love it as a filling on a crunchy baguette.

INGREDIENTS:

- 2 Tbsp olive oil
- ⅛ tsp crushed red pepper flakes
- 1 eggplant, cut into ½-inch cubes
- 2 celery stalks, thinly sliced
- 1 onion, diced
- 1 red bell pepper, diced
- Sea salt and ground black pepper, to taste
- 3 Tbsp dried currants
- 2¼ cups diced tomatoes
- 3 Tbsp red wine vinegar
- 1 Tbsp drained capers
- 4 oz chèvre (soft goat cheese)
- 4 whole-grain rolls or mini baguettes, cut crosswise
- 20 fresh basil leaves or as desired

INSTRUCTIONS:

ONE: Heat oil in a very large skillet over high heat. Add pepper flakes and eggplant and cook until eggplant starts to soften, about three minutes. Add celery, onion and bell pepper, season with salt and black pepper, and cook until vegetables start to soften, about five minutes. Stir in currants and tomatoes with their juice.

TWO: Partially cover skillet and simmer over low heat until vegetables are soft and mixture thickens, stirring occasionally, about 15 minutes. Stir in vinegar and capers.

THREE: To assemble sandwiches, open up each roll, spread on one ounce chèvre, fill with caponata mixture, dividing evenly, and top with five basil leaves. Enjoy your sandwich warm or take it to go. (NOTE: If you plan on taking your sandwich to go, pack all elements separately and assemble at mealtime.)

Nutrients per sandwich: Calories: 451, Total Fat: 16 g, Sat. Fat: 5.5 g, Carbs: 64 g, Fiber: 14 g, Sugars: 20 g, Protein: 17 g, Sodium: 1038 mg, Cholesterol: 13 mg

Caponata Sandwiches

Flank
Steak
Roll

Flank Steak Roll
WITH SPINACH & GARLIC

*Serves 4. **Hands-on time:** 25 minutes. **Total time:** 1 hour, 15 minutes.*

Easy enough for everyday family sit-downs yet impressive enough for a more elaborate occasion, our gussied-up flank steak is delicious and visually appealing on your plate.

INGREDIENTS:

- Olive oil cooking spray
- ¼ cup whole-wheat panko
- 1 Tbsp pine nuts, toasted
- 2 tsp red wine vinegar
- 2 cloves garlic, minced
- ¼ tsp fine sea salt
- ¼ tsp dried red pepper flakes
- 1 (1 lb) flank steak, trimmed of visible fat
- 3 oz spinach leaves (about 6 cups)

EQUIPMENT:

- Kitchen string

OPTION: Add a new twist to this recipe by switching up the greens: Arugula and even chard (minus the tougher stems) are perfect alternatives to spinach. Plus, you can sprinkle some shredded carrot into the mix before rolling your steak for added texture and a pop of color.

INSTRUCTIONS:

ONE: Preheat oven to 400°F. Arrange a rack in a baking pan and coat with cooking spray.

TWO: In a small bowl, combine panko, nuts, vinegar, garlic, salt and pepper flakes. Set aside.

THREE: Place steak on a work surface. Holding a sharp knife (ideally a carving knife with a thinner blade than a chef's knife) parallel to the work surface and positioned along one of the longer sides, cut steak almost in half horizontally, so it opens like a book. Spread steak open with the "spine of book" parallel to you.

FOUR: Sprinkle panko mixture evenly over steak, leaving a one-inch border along the farthest edge. Arrange spinach on top of panko mixture. Beginning with the closest edge, roll steak up, gently pressing down on spinach. Rotate steak roll so it's vertical to you and tie crosswise at one-inch intervals with kitchen string. Place steak on rack in prepared baking pan and bake until a meat thermometer inserted into the thickest part of steak registers 150°F for medium doneness, about 35 minutes, or 130°F for medium rare, about 30 minutes. Transfer steak roll to a cutting board, cover loosely with foil and let rest for 10 minutes (internal temperature will continue to rise to about 160°F for medium and 140°F for medium rare).

FIVE: Remove foil and string and carefully cut steak crosswise into half-inch slices. Serve drizzled with any juices accumulated on cutting board.

Nutrients per 4 oz flank steak roll: Calories: 230, Total Fat: 11 g, Sat. Fat: 3.5 g, Carbs: 8 g, Fiber: 2 g, Sugars: 0 g, Protein: 26 g, Sodium: 220 mg, Cholesterol: 40 mg

How to assemble your steak roll:

ONE: Place steak on a work surface. Holding a sharp carving knife parallel to the work surface and positioned along one of the longer sides, cut steak almost in half horizontally, so it opens like a book.

TWO: Spread steak open with the "spine of book" parallel to you. Sprinkle panko mixture evenly over steak, leaving a one-inch border along the farthest edge. Arrange spinach on top of panko mixture.

THREE: Beginning with the closest edge, roll steak up, gently pressing down on spinach.

FOUR: Rotate steak roll so it's vertical to you. Tie crosswise at one-inch intervals with kitchen string. Place steak on rack in a prepared baking pan and bake according to recipe instructions.

FIVE: Transfer cooked steak roll to a cutting board, loosely cover with foil and let rest for 10 minutes.

SIX: Remove foil and string and carefully cut steak crosswise into half-inch slices.

Garden Egg Scramble

*Serves 6. **Hands-on time:** 10 minutes. **Total time:** 15 minutes.*

Cooking up eggs for breakfast doesn't have to mean a platter of greasy bacon and eggs. Keep it light and refreshing by dishing up a colorful and flavorful egg white and mixed vegetable combination. Look for rehydrated sun-dried tomatoes in zip-lock packages in the produce section of your grocery store. They help keep this recipe's fat content low since they aren't soaked in oil like the traditional jarred varieties.

INGREDIENTS:

- 1½ cups chopped asparagus
- 2 tsp olive oil
- ¼ cup diced onion
- 2 cloves garlic, minced
- 1 (8-oz) pkg fresh mushrooms, sliced
- 3 cups fresh baby spinach
- 6 egg whites
- ½ cup chopped fresh basil
- ¼ cup rehydrated sun-dried tomatoes

INSTRUCTIONS:

ONE: Bring water to a boil in a medium saucepan. Add asparagus and cook until crisp and bright, about one to two minutes. Immediately remove and plunge asparagus into a bowl of ice water until cooled.

TWO: Heat oil in a large skillet over medium heat. Add onion, garlic and mushrooms and cook for about five minutes or until tender. Add spinach and asparagus and cook until spinach is wilted, about three to five minutes. Stir in egg whites, basil and tomatoes and cook, mixing well to scramble, about three to five more minutes. Serve immediately.

Nutrients per 1-cup serving: Calories: 60, Total Fat: 2 g, Sat. Fat 0 g, Carbs: 6 g, Fiber: 2 g, Sugars: 3 g, Protein: 6 g, Sodium: 125 mg, Cholesterol: 0 mg

Nutritional Bonus:

Well touted for its impressive iron content, spinach is also host to vitamin C, fiber, flavonoids and calcium, which is important for strengthening bones and protecting against memory loss. And, if you thought only bright orange produce offers rich amounts of beta-carotene, think again: The vitamin A precursor and carotenoid is also found in Popeye's favorite food.

A Better Monte Cristo Sandwich

*Serves 4. **Hands-on time:** 15 minutes. **Total time:** 15 minutes.*

The Monte Cristo is usually assembled with ham, turkey or chicken and full-fat cheese sandwiched between two slices of white bread, then dipped in a beaten whole egg and fried in butter. Better for your health and better on taste, our sandwich is a much lighter, more nutritious fat-sparing meal.

INGREDIENTS:

- 1 lb turkey breast scaloppine (thinly sliced turkey), cut into 4-oz pieces
- 2 tsp olive oil, divided
- 1½ tsp dried oregano
- Sea salt and fresh ground black pepper, to taste
- ½ cup egg whites
- 2 Tbsp skim milk
- Cayenne pepper, to taste
- 3 Tbsp Dijon mustard
- 8 slices whole-grain bread
- 1 cup baby spinach leaves
- 1 pear, thinly sliced
- 4 (1-oz) slices low-fat Swiss cheese

INSTRUCTIONS:

ONE: In a small bowl, season turkey with one teaspoon oil, oregano, salt and black pepper.

TWO: Heat a nonstick sauté pan over medium-high heat. Add turkey and sauté until light golden at edges and fully cooked throughout, about two to three minutes per side. Remove from heat and set aside.

THREE: In a shallow dish, whisk together egg whites and milk. Season with salt, black pepper and cayenne. Set aside.

FOUR: Spread about one teaspoon (adjust to taste) Dijon mustard on one side of each bread slice and place, mustard-side-up, onto a flat work surface. Layer equal parts spinach, pear and turkey onto four slices of bread. Top each stack with one slice cheese and another slice of bread, mustard-side-down, pressing gently.

FIVE: In a medium nonstick sauté pan, heat remaining teaspoon of oil over medium heat.

SIX: Using a spatula, carefully dip one side of a sandwich into egg mixture (egg mixture should go about halfway up the bread slice when immersed). With your hand on the top of the sandwich and spatula underneath, carefully flip to immerse the other side in egg, then gently transfer to hot pan. Sauté sandwich, turning once, until golden brown and crisp, about five minutes total. Remove from pan. Repeat with remaining sandwiches. Cut sandwiches in half and serve immediately.

Nutrients per sandwich: Calories: 420, Total Fat: 7 g, Sat. Fat: 2 g, Carbs: 34 g, Fiber: 6 g, Sugars: 9 g, Protein: 53 g, Sodium: 750 mg, Cholesterol: 105 mg

Nutritional Bonus:
A traditional Monte Cristo has an average 35 grams of total fat and offers little in the way of nutritional value. Our Monte makeover – under 10 grams of fat – is fresh, delicious and loaded with lean protein, calcium, manganese and selenium.

Tip:
Monte Cristo sandwiches are traditionally served with jelly for dipping. While the pear, Dijon and cayenne pepper in this sandwich will probably satisfy your flavor fancy, opt for an unsweetened all-fruit spread or applesauce if you're hankering for some dipping action.

A Better Monte Cristo Sandwich

Shepherd's Pie

Shepherd's Pie
WITH BUTTERMILK CHIVE MASHED POTATO CRUST

Serves 6. ***Hands-on time:*** *25 minutes.* ***Total time:*** *1 hour.*

Lean ground turkey and buttermilk-mashed Yukon gold potatoes give this seasonal family favorite all the flavor and creaminess you'd expect from a shepherd's pie – with none of the actual butter or cream. Translation: a low-cal, low-fat meal sure to soothe any wintertime craving, guilt free.

INGREDIENTS:

• 1 lb Yukon gold potatoes, peeled and cut into 2-inch pieces

• 1 clove garlic, whole, plus 1 tsp minced garlic, divided

• ⅔ cup buttermilk

• 1 Tbsp chopped chives

• Sea salt and ground black pepper, to taste

• 4 tsp olive oil, divided

• 1 lb lean ground turkey breast

• 1 yellow onion, finely chopped (1 cup)

• 3 medium carrots, halved lengthwise and cut into half moons (about 1 cup)

• 1 celery stalk, diced (about ⅓ cup)

• 1 tsp finely chopped fresh rosemary leaves

• 1 cup low-sodium chicken broth

• 1 Tbsp tomato paste

• ½ cup frozen peas

INSTRUCTIONS:

ONE: Preheat oven to 375°F.

TWO: Bring potatoes and whole garlic clove to a boil in a pot of water set over high heat. Cook until potatoes are tender, about 15 to 20 minutes, then drain well. Mash potatoes and garlic with a potato masher, ricer or food mill until smooth. Add buttermilk and chives and season with salt and pepper. Set aside.

THREE: Meanwhile, heat one teaspoon of oil in a large nonstick skillet over medium-high heat. Add turkey and cook, stirring often and breaking meat into small pieces with a wooden spoon. Cook until no pink remains, about eight minutes. Drain and discard fat; set turkey aside.

FOUR: Heat two teaspoons oil in same skillet. Add onion, carrots, celery and rosemary, and cook, stirring occasionally, until vegetables are soft, about eight minutes. Add reserved turkey, broth and tomato paste and continue to cook until most of liquid is absorbed, about five minutes. Stir in peas, transfer mixture to a shallow baking dish and cover with mashed potatoes in an even layer. Run a fork over top of potatoes in a crosshatch pattern or swirl with a spatula or the back of a spoon. Brush top with remaining teaspoon oil and bake in oven until filling is bubbling and top is golden brown, about 30 minutes. Let stand five minutes before serving.

Nutrients per 1½-cup serving: Calories: 160, Total Fat: 4 g, Sat. Fat: 0.5 g, Carbs: 10 g, Fiber: 2 g, Sugars: 4 g, Protein: 20 g, Sodium: 150 mg, Cholesterol: 40 mg

How to assemble your shepherd's pie:

ONE: Transfer turkey-vegetable mixture to a shallow baking dish and cover with mashed potatoes in an even layer.

TWO: Run a fork over top of potatoes in a crosshatch pattern or swirl with a spatula or the back of a spoon. Brush top with one teaspoon oil and bake at 375°F for about 30 minutes.

Paella

*Serves 4. **Hands-on time:** 30 minutes. **Total time:** 1 hour, 15 minutes.*

Paella is composed of rice, meat and vegetables. In Valencia, where it's said to have originated, paellas are almost always single-protein dishes. Here in America, however, we like to mix fish, chicken and pork. Throw in some vegetables and you have a complete good-for-you one-dish meal.

INGREDIENTS:

- 8 oz boneless, skinless chicken breasts
- 4 oz deli-fresh, low-fat smoked turkey sausage, cut into bite-size pieces
- 1 tsp olive oil
- ½ medium onion, diced (about ½ cup)
- 1 medium tomato, chopped
- ½ red bell pepper, diced (½ cup)
- ½ green bell pepper, diced (½ cup)
- 1 tsp sweet paprika
- 2 cloves garlic, smashed
- 2 Tbsp chopped fresh parsley
- ½ tsp saffron (optional)
- 1 cup brown rice
- 1 cup low-sodium chicken stock
- ½ cup frozen peas, thawed
- 12 little neck clams, cleaned

INSTRUCTIONS:

ONE: Simmer three cups water in a small saucepan over medium heat. Add chicken and cook for 10 to 15 minutes, depending on thickness. Remove chicken with strainer or slotted spoon and set aside. When cool, cut chicken into bite-size pieces. Bring same water to simmer again over medium heat, then add sausage; cook five minutes. Remove sausage and set aside, reserving poaching liquid in a bowl or measuring cup.

TWO: Heat oil in a large nonstick sauté pan over medium-high heat. Add onion and cook for two minutes. Add tomato, peppers and paprika. Cook for another two to three minutes, until vegetables start to soften.

THREE: Mash garlic, parsley and saffron, if desired, together in a small bowl with the back of a spoon or fork until it makes a thick paste.

FOUR: Stir garlic-parsley mash into vegetables in pan. Mix in rice and toss together for two minutes, until rice is coated.

FIVE: Add enough chicken stock to reserved poaching liquid to make four cups. Save any extra stock, as you may need it later. Add stock mixture to rice in pan and bring to boil over medium-high heat. Reduce heat to medium-low, until mixture just simmers. Cover and cook for 35 minutes.

SIX: Add chicken, sausage, peas and clams to rice. Cover and cook for another 10 to 12 minutes, until rice is tender and clams open up. If rice gets too dry and begins to stick, add extra broth. Serve in large bowls.

Nutrients per 1½-cup serving: Calories: 260, Total Fat: 7 g, Sat. Fat: 1.5 g, Carbs: 25 g, Fiber: 4 g, Sugars: 4 g, Protein: 25 g, Sodium: 270 mg, Cholesterol: 70 mg

Three-Grain Tabouli

*Serves 6. **Makes** 6 cups. **Hands-on time:** 30 minutes. **Total time:** 30 minutes.*

Millet and kasha give a chewier texture and more substantial bite to this refreshing Lebanese grain salad, while shrimp pumps up the protein. If you don't have kasha and millet on hand, just double the bulgur and increase the water to three cups.

INGREDIENTS:

- ¼ cup millet
- ¼ cup roasted whole buckwheat groats (known as kasha)
- ½ cup fine bulgur
- ½ cup coarsely chopped mint leaves
- 4 green onions, chopped
- 1 bunch parsley, finely chopped (about 1 cup)
- 1 medium tomato, diced
- 8 oz large precooked shrimp, thawed from frozen
- Juice of 2 lemons (about 5 Tbsp)
- 2 tsp lemon zest
- 3 Tbsp low-sodium chicken broth
- 2 Tbsp olive oil
- ½ tsp kosher salt

INSTRUCTIONS:

ONE: Heat millet in a nonstick saucepan over medium-high heat until it begins to brown and pop, about five to ten minutes. Then add half-cup plus two tablespoons water and bring to a simmer, covered. Simmer for eight minutes. Set aside. In another pot, bring half-cup water to boil over high heat. Add kasha, lower heat to medium, cover and cook for 10 minutes, until kasha becomes soft and more than doubles in size. Set aside. While millet and kasha are cooking, soak bulgur in one-and-a-half cups warm water for 10 minutes in a separate bowl. Drain.

TWO: In a large bowl, blend all three grains together. Add mint, onions, parsley and tomato, and gently mix. Cut each shrimp in half and mix into grain mixture.

THREE: In a separate bowl, whisk together lemon juice, zest, broth, oil and salt. Pour over grain mixture; toss and serve.

Nutrients per 1-cup serving: Calories: 210, Total Fat: 6 g, Sat. Fat: 1 g, Carbs: 27 g, Fiber: 6 g, Sugar: 1 g, Protein: 12 g, Sodium: 240 mg, Cholesterol: 55 mg

NOTE: Bulgur is typically found in three grades: fine, medium and coarse, depending on how it's cut. The fine grain is best for salads and can be eaten uncooked if soaked first. Medium and coarse grains, often used in pilafs and stews, do not need to be soaked but must be cooked.

Three-Grain
Tabouli

Quinoa &
Vegetable
Sauté

THE BEST OF CLEAN EATING

Quinoa & Vegetable Sauté

*Serves 4. **Hands-on-time:** 15 minutes. **Total time:** 15 minutes.*

A relatively unknown superfood, quinoa has a nutty flavor and light crunchy texture when cooked. It's considered a grain, but it's actually the seed of a type of leafy green vegetable!

INGREDIENTS:

- ½ cup uncooked quinoa
- 1 cup water
- 1 Tbsp canola oil
- 1 cup finely diced red onion
- ¾ red bell pepper, finely chopped
- 2 cups chopped green cabbage
- 1 Tbsp Herbes de Provence (or substitute 1 tsp each: marjoram, thyme, basil and rosemary)
- ¼ tsp sea salt
- 1 cup frozen shelled peas
- ½ cup vegetable broth or water
- 6 oz extra-firm tofu, cut into bite-size cubes

INSTRUCTIONS:

ONE: Rinse quinoa in a fine-mesh strainer. In a small saucepan, combine quinoa with water. Cover and bring to a boil over high heat; reduce heat and continue cooking for 10 minutes.

TWO: While quinoa cooks, heat oil in a sauté pan over medium-high heat. Add onion, bell pepper, cabbage, Herbes de Provence and sea salt. Continue to stir and sauté for five minutes, then add peas and broth. Cover pan and cook five more minutes.

THREE: Add cooked quinoa to vegetables, with any remaining cooking liquid. Stir in tofu. Cover and let stand for one minute before serving.

Nutrients per 1¼ cup serving: Calories: 172, Total Fat: 7 g, Sat. Fat: 1 g, Trans Fat: 0 g, Carbs: 21 g, Fiber: 5 g, Protein: 9 g, Sugars: 7 g, Sodium: 307 mg, Cholesterol: 0 mg

Lemon Artichoke Chicken

*Serves 4. **Hands-on time:** 32 minutes. **Total time:** 32 minutes.*

Your regular old chicken is brought to the next level of delicious with the addition of our fresh, zesty lemon-artichoke mixture.

INGREDIENTS:

- ¼ cup whole-wheat flour
- ½ Tbsp dried oregano
- Fresh ground black pepper, to taste
- ¼ tsp sea salt or coarse kosher salt (plus additional for seasoning to taste)
- 1 lb thin chicken breast cutlets
- Olive oil cooking spray
- ½ Tbsp extra-virgin olive oil
- 1 medium onion, cut lengthwise and thinly sliced
- 1 clove garlic, minced
- ¼ cup low-sodium chicken broth
- 1 (14-oz) jar artichoke hearts, drained and cut into sixths
- ¼ cup fresh lemon juice (about 2 lemons)
- 1 tsp lemon zest
- 2 Tbsp chopped fresh parsley for garnish

INSTRUCTIONS:

ONE: In a shallow bowl, thoroughly combine flour, oregano, pepper and salt. Dredge each chicken cutlet in flour mixture, shake off excess and place on a plate.

TWO: Coat a large nonstick skillet with cooking spray and heat on medium to medium-high, so skillet is hot but not smoking. Add half the chicken cutlets and cook three to five minutes per side, until lightly browned and cooked through. Transfer to a clean serving plate and repeat with remaining cutlets, first coating skillet once more with cooking spray. Cover your serving plate with foil to keep chicken warm.

THREE: Adjust temperature to medium-low and heat oil. Place onion in pan and cook, stirring frequently, until soft and golden – five to six minutes. Add garlic, cooking for one minute, stirring constantly; then chicken broth, bringing it to a simmer; followed by artichokes, lemon juice and zest, simmering for two to three minutes until heated through and slightly thickened. Season to taste with salt and pepper.

FOUR: Pour artichoke mixture over chicken cutlets, sprinkle with parsley and serve.

Nutrients per serving (4 oz chicken, ½ cup artichoke mixture): Calories: 220, Total Fat: 4.5 g, Sat. Fat: 1 g, Carbs: 20 g, Fiber: 2 g, Sugars: 2 g, Protein: 27 g, Sodium: 420 mg, Cholesterol: 65 mg

Cobb Salad
WITH WHITE FISH

Serves *4.* **Makes** *about ½ cup dressing.* **Hands-on time:** *30 minutes.*
Total time: *30 minutes.*

Cobb salad may be a classic, but is often far from light and refreshing. We've ditched the mass of egg yolks and allowed the egg whites to appear solo, substituted in lean white fish fillets for additional clean protein, opted for low-fat feta and added our own homemade Dijon vinaigrette.

INGREDIENTS:

- 4 eggs
- 4 fillets white fish (about 1 lb), preferably cod or pollock
- ½ tsp paprika
- Sea salt and fresh ground black pepper, to taste
- 1 large head green leaf or romaine lettuce, cleaned and torn into pieces
- 1 avocado, peeled, pitted and diced
- 2 oz Kalamata olives, pitted and diced
- 2 tomatoes, preferably Roma, seeded and chopped
- 2 oz low-fat feta cheese, crumbled
- 2 tsp extra-virgin olive oil
- ¼ cup balsamic vinegar
- 1 tsp raw honey
- 1 clove garlic, minced
- 1 tsp Dijon mustard
- Juice of 1 lemon

INSTRUCTIONS:

ONE: Place eggs in a small pot, cover with water and bring to a boil over medium-high heat. Boil for 10 minutes. Remove eggs from heat and water and place in an ice-water bath for at least five minutes. Peel, remove and discard yolks, and chop egg whites.

TWO: Preheat broiler on high. Line a cookie sheet with aluminum foil and place fillets on sheet. Sprinkle with paprika and season with salt and pepper. Broil for five minutes, remove from heat and let cool for five minutes, then cut fillets into half-inch square chunks.

THREE: Divide lettuce evenly among four bowls or plates. In individual sections over each bed of lettuce, portion out a quarter of fish, a quarter of egg whites, a quarter of avocado, a half-ounce of olives, a quarter of tomatoes and a half-ounce of feta. (Each salad topping should be arranged in its own section over lettuce instead of tossed together.)

FOUR: In a small bowl, whisk together oil, vinegar, honey, garlic, Dijon mustard and lemon juice. Season with salt and pepper. Drizzle dressing over four salads, dividing evenly, and serve immediately. Leftover dressing can be kept, covered, in refrigerator for up to four days.

Nutrients per salad (1 fish fillet, 1 egg white, ¼ avocado, ½ oz olives, ½ tomato, ½ oz cheese, 3 Tbsp dressing): *Calories: 280, Total Fat: 13 g, Sat. Fat: 2.5 g, Carbs: 13 g, Fiber: 3 g, Sugars: 5 g, Protein: 28 g, Sodium: 503 mg, Cholesterol: 54 mg*

Nutritional Bonus:
Not only do avocados contain nearly 20 assorted vitamins, minerals and beneficial phytonutrients, they're also one of the best fruit sources of lutein, a plant carotenoid and antioxidant that promotes eye health and may help reduce the risk of arteriosclerosis (hardening of the arteries).

Tuna Niçoise Stovetop Casserole

Serves 8. **Hands-on time:** *30 minutes.* **Total time:** *30 minutes.*

To make a classic salad a bit heartier for a weeknight family meal, we've transformed a tuna Niçoise into a stovetop couscous casserole. Bonus: The recipe serves eight, so you'll have more than enough to spare for lunches or a leftovers dinner.

INGREDIENTS:

- 2 cups couscous
- 8 small red potatoes, cut into halves, or 4 large red potatoes, cut into quarters
- 2 (6-oz) pouches or cans unsalted water-packed tuna
- ½ lb frozen green beans, thawed
- ½ cup pitted Kalamata olives, sliced
- Juice and zest of 1 lemon
- 1 Tbsp Dijon mustard
- 1 Tbsp finely diced white onion
- 1 clove garlic, minced
- 1 Tbsp apple cider vinegar
- 2 tsp extra-virgin olive oil
- 2 tsp minced fresh flat-leaf parsley
- Sea salt and fresh ground black pepper, to taste
- Olive oil cooking spray

INSTRUCTIONS:

ONE: Cook couscous according to package directions.

TWO: Over medium-high heat, bring a medium-size pan filled with water to boil. Cook potatoes for 10 minutes; drain. In a large bowl, mix together tuna, green beans, olives and potatoes. Once couscous is cooked, mix it into tuna-vegetable mixture.

THREE: In a medium bowl, whisk together lemon juice and zest, Dijon mustard, onion, garlic, vinegar, oil, parsley, salt and pepper. Pour dressing over tuna-couscous mixture.

FOUR: Heat large nonstick or cast-iron skillet over high heat for one minute. Reduce heat to medium-high, mist pan with cooking spray and sauté tuna-couscous mixture for about five minutes or until thoroughly warmed. Remove from heat and serve immediately.

Nutrients per 1-cup serving: *Calories: 430, Total Fat: 6 g, Sat. Fat: 1 g, Carbs: 70 g, Fiber: 11 g, Sugars: 4 g, Protein: 25 g, Sodium: 350 mg, Cholesterol: 15 mg*

TIP:
Tuna is an excellent protein choice; it's low in fat and the fat it does contain is made up of omega 3 fatty acids. However, tuna can be high in mercury. To enjoy this healthful fish more often, choose chunk light or skipjack tuna. Albacore, yellowfin and bigeye (ahi) contain considerably more mercury, so eat these varieties only occasionally, and avoid entirely if you're pregnant.

Turkey Ragout

*Serves 4. **Hands-on time:** 10 minutes. **Total time:** 25 minutes.*

Thank France for this thick, well-seasoned stew that incorporates a bounty of vegetables with lean, soul-satisfying protein. Sizzle meaty chunks of turkey with a variety of quick-cooking veggies and, yes, garlic bread on the side.

INGREDIENTS:

TURKEY RAGOUT

- Olive oil spray
- 1 lb boneless, skinless turkey breast cutlets, cut into 2-inch pieces
- 2 cloves garlic, minced
- 1 (10 oz) pkg mushrooms, halved
- 1 small zucchini, halved and cut into ½-inch slices
- 1 (14.5 oz) jar no-salt-added diced tomatoes with juice
- ½ tsp sea salt
- ½ tsp fresh ground pepper
- ½ tsp thyme
- ½ tsp oregano

GARLIC BREAD

- 4 cloves garlic, minced
- 1 tsp extra-virgin olive oil
- 1 (16- to 20-inch) whole-wheat or multigrain ciabatta (about 12 oz)

INSTRUCTIONS:

ONE: Preheat oven to 400°F. On the stovetop, mist a large nonstick skillet with olive oil spray and place over medium heat. Add turkey and brown for two to three minutes. Turn turkey pieces with spatula and add garlic, mushrooms, zucchini, tomatoes, salt and remaining spices.

TWO: Sauté for five minutes, stirring once or twice so the meat is browned on top and the veggies begin to sizzle. Cover with a lid, turn heat to low and simmer for 10 to 12 minutes.

THREE: Meanwhile, prepare garlic bread: In a small bowl, stir together minced garlic and olive oil. Cut ciabatta in half lengthwise and spread garlic oil in center. Close loaf and cut into two-inch pieces. Wrap entire loaf loosely in foil and place in oven for eight to nine minutes to warm while ragout finishes cooking.

Nutrients per 1½ cups ragout and 3 oz bread: *Calories: 397, Total Fat: 7 g, Sat. Fat: 0 g, Carbs: 45 g, Fiber: 9.5 g, Sugars: 9 g, Protein: 41.5 g, Sodium: 744 mg, Cholesterol: 45 mg*

Baja-Style Fish Tacos
WITH FAUX CREAM

*Serves 4. **Hands-on time:** 20 minutes. **Total time:** 35 minutes.*

Typically, the fish in a Baja-style fish taco is beer-battered and fried, then topped with a white sauce, usually mayonnaise thinned with water, before being wrapped in a cabbage-filled tortilla. Here, we've cut fat and calories by baking the fish instead of frying. The white sauce gets lightened with tangy Greek-style yogurt, seasoned with Mexican spices.

INGREDIENTS:

- 4 whole-grain tortillas
- 1 lb fresh tilapia fillets
- ½ fresh lime
- ¼ tsp kosher salt
- ⅛ tsp ground black pepper
- ½ cup plain, low-fat, Greek-style yogurt
- 1 small jalapeño pepper, minced
- ¼ tsp dried oregano
- ¼ tsp ground cumin
- 1 cup shredded cabbage
- 1 avocado, seeded and cut into slices

INSTRUCTIONS:

ONE: Preheat oven to 350°F. Stack tortillas and wrap them in a sheet of aluminum foil. Line a rimmed baking sheet with aluminum foil. Place fish fillets on baking sheet and squeeze lime juice evenly over each. Sprinkle with salt and black pepper. Place tortillas and fish in oven. Remove tortillas after five minutes and set aside. Bake fish until it's just cooked through, about seven to ten minutes.

TWO: While fish is baking, stir together yogurt, jalapeño pepper, oregano and cumin. If you like a thinner sauce, stir in a tablespoon or two of water.

THREE: Break up the fish with a fork and divide into four equal portions. Fill each warmed tortilla with shredded cabbage and fish, and top each with one-quarter of the avocado and two tablespoons of yogurt sauce.

Nutrients per taco: *Calories: 360, Total Fat: 13 g, Sat. Fat: 2.5 g, Carbs: 29 g, Fiber: 6 g, Sugars: 2 g, Protein: 31 g, Sodium: 370 mg, Cholesterol: 55 mg*

Baja-Style
Fish Tacos

Turkey
Paninis

Turkey Paninis
WITH SUN-DRIED TOMATOES

Serves 4. ***Hands-on time:*** *10 minutes.* ***Total time:*** *20 minutes.*

Sassier than sandwiches, paninis make for a delicious, clean quick-fix meal. If you don't have a countertop grill, put paninis in a hot skillet and use another heavy skillet to press them down as they toast.

INGREDIENTS:

- 1 whole-wheat baguette, cut crosswise in fourths
- 12 sun-dried tomatoes (packed in olive oil), patted dry and halved
- 2 oz part-skim mozzarella cheese, thinly sliced
- 6 (1-oz) slices reduced-sodium fresh deli turkey
- 1½ cups arugula leaves

INSTRUCTIONS:

ONE: Split open baguette sections and layer each bottom half with six pieces tomato, half-ounce cheese, one-and-a-half slices turkey and top half of bread. Toast sandwich on a countertop grill or panini press on medium heat, lid down, until lightly browned, about six minutes. If using stovetop method, toast about three minutes per side, or until lightly browned.

TWO: As soon as paninis are done toasting, open each and add one-third cup arugula. Slice each panini on the diagonal and serve immediately.

Nutrients per panini: Calories: 260, Total Fat: 6 g, Sat. Fat: 2 g, Carbs: 34 g, Fiber: 5 g, Sugars: 4 g, Protein: 16 g, Sodium: 830 mg, Cholesterol: 25 mg

Roasted Rainbow Tomato Salad

Serves 4. ***Makes*** *4 cups.* ***Hands-on time:*** *10 minutes.* ***Total time:*** *45 minutes.*

A simple Caprese salad is a quintessential summer dish and ours is a show-stopping addition to any table with its gorgeous rainbow of tomatoes.

INGREDIENTS:

- 8 cups heirloom-style grape and cherry tomatoes (combination of red, yellow, orange and/or tiger-striped)
- 6 cloves garlic, sliced in half lengthwise
- 1 Tbsp olive oil
- 2 Tbsp balsamic vinegar
- Sea salt and fresh ground black pepper, to taste
- 2 oz low-fat mini bocconcini cheese, sliced in half (about ⅓ cup)
- 12 large leaves fresh basil, thinly sliced

TIP: Little heirloom tomatoes are usually available at supermarkets during the summer season. If you can't find them at your local grocer, try regular grape and cherry tomatoes in their place. They won't be as colorful, but they're still tasty!

INSTRUCTIONS:

ONE: Preheat oven to 350°F.

TWO: In a large mixing bowl, toss tomatoes with garlic, oil and vinegar. Season with salt and pepper.

THREE: Prepare four foil pouches as per the "How to Make a Foil Pouch" guide below. Divide seasoned tomatoes evenly among foil pouches and seal. Using a knife, carefully pierce six small holes in the top of each pouch. Place pouches on a baking tray and slide onto middle rack of preheated oven. Roast for 20 minutes or until tomatoes are soft and fragrant. Remove from oven, carefully open pouches and drain excess liquid from tomatoes with a strainer. Add half-ounce cheese to each pouch, close and cook for five more minutes. Let cool for five minutes.

FOUR: To serve, divide tomato mixtures evenly among four plates. Top each with about one teaspoon sliced basil. Serve immediately.

Nutrients per 1-cup serving: Calories: 135, Total Fat: 7 g, Sat. Fat: 2 g, Carbs: 15 g, Fiber: 4 g, Sugars: 9 g, Protein: 5.5 g, Sodium: 58 mg, Cholesterol: 0 mg

HOW TO MAKE A FOIL POUCH:

ONE: Tear off a piece of heavy-duty aluminum foil about 20 inches in length and place on a flat surface, long side facing you. If you'll be adding liquid to the pouch, fold over long edges of foil parallel to your counter by about a half-inch so liquid will not run off.

TWO: Place food to be cooked in center of foil.

THREE: Grasp top and bottom edges of the foil (the long sides) and pull up over the food, pinching together at the top.

FOUR: Begin folding foil down toward the food until it is about two inches from the food.

FIVE: Grasp the right side of the foil and fold over a few times toward the center to seal. Take hold of the left side of the foil and repeat.

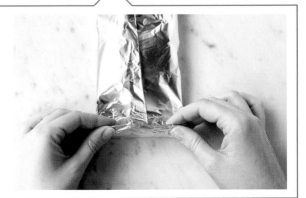

Baked Salmon
WITH BLACK BEAN SALSA & QUICK CORN SAUTÉ

Serves 4. ***Hands-on time:*** *20 minutes.* ***Total time:*** *20 minutes.*

This Mexican-inspired seafood meal includes a corn sauté that's cooked for only five minutes to boost health and taste. Less time over the heat helps the vegetable retain more nutrients while maintaining its crisp texture.

INGREDIENTS:

- 4 (4-oz) wild-caught salmon fillets, rinsed in cold water and patted dry
- 1 cup fresh corn or 1 cup frozen corn, thawed
- ½ cup minced red bell pepper
- 1 medium onion, diced, divided
- 1 tsp chile powder, plus additional for garnish
- 1 Tbsp extra-virgin olive oil
- 1 large tomato, chopped
- 1 clove garlic, minced
- 1 cup cooked black beans or 1 cup canned black beans, drained and rinsed well (NOTE: Look for beans that are packed in bisphenol-A-free cans, such as Eden Organic Black Beans.)
- Juice of ½ lemon
- 1 cup loosely packed cilantro, chopped, divided

INSTRUCTIONS:

ONE: Preheat oven to 350°F. Arrange salmon on a baking sheet lined with aluminum foil and bake for 12 minutes, using a fork to test doneness. If center flakes easily and is opaque, salmon is done; if not, bake for another two to three minutes and check again.

TWO: In a bowl, combine corn, pepper, half of onion and chile powder. Heat oil over medium heat and sauté corn mixture for five minutes, stirring occasionally.

THREE: In another bowl, combine tomato, garlic, beans, lemon juice, half of cilantro and remaining half of onion. Toss gently.

FOUR: Just before serving, toss remaining half of cilantro with corn sauté. Top each salmon fillet with a half-cup of bean salsa. Then dust corn sauté with additional chile powder and serve alongside salmon and salsa.

Nutrients per serving (4 oz salmon, ½ cup bean salsa, ½ cup corn sauté): *Calories: 302, Total Fat: 11.5 g, Sat. Fat: 2 g, Carbs: 21.5 g, Fiber: 7 g, Sugars: 4 g, Protein: 28 g, Sodium: 68 mg, Cholesterol: 62 mg*

NUTRITIONAL BONUS: This dish offers a heaping serving of antioxidants – more than half of your daily recommended need of vitamin C alone. The immunity-boosting vitamin also ensures that you make the most use out of the iron in your dinner, as vitamin C aids your body in iron absorption.

Sautéed Sole Sandwiches
WITH CITRUS SLAW

Serves 4. ***Hands-on time:*** *20 minutes.* ***Total time:*** *20 minutes.*

Citrus slaw gives these fish sandwiches a crunchy, healthy twist. Our recipe steers away from heavy mayonnaise using lighter ingredients with a hint of lemon infusion.

INGREDIENTS:

- 1 tsp olive oil
- 4 (5-oz) fillets of sole (or similar fish such as cod), skin and bones removed
- Sea salt and freshly ground black pepper, to taste
- ¼ tsp cayenne pepper
- 2 Tbsp fresh lemon juice
- 1 tsp Dijon mustard
- 2 Tbsp nonfat plain Greek-style yogurt
- 2 tsp raw honey
- ¼ tsp celery seed
- 2 Tbsp chopped fresh dill
- ¼ head green cabbage, finely shredded
- 1 stalk celery, thinly sliced crosswise
- 1 large carrot, peeled and grated
- 1 orange, peel and pith removed, segmented
- 4 whole-grain buns, split in half and toasted

INSTRUCTIONS:

ONE: Heat oil in large skillet over medium-high heat. Season both sides of fillets with salt, black pepper and cayenne. Place fillets in pan. Cook until golden brown on the outside and center turns lightly opaque, about two minutes per side.

TWO: In a large bowl, whisk together lemon juice, Dijon mustard, yogurt, honey, celery seed and dill. Add cabbage, celery, carrot and orange segments and toss together. Season with salt and black pepper.

THREE: To assemble each sandwich, place fillet on bottom half of bun, pile slaw on top of fish and cover with top half of bun. Place a big napkin across your lap and enjoy!

Nutrients per serving (1 sandwich with ¾ cup slaw): *Calories: 315, Total Fat: 5 g, Sat. Fat: 1.4 g, Carbs: 37 g, Fiber: 7 g, Sugars: 11 g, Protein: 35 g, Sodium: 594 mg, Cholesterol: 50 mg*

Nutritional Bonus:
White-fleshed fish, such as haddock, cod and sole, are some of the best sources of animal protein. These fish are low in fat and calories and packed with vitamins and minerals, including vitamins B6 and B12, as well as iodine, which is a metabolism booster.

Sautéed Sole Sandwiches

Turkey
Meatballs

Nutritional Bonus:
Select ground turkey that is at least 95 percent lean with less than four grams of saturated fat per serving. This way you can enjoy the ease of using a ground meat without loading up on saturated fat.

Turkey Meatballs
WITH WHOLE-WHEAT SPAGHETTI, SPINACH & RICOTTA

*Serves 4. **Hands-on time:** 20 minutes. **Total time:** 40 minutes.*

Spinach and ricotta is a popular addition to pasta dishes. By choosing low-fat ricotta instead of the full-fat version, you'll still get that creamy taste you love without compromising your healthy lifestyle.

INGREDIENTS:

- 1 tsp olive oil
- ½ yellow onion, finely chopped
- 2 cloves garlic, minced
- 1 lb extra-lean ground turkey
- ¼ cup finely chopped fresh basil
- ¼ cup finely chopped fresh marjoram or oregano
- ½ cup whole-grain breadcrumbs
- 1 Tbsp tomato paste
- 1 egg
- ½ tsp sea salt
- ½ tsp fresh ground black pepper
- 8 oz whole-wheat spaghetti
- 4 cups baby spinach
- ¾ cup low-fat ricotta cheese
- Juice and zest of 1 lemon

INSTRUCTIONS:

ONE: Preheat oven to 400°F. Heat oil in a nonstick skillet over medium heat. Add onion and garlic and cook until soft but not browned, three to five minutes.

TWO: In a large bowl, place turkey, onion-garlic mixture, basil, marjoram, breadcrumbs, tomato paste, egg, salt and pepper. Using your hands or a large spoon, gently mix together until combined.

THREE: Using a small ice cream scoop or a tablespoon, portion out turkey mixture in golf-ball-sized increments. Use clean hands to roll mixture into 20 meatballs and place on a parchment-lined baking sheet. Bake until lightly browned and cooked through, about 20 minutes.

FOUR: Meanwhile, cook spaghetti according to package directions, until al dente – tender but still firm to the bite. Drain pasta, reserving half-cup pasta water.

FIVE: In a large serving bowl, add spaghetti, spinach, cheese, lemon zest and juice, and quarter-cup reserved pasta water. Gently toss to combine, allowing heat of spaghetti to wilt spinach and cooking water to melt ricotta to a creamy sauce. Add more reserved pasta water, if necessary, to reach desired consistency. Taste and adjust seasoning if desired. Add meatballs and serve immediately.

Nutrients per serving (5 meatballs, 2 oz pasta): *Calories: 477, Total Fat: 8 g, Sat. Fat: 3 g, Carbs: 63 g, Fiber: 10 g, Sugars: 3.5 g, Protein: 44 g, Sodium: 787 mg, Cholesterol: 126 mg*

Cajun Jambalaya

*Serves 4. **Makes** 6 cups. **Hands-on time:** 20 minutes. **Total time:** 45 minutes.*

Opting to make your jambalaya in a foil pouch translates to cleanup in a snap! By using instant brown rice, your grains steam perfectly without the need for a pot to be pulled from your cabinet or water to be boiled.

INGREDIENTS:

- ½ lb raw shrimp, 26/30 size, peeled and deveined, tail on
- 4 oz boneless, skinless chicken breast, diced into 1-inch pieces
- 1 all-natural low-sodium turkey sausage, sliced
- ½ medium white onion, diced
- 1 medium green bell pepper, stem and seeds removed and discarded, diced
- 1 rib celery, diced
- 1½ medium vine-ripe tomatoes, cored and diced
- 2 cloves garlic, minced
- 1½ Tbsp salt-free Cajun seasoning
- 1 cup all-natural instant brown rice
- ½ cup low-sodium chicken broth
- Sea salt and fresh ground black pepper, to taste
- Olive oil cooking spray

INSTRUCTIONS:

ONE: Preheat oven to 400°F.

TWO: In a large mixing bowl, toss together all ingredients except cooking spray, mixing well until combined.

THREE: Prepare two foil pouches as per the "How to Make a Foil Pouch" guide on p. 41, paying close attention to pouch modifications for liquid ingredients. Spray each piece of foil with cooking spray. Divide mixture evenly among both pieces of foil and seal.

FOUR: Place pouches on a baking tray and slide onto middle rack of preheated oven for 25 minutes or until rice and proteins are fully cooked. (When cooked, rice will be soft and proteins will be firm and opaque.) To test for doneness, carefully open one pouch and taste a few grains of rice from the center. If necessary, close pouch and bake for five more minutes.

FIVE: When meal is properly cooked, carefully open pouch and pour mixture into a large serving bowl; serve immediately.

Nutrients per 1½-cup serving: *Calories: 339, Total Fat: 5 g, Sat. Fat: 1 g, Carbs: 24 g, Fiber: 3 g, Sugars: 3 g, Protein: 46 g, Sodium: 354 mg, Cholesterol: 171 mg*

Curry Coconut Chickpeas

*Serves 2. **Hands-on time:** 10 minutes. **Total time:** 10 minutes.*

Chickpeas are full of protein and nutrients, which makes them an excellent meat alternative. You'll love this Thai-inspired vegetarian dish!

INGREDIENTS:

- Olive oil cooking spray
- 1 cup of napa cabbage or bok choy, sliced
- ½ cup diced onion
- ½ cup diced red bell pepper
- ½ cup light coconut milk (shake can first)
- 1 tsp minced fresh garlic
- 1 tsp grated fresh ginger
- 1 tsp curry powder
- ¾ cup cooked chickpeas
- ¼ tsp sea salt
- Pinch fresh ground black pepper
- 1 Tbsp thinly sliced fresh basil

INSTRUCTIONS:

ONE: Preheat a nonstick frying pan, lightly coated with spray, over medium heat. Add napa cabbage; sauté until cabbage shrinks down. Add onion and pepper; sauté for two to four minutes.

TWO: Add one tablespoon coconut milk along with garlic, ginger and curry powder; sauté for two minutes . Add remaining coconut milk, chickpeas, salt and pepper; heat until warm. Add fresh basil and serve.

Nutrients per 1-cup serving: Calories: 179, Total Fat: 5 g, Sat. Fat: 3 g, Carbs: 27 g, Fiber: 6 g, Sugars: 5 g, Protein: 7.5 g, Sodium: 300 mg, Cholesterol: 0 mg

---

NEW!

Light & Healthy Pork "Fried" Rice

*Makes 8 cups. **Hands-on time:** 30 minutes. **Total time:** 30 minutes.*

Fried rice dishes are usually made with vast quantities of oil. Better for your health and better on taste, our pork dish is "fried" in a small amount of safflower oil, a heart-healthy oil that may reduce cholesterol and help you slim down at the same time.

INGREDIENTS:

- 1 tsp plus 1 Tbsp safflower oil, divided
- ½ lb pork tenderloin cutlets, trimmed of visible fat, cut into ¼-inch strips
- Fresh ground black pepper, to taste
- 2 tsp plus 2 Tbsp low-sodium soy sauce, divided
- ½ yellow onion, very thinly sliced
- ½ red bell pepper, finely chopped
- 1 carrot, peeled and finely chopped
- 1 bunch broccoli, cut into small bite-sized pieces (1 cup)
- 1 Tbsp grated fresh ginger
- Sea salt, to taste
- 3 cloves garlic, minced
- ½ cup frozen peas, thawed
- 3 cups cooked brown rice
- 1 egg plus 3 egg whites, beaten
- 1 Tbsp Asian fish sauce
- ¼ cup thinly sliced green onions
- Fresh cilantro for garnish
- Chile sauce for garnish, optional

INSTRUCTIONS:

ONE: In a very large nonstick skillet or wok, heat one teaspoon oil over medium-high heat. Add pork in a single layer and season with black pepper. Brown pork, stirring occasionally until cooked through, three to five minutes. Stir in two teaspoons soy sauce. Remove pork and set aside.

TWO: Return skillet to stove and add remaining tablespoon of oil. Add onion, red pepper, carrot, broccoli and ginger, and season with salt and black pepper. Cook over medium-high heat until vegetables are slightly soft, about five minutes. Add garlic and cook for two more minutes.

THREE: Stir in peas and rice, and cook until completely heated through, about five minutes.

FOUR: Push rice mixture over to one side of pan and add eggs to now-empty side. Allow eggs to fully cook, stirring occasionally, three to five minutes, and then stir eggs into rice mixture.

FIVE: Add pork and any accumulated juices to skillet. Stir in fish sauce, remaining two tablespoons soy sauce and green onions. Garnish with cilantro and chile sauce, if desired.

Nutrients per 1-cup serving: Calories:188, Total Fat: 5 g, Sat. Fat: 1.1 g, Carbs: 23 g, Fiber: 3 g, Sugars: 2 g, Protein: 12 g, Sodium: 451 mg, Cholesterol: 43 mg

Pork "Fried" Rice

Spanish
Pork

THE BEST OF CLEAN EATING

Spanish Pork
WITH REDSKINS

Serves 4. **Hands-on time:** *20 minutes.* **Total time:** *20 minutes.*

Leaving the skins on the potatoes maximizes their nutrition and flavor. And tossing them with extra-virgin olive oil, goat cheese and herbs creates a much lighter side-dish than if you were to mash them with full-fat milk, cream or butter.

INGREDIENTS:

- 2 redskin potatoes, cut into 1-inch pieces
- 1 zucchini, sliced into ½-inch rounds
- 1 medium onion, sliced into ½-inch rounds
- 3 tsp extra-virgin olive oil, divided
- 4 cloves garlic, chopped into slivers
- ¾ lb extra-lean ground pork
- 1 cup frozen peas
- 1 cup frozen corn
- 1 Tbsp sweet paprika
- 1 red bell pepper, minced
- 1 medium tomato, chopped
- Juice of ½ lemon
- ½ tsp dried sage
- ½ tsp dried thyme
- Sea salt and fresh ground black pepper, to taste
- 1 oz goat cheese

INSTRUCTIONS:

ONE: Fill a medium pot with water and bring to a boil. Add potatoes, cover, reduce heat to medium-low and cook for 10 minutes. Pierce potatoes with a knife to make sure they're tender, then remove from heat and drain.

TWO: While potatoes are cooking, sauté zucchini and onion in half of the oil over medium heat for three minutes. Add garlic and cook for another minute, stirring constantly to prevent garlic from burning. Stir in pork, peas, corn and paprika. Cook for five more minutes, making sure all ingredients are evenly distributed across surface of pan.

THREE: Remove pork mixture from heat and stir in bell pepper, tomato and lemon juice. Cover with lid to keep warm while finishing potatoes.

FOUR: Gently toss potatoes with remaining oil. Add sage and thyme and season with salt and black pepper. Place about a half-cup potatoes alongside a quarter of pork mixture on each plate, then crumble a quarter of cheese over top of each dish before serving.

Nutrients per serving (½ cup potato, 1½ cups vegetables, 3 oz pork, ¼ oz cheese): *Calories: 350, Total Fat: 9 g, Sat. Fat: 3 g, Carbs: 35 g, Fiber: 6 g, Sugars: 6 g, Protein: 33 g, Sodium: 156 mg, Cholesterol: 26 mg*

Asian Lettuce Cups

Serves 4. **Hands-on time:** *20 minutes.* **Total time:** *20 minutes.*

Romaine lettuce leaves make these Asian Lettuce Cups a crispy appetizer to easily eat out of hand when mingling at your next get-together. Or try serving the individual portions as a side to a stir-fry entrée for a complete Asian-inspired meal.

INGREDIENTS:

LETTUCE CUPS

- 4 Romaine lettuce leaves
- 2 cups bean sprouts
- 2 green onions, sliced
- 2 celery stalks, cut into strips (about 2 x ¼-inch)
- 2 medium carrots, peeled and cut into strips (about 2 x ¼-inch)
- ½ cup baby corn, chopped
- ¼ cup chopped cooked or raw broccoli
- ¼ cup cooked, sliced asparagus (½-inch slices)
- 2 Tbsp chopped fresh cilantro
- Sea salt and fresh ground black pepper, to taste (optional)
- 1 recipe Rice Vinegar & Wasabi Dressing (about ¼ cup; at right)
- 2 Tbsp chopped unsalted peanuts

RICE VINEGAR & WASABI DRESSING:

- 2 Tbsp rice vinegar
- 1 Tbsp extra-virgin olive oil
- ½ tsp wasabi paste (or to taste)
- ½ tsp pure sesame oil
- ¼ tsp toasted unsalted sesame seeds
- Sea salt, to taste

INSTRUCTIONS:

ONE: Wash and trim lettuce and arrange leaves on four individual serving plates.

TWO: In a medium-sized mixing bowl, combine sprouts, onions, celery, carrots, corn, broccoli, asparagus and cilantro, and season with salt and pepper, if desired. Add Rice Vinegar & Wasabi Dressing and toss to combine.

THREE: Divide vegetable mixture evenly among lettuce leaves and top each with half a tablespoon of peanuts. Serve immediately.

INSTRUCTIONS (RICE VINEGAR & WASABI DRESSING):

Whisk together in a small mixing bowl until blended. Refrigerate until serving or use immediately.

Nutrients per 1 cup salad (including 1 Tbsp dressing): *Calories: 160, Total Fat: 10 g, Sat. Fat: 1.5 g, Carbs: 14 g, Fiber: 3 g, Sugars: 3 g Protein: 7 g, Sodium: 140 mg, Cholesterol: 0 mg*

Country-Fried Steak
WITH MUSHROOM GRAVY

Serves 4. ***Hands-on time:*** *10 minutes.* ***Total time:*** *20 minutes.*

You'll love our healthy take on this Southern classic!

INGREDIENTS:

- ½ oz dried porcini or shiitake mushrooms
- 1 lb lean round steak, trimmed of fat and cut into 4 equal pieces (about 4 oz each)
- Sea salt and ground black pepper, to taste
- 3 Tbsp whole-wheat flour, divided
- 2 large egg whites
- 4 slices whole-wheat toast, crusts removed and toast cut into 2-inch pieces
- 1 Tbsp dried minced onion
- 1 tsp dried oregano
- 1 tsp dried thyme
- ½ tsp garlic powder
- 3 tsp olive oil, divided
- 6 oz cremini mushrooms, thinly sliced
- 1 cup low-sodium beef broth
- ½ cup 1% milk

INSTRUCTIONS:

ONE: Place dried mushrooms in a bowl and pour half-cup boiling water over top. Let stand 10 to 15 minutes.

TWO: Using a meat mallet, rolling pin or bottom of a heavy skillet, pound steaks to quarter-inch thickness. Season both sides of steaks with salt and pepper. Set aside.

THREE: Place two tablespoons of flour in a shallow dish. Place egg whites in a separate shallow dish. In a food processor, combine toast, onion, oregano, thyme and garlic powder. Process until mixture resembles bread crumbs. Transfer crumbs to a third shallow dish.

FOUR: Add steaks to dish with flour and turn to coat both sides. Shake off excess flour and transfer steaks to egg whites. Turn to coat both sides and transfer steaks to bread-crumb mixture. Again, turn to coat both sides.

FIVE: Heat two teaspoons of oil in a large skillet over medium-high heat. Add steaks and cook two to three minutes per side, until brown on the outside and pink on the inside (cook slightly longer for well-done meat).

SIX: Prepare gravy: Drain rehydrated mushrooms, reserving soaking liquid, and chop mushrooms. Heat remaining teaspoon of oil in a medium saucepan over medium-high heat. Add both chopped and cremini mushrooms and sauté three to five minutes, until mushrooms soften and release liquid. Add reserved mushroom-soaking liquid and beef broth and bring to a simmer. In a medium bowl, whisk together milk and remaining tablespoon of flour. Add milk mixture to mushrooms and simmer three to five minutes, until mixture thickens. Spoon gravy over steaks just before serving.

Nutrients per serving (4 oz steak and ½ cup gravy): Calories: 313, Total Fat: 9 g, Sat. Fat: 3 g, Carbs: 27 g, Fiber: 5 g, Sugars: 5 g, Protein: 35 g, Sodium: 302 mg, Cholesterol: 52 mg

Asparagus Primavera
WITH COUSCOUS, WHITE BEANS & CHAMPAGNE VINAIGRETTE

Serves 4. ***Hands-on time:*** *20 minutes.* ***Total time:*** *20 minutes.*

When spring arrives, and with it fresh young vegetables, it's a perfect time to make a primavera dish. (*Primavera* means "spring" in both Spanish and Italian.) Not only is this vegetarian dinner rich in complete protein thanks to the complementary pairing of grains and beans, it's also chock-full of antioxidants and fiber.

INGREDIENTS:

- 1½ cups dry whole-grain couscous
- 1 lb asparagus, rinsed and bottom thirds snapped off (stalks will naturally snap when you bend them)
- 8 oz carrots, cut into 2-inch-long sticks
- 4 oz baby corn, cut in half lengthwise
- 15 oz cooked white Northern beans or 1 (15-oz) can white Northern beans, drained and rinsed well (NOTE: Look for beans that are packed in bisphenol-A-free cans, such as Eden Organic Great Northern Beans.)
- 2 cups loosely packed baby spinach, cut into strips
- 2 Tbsp extra-virgin olive oil
- 2 Tbsp champagne vinegar
- 2 Tbsp fresh orange juice
- 1 tsp dried dill or 1 Tbsp fresh dill, plus additional dill for garnish
- Sea salt and fresh ground black pepper, to taste
- ¼ cup grated Parmesan cheese

INSTRUCTIONS:

ONE: Fill a shallow pot with about one inch of water and bring to a boil.

TWO: In a separate medium pot, bring one-and-a-half cups of water to a boil, then add couscous. Remove from heat, stir and cover. Couscous will be ready in five minutes.

THREE: Use a vegetable peeler to peel the bottom half of the asparagus (after you've snapped off bottom third). Cut stalks in half. Place carrots and asparagus into shallow pot of boiling water, reduce heat to low, cover and simmer for five minutes. Remove from heat and drain immediately.

FOUR: In a large salad bowl, toss corn with remaining ingredients, except Parmesan. Add asparagus and carrots and toss again.

FIVE: To serve, fluff couscous with a fork before spooning about one cup couscous onto each of four plates. Spoon salad over top, dividing evenly, and garnish with Parmesan and a little dill, if desired.

Nutrients per 1½-cup serving: Calories: 462, Total Fat: 10 g, Sat. Fat: 2 g, Carbs: 76 g, Fiber: 16 g, Sugars: 6 g, Protein: 21 g, Sodium: 252 mg, Cholesterol: 5 mg

Asparagus Primavera

Thai
Coconut
Shrimp

Thai Coconut Shrimp
WITH BROWN RICE PASTA

*Serves 4. **Hands-on time:** 20 minutes. **Total time:** 20 minutes.*

Thai cuisine is beloved for its pungent flavors and fiery curries. In this noodle bowl, we've used the sweet creaminess of light coconut milk and the good-for-you monounsaturated fat of natural peanut butter to balance the sharper tastes of garlic, ginger and spicy red pepper.

INGREDIENTS:

- 8 oz dry brown rice noodles or pasta of your choice
- 2 cups broccoli florets
- ⅔ cup light coconut milk (shaken to combine)
- 1 Tbsp tomato paste
- 3 Tbsp natural peanut butter with sea salt
- 1 tsp ground ginger
- 4 cloves garlic, minced
- ¼ tsp red pepper flakes
- Juice of ½ lime
- 1 red bell pepper, sliced into thin strips
- 1 cup bean sprouts
- 24 medium raw shrimp, peeled, deveined and rinsed under cold running water

INSTRUCTIONS:

ONE: Bring two medium pots of water to a boil over high heat. In one pot, cook pasta according to package directions, then rinse with hot water to ensure pasta doesn't get sticky when left to stand. (NOTE: Hot water washes away the starch better than cold water.) Fluff pasta with your fingers or a fork to further de-clump noodles, then set aside. In the second pot of boiling water, add broccoli, cover, turn heat down to low and simmer for five minutes. Drain and set aside.

TWO: Meanwhile, in a bowl, add coconut milk, tomato paste, peanut butter, ginger, garlic, pepper flakes and lime juice. Use a fork or whisk to thoroughly combine.

THREE: Simmer coconut mixture, bell pepper and bean sprouts in a nonstick pan over medium-low heat for five minutes, stirring often to prevent clumping. Add shrimp and cook for another two minutes, then flip shrimp over and continue to cook for a final minute.

FOUR: Toss noodles and broccoli with coconut-shrimp mixture and serve piping hot.

Nutrients per serving (½ cup pasta, 6 shrimp, 1 cup vegetables, 3 Tbsp coconut sauce): Calories: 338, Total Fat: 9 g, Sat. Fat: 2 g, Carbs: 48 g, Fiber: 6 g, Sugars: 2.5 g, Protein: 20 g, Sodium: 286 mg, Cholesterol: 55 mg

Shrimp, Edamame & Cellophane Noodle Salad

*Serves 4. **Hands-on time:** 15 minutes. **Total time:** 20 minutes.*

Cellophane noodles are also known as "bean thread" or "mung bean" noodles or sticks. Popular in stir-fries and soups, you'll love their texture in this East-Asian-inspired salad.

INGREDIENTS:

- 2½ Tbsp balsamic vinegar
- 2 Tbsp low-sodium soy sauce
- 1 Tbsp agave nectar
- 2 cloves garlic, smashed
- 12 oz raw shrimp, peeled and deveined
- 8 oz dried cellophane noodle
- 1½ cups shelled edamame (unthawed if frozen)
- 1 Tbsp refined safflower oil
- 3 shallots, sliced into ¼-inch pieces
- ¼ cup sunflower sprouts

INSTRUCTIONS:

ONE: In a small bowl, combine vinegar, soy sauce and agave. Set aside.

TWO: Fill a large pot with water. Add garlic and bring to a boil over high heat. Remove from heat and add shrimp and noodles. Cover and let stand until shrimp are barely opaque, about three minutes. Stir in edamame. Drain, rinse with cold water and drain again. Remove garlic and set aside.

THREE: In a large wok or skillet, heat oil over medium-high heat until it shimmers. Add shallots and stir-fry for two minutes, until tender. Remove wok from heat and stir in vinegar mixture. Stir in noodle mixture.

FOUR: Serve warm or at room temperature, topped with sprouts.

Nutrients per 1-cup serving: Calories: 290, Total Fat: 7 g, Sat. Fat: 0.5 g, Carbs: 30 g, Fiber: 3 g, Sugars: 7 g, Protein: 25 g, Sodium: 455 mg, Cholesterol: 129 mg

NUTRITIONAL BONUS: While you might be aware that edamame, or soybeans, are high in protein, you might not know that their folate content is super high, with half a cup (prepared from frozen) providing over 60 percent of your recommended daily intake. Folate, also known as vitamin B9 or folic acid, is particularly important for unborn children. In kids and adults, folate deficiency can affect cell regeneration and even lead to anemia.

Tricolore Linguine with Sun-Dried Tomatoes

Serves 4. ***Hands-on time:*** *20 minutes.* ***Total Time:*** *20 minutes.*

INGREDIENTS:

- 2 cups fresh green peas (or 1 cup green peas and 1 cup edamame)
- 1 lb tricolored whole-wheat linguine
- 6 Tbsp extra-virgin olive oil
- 6 cloves garlic, peeled and minced
- 2 shallots, peeled and minced
- 1 cup chopped sundried tomatoes, not in oil
- ½ cup low-sodium, low-fat chicken or vegetable broth
- Sea salt and freshly ground pepper to taste
- ½ cup chopped fresh Italian parsley

INSTRUCTIONS:

ONE: Flash-cook peas and/or edamame until just tender but firm. Drain and set aside. Cook pasta al dente. Drain.

TWO: In a large skillet, sauté garlic and shallots in olive oil. Add sundried tomatoes, peas and chicken broth. Bring to a boil. Remove from heat and immediately add drained pasta to the skillet. Toss lightly until sauce and vegetables cover the linguine.

THREE: Add sea salt and freshly ground black pepper and garnish with chopped Italian parsley.

Nutrients per serving: *Calories: 490, Total Fat: 17 g, Sat. Fat: 3 g, Carbs: 75 g, Fiber: 11 g, Sugars: 7 g, Protein: 17 g, Sodium: 257 mg, Cholesterol: 0 mg*

Curried Chicken Salad
WITH TROPICAL FRUIT

Serves 4. ***Hands-on time:*** *20 minutes.* ***Total time:*** *20 minutes.*

This protein-packed salad couldn't be easier on your schedule – or zingier on your taste buds. It also happens to be high in vitamin C.

INGREDIENTS:

- ¼ cup low-fat yogurt
- Juice of ½ lime
- ½ tsp curry powder
- ½ (15-oz) can mixed tropical fruit packed in juice, unsweetened, drained
- 1 leftover cooked chicken breast, diced into 1-inch pieces
- 1 bag pre-washed mixed greens

INSTRUCTIONS:

ONE: In a small bowl, stir together yogurt, lime juice and curry powder.

TWO: Place tropical fruit and chicken breast in a medium mixing bowl. Add yogurt dressing and stir to coat.

THREE: Divide mixed greens between four plates and top each with chicken salad.

Nutrients per serving: *Calories: 134, Total Fat: 2 g, Sat. Fat: 1 g, Carbs: 11.5 g, Fiber: 2 g, Sugars: 9 g, Protein: 16 g, Sodium: 60 mg, Cholesterol: 39 mg*

TIP: Use the leftover Curried Chicken Salad to fill a wrap, pita or hollowed-out submarine bun for a quick and easy brown-bag lunch!

Nutritional Bonus

This fruity entrée contains 30 milligrams of vitamin C, almost 50 percent of the recommended daily amount. Vitamin C aids in the body's absorption of iron.

Curried Chicken Salad

56

Sautéed
Halibut

Nutritional Bonus:

**Halibut is truly a nutrient-dense
fish. Not only does it provide
omega-3 fatty acids, which offer
a broad array of cardiovascular
benefits, but it also supplies a
significant dose of important
minerals, including magnesium,
selenium, phosphorous
and potassium.**

Sautéed Halibut

WITH ARTICHOKE HEARTS, CHERRY TOMATOES
& CANNELLINI BEANS

Serves 4. *Hands-on time:* 20 minutes. *Total time:* 20 minutes.

Halibut and tomatoes are a match made in heaven. This summery recipe tastes light and refreshing, but the halibut and hearty beans pack an extra punch of protein.

INGREDIENTS:

- 2 tsp olive oil, divided
- 4 (5-oz) halibut fillets, skin removed
- Sea salt and fresh ground black pepper, to taste
- 2 cloves garlic, minced
- 1 to 1½ cups cooked cannellini beans (15-oz can, drained and rinsed)
- 1 cup frozen artichoke hearts, thawed
- 2 tsp capers, drained and chopped
- ¼ cup low-sodium chicken or vegetable broth
- 1 cup halved cherry tomatoes
- 2 Tbsp thinly sliced fresh basil
- Juice of ½ lemon

INSTRUCTIONS:

ONE: Heat one teaspoon oil in a large nonstick skillet over medium-high heat. Season halibut on both sides with salt and pepper then place in pan, presentation-side-down. Cook for three to four minutes per side, or until halibut begins to turn opaque in the middle. Remove from pan, set aside and cover to keep warm while standing.

TWO: Add remaining one teaspoon oil, garlic, beans and artichoke hearts to skillet over medium-high heat; season with salt and pepper. Cook until garlic is fragrant, and beans and artichokes are heated through, about three minutes. Stir in capers and broth, then remove skillet from heat.

THREE: Add tomatoes and basil, tossing to combine. Taste and make adjustments to seasoning, if desired.

FOUR: To serve, divide bean mixture equally among four plates, place each halibut fillet overtop and finish with lemon juice.

TIP: We've opted for cooked beans instead of canned to avoid chemicals such as bisphenol A (BPA), which may be hiding in the can's lining and can leach into your food. If you're running short on time, feel free to go with canned beans but take a few safe-guarding steps: Look for brands that choose BPA-free cans for their produce, such as Eden Foods. And remember to drain and rinse the beans well first.

Nutrients per serving (5 oz halibut, ¾ cup bean mixture): *Calories: 308, Total Fat: 6 g, Sat. Fat: 0.7 g, Carbs: 24 g, Fiber: 9 g, Sugars: 3.5 g, Protein: 38 g, Sodium: 668 mg, Cholesterol: 46 mg*

Quick White Bean & Spinach Ravioli

Serves 4. *Hands-on Time:* 15 minutes. *Total Time:* 15 minutes.

The canned ravioli and pastas your kids may love are, unfortunately, loaded with sodium, unhealthy fats and a long list of unpronounceable ingredients. You can do much better with homemade ravioli. Wonton wrappers, which are usually found in the produce section at grocery stores, are essentially fresh pasta squares. Just fill and seal them, cook and toss with your kids' favorite pasta sauce.

INGREDIENTS:

- ¼ cup frozen chopped spinach
- ½ cup cannellini (white kidney) beans
- ½ cup reduced-fat ricotta cheese
- 2 Tbsp shredded reduced-fat mozzarella cheese
- ¼ tsp kosher salt
- 32 square wonton wrappers
- 1 cup unsalted or reduced-sodium tomato sauce

INSTRUCTIONS:

ONE: Fill a medium saucepan with hot water; cover and bring to a boil.

TWO: While water is heating, defrost the spinach in a microwave oven. Squeeze as much water as you can out of the thawed spinach and place in the bowl of a food processor. Add the beans, cheeses and salt. Process the bean and cheese mixture until smooth, approximately one minute. You should have approximately three-quarters cup of ravioli filling.

THREE: Fill a small bowl with warm water. Lay out 16 wonton wrappers. Dip your finger in the water and moisten edges of each wrapper. Place one teaspoon of bean-and-cheese filling in center of each square. From the leftover 16 wrappers, take another wrapper, place it on top of filling, and seal by pressing firmly along edges of ravioli. Repeat until all wrappers or filling are used up.

FOUR: Gently place ravioli in boiling water and cook for approximately two minutes. The ravioli is ready when you can see the green of the filling through the wrappers. While pasta cooks, warm tomato sauce in a small saucepan. Drain pasta, place four ravioli on each plate, and top with a quarter-cup of sauce.

Nutrients per 4 ravioli and ¼-cup sauce: *Calories: 343, Total Fat: 3 g, Sat. Fat: 1 g, Carbs: 60 g, Fiber: 6 g, Sugars: 4 g, Protein: 18 g, Sodium: 621 mg, Cholesterol: 17 mg*

NUTRITIONAL BONUS: The wonton wrappers and cannellini (white kidney) beans in the filling give kids a good boost of protein. And because the beans have been blended, your children won't complain about the texture.

Mixed Mushrooms, Bok Choy & Black Bean Sauce
WITH SOBA NOODLES

Serves 4. *Hands-on time:* 10 minutes. *Total time:* 20 minutes.

INGREDIENTS:

- 6 oz no-salt-added buckwheat soba noodles
- 2 Tbsp refined safflower oil, divided
- ¾ cup low-sodium chicken or vegetable stock
- 2 Tbsp prepared, all-natural black bean garlic sauce
- 1 Tbsp low-sodium soy sauce
- 1 Tbsp arrowroot powder
- ½ onion, halved and cut into ¼-inch slices
- 4 heads baby bok choy (about 12 oz), sliced crosswise into ½-inch pieces
- 1 portobello mushroom, halved and sliced into ¼-inch pieces
- 8 shiitake mushrooms, stemmed and thinly sliced
- 8 large cremini (brown) or white mushrooms, thinly sliced
- 2 oz enoki mushrooms
- 4 green onions, including half of greens, thinly sliced on the diagonal

INSTRUCTIONS:

ONE: Cook noodles according to package directions. Drain and return to pot. Toss with one tablespoon oil, cover and set aside.

TWO: In a small bowl, combine stock, black bean sauce, soy sauce and arrowroot. Set aside.

THREE: In a large wok or skillet, heat remaining oil over medium-high heat until it shimmers. Add onion and stir-fry for one minute. Add bok choy and stir-fry for one minute. Add portobello mushroom and stir-fry for one minute. Add shiitake and cremini mushrooms, and stir-fry for two minutes, or until all mushrooms in wok are tender. Add stock mixture and enoki mushrooms. Cook, stirring occasionally, until sauce comes to a boil and thickens, about one minute.

FOUR: Serve stir-fry over noodles, sprinkled with green onions.

Nutrients per 2-cup serving: *Calories: 296, Total Fat: 8 g, Sat. Fat: 0.5 g, Monounsaturated Fat: 5.5 g, Polyunsaturated Fat: 1 g, Carbs: 51 g, Fiber: 6 g, Sugars: 7 g, Protein: 9 g, Sodium: 621 mg, Cholesterol: 0 mg*

NUTRITIONAL BONUS: Mushrooms – and this recipe is loaded with them! – are a great source of selenium, an essential trace mineral thought to help fight cancer and contribute to a healthy immune system.

Chicken & Summer Vegetable Cacciatore
WITH POLENTA

Serves 6. *Hands-on time:* 25 minutes. *Total time:* 25 minutes.

Cacciatore means "hunter" in Italian. Cooking *"alla cacciatore"* refers to a meal prepared hunter-style, usually with herbs, tomatoes, bell peppers and other seasonal vegetables. We've teamed this classic with ever-versatile polenta, a dish made of boiled cornmeal that is a staple in the Northern Italian diet.

INGREDIENTS:

CACCIATORE

- 2 tsp olive oil, divided
- 2 (4-oz) boneless, skinless chicken breasts, cut into ½-inch chunks
- Sea salt and ground black pepper, to taste
- 1 small zucchini, sliced into ¼-inch pieces
- 1 small yellow squash, sliced into ¼-inch pieces
- 1 red bell pepper, thinly sliced
- 1 orange bell pepper, thinly sliced
- 2 cloves garlic, minced
- 2 tomatoes, cores removed and sliced into ½-inch chunks
- ½ cup low-sodium chicken broth
- 1 Tbsp finely chopped fresh oregano
- ¼ cup thinly sliced fresh basil

POLENTA

- 2 cups low-sodium chicken broth
- 1 cup polenta
- Sea salt and ground black pepper, to taste

INSTRUCTIONS:

ONE: Prepare cacciatore: Heat one teaspoon oil in a large nonstick skillet over medium-high heat. Season chicken with salt and black pepper and place chicken in skillet in a single layer. Cook, turning once, until no pink remains, about five minutes. Remove chicken and set aside.

TWO: Return skillet to medium-high heat and add remaining one teaspoon oil. Add zucchini, squash, bell peppers and garlic; season with salt and black pepper. Sauté vegetables until they start to soften, about three to five minutes.

THREE: Return chicken to skillet. Add tomatoes, half cup broth and oregano; stir to combine. Simmer for five minutes, until vegetables are cooked and flavors melded.

Continued ▶

FOUR: Meanwhile, prepare polenta: Bring two cups broth and two cups water to a boil in a medium saucepan over high heat. Add polenta, reduce heat to low and whisk until polenta has absorbed all liquid and is cooked, five minutes. Season with salt and black pepper.

FIVE: To serve, divide polenta evenly into six large, shallow serving bowls, top with equal amounts cacciatore mixture and sprinkle with basil. Serve immediately.

Nutrients per serving ($^2/_3$ cup polenta, 1 cup chicken and veggies with sauce):
Calories: 115, Total Fat: 5 g, Sat. Fat: 0.8 g, Carbs: 6 g, Fiber: 1.7 g, Sugars: 3.8 g, Protein: 10 g, Sodium: 169 mg, Cholesterol: 22 mg

Chicken & Summer Vegetable Cacciatore

Nutritional Bonus:

Cumin provides iron, which helps deliver oxygen to your cells. Not getting enough of the mineral can result in fatigue and low immunity.

Chinese
Five Spice
Flank Steak

Chinese Five Spice Flank Steak
WITH GRILLED PEPPERS

*Serves 4. **Hands-on time:** 20 minutes. **Total time:** 20 minutes.*

Typically used as a rub for fattier meats, Chinese Five Spice powder is a mixture of five spices: anise, cloves, cinnamon, Sichuan pepper and ground fennel, each with a very distinct flavor. Sweet, sour, bitter, pungent and salty come together harmoniously to bring an East Asian flair to your traditional steak. This powder is intense and can overwhelm a dish, so be sure to use sparingly!

INGREDIENTS:

- 1 (1-lb) flank steak, trimmed of any visible fat
- 2 tsp olive oil, divided
- Sea salt and fresh ground black pepper, to taste
- 1 tsp Chinese Five Spice powder
- 1 tsp ground cumin
- 1 tsp garlic powder
- 1 red bell pepper, sliced
- 1 yellow bell pepper, sliced
- ¼ cup fresh cilantro leaves

INSTRUCTIONS:

ONE: Heat a grill or grill pan to medium-high heat. Coat both sides of steak with one teaspoon oil and season with salt and black pepper. In a small bowl, combine Five Spice powder, cumin and garlic powder; rub spice mixture on both sides of steak.

TWO: Place steak on grill or grill pan and cook, turning once, for about two minutes per side for medium doneness (steak will be slightly pink but not red in center). Remove steak from heat and let rest for at least five minutes.

THREE: In a large bowl, toss bell peppers with remaining one teaspoon oil and season with salt and black pepper. Add bell peppers to grill or grill pan and cook on medium-high until slightly soft, two minutes per side (if using grill pan, wipe clean with paper towel first).

FOUR: Transfer steak to a cutting board and thinly slice against the grain. To serve, place bell peppers on a plate, arrange steak on top and garnish with cilantro.

Nutrients per serving (4 oz steak, ½ cup peppers): Calories: 236, Total Fat: 11 g, Sat. Fat: 3.8 g, Carbs: 6 g, Fiber: 1.4 g, Sugars: 2 g, Protein: 26 g, Sodium: 238 mg, Cholesterol: 45 mg

Thai-Style Tofu & Noodles

*Serves 4. **Hands-on time:** 15 minutes. **Total time:** 20 minutes.*

Imagine the rich flavor of a creamy, spicy peanut sauce over noodles and fire-seared ripe bell peppers. Whole-wheat pasta makes a tantalizing twist with this colorful plate of international fare. Add more or less dried red pepper flakes according to your taste. You can also splash on your favorite hot sauce right at the table.

INGREDIENTS:

TOFU & NOODLES

- 2 quarts, plus 1 Tbsp water
- ½ lb whole-wheat linguine
- Olive oil spray
- 1 (14 oz) pkg extra-firm tofu, drained and cut into ½-inch cubes
- 4 cloves garlic, minced
- 1 tsp low-sodium soy sauce
- 1 medium red pepper, cut into ½-inch slices
- 1 medium green pepper, cut into ½-inch slices
- ⅛ tsp sea salt

INGREDIENTS:

SAUCE

- 2 Tbsp natural, unsalted peanut butter
- ⅓ cup salsa
- ¼ tsp dried red pepper flakes
- ⅓ cup water

INSTRUCTIONS:

ONE: In a large pot, bring two quarts water to a boil; add linguine and cook for about 10 minutes.

TWO: Meanwhile, purée sauce ingredients in a blender for about 15 seconds until creamy; set aside.

THREE: Mist a large nonstick skillet with olive oil spray and place over medium heat. Add tofu and spoon minced garlic and soy sauce evenly over all pieces. Sauté tofu, stirring frequently, for about five minutes.

FOUR: While the tofu is cooking, spray a separate medium nonstick skillet with olive oil spray and place over medium-high heat. Add peppers and sprinkle with salt. Sauté peppers for two to three minutes; pour one tablespoon water into the pan and immediately cover with lid. Cook for three or four minutes, until peppers are tender and slightly blackened.

FIVE: After cooking the tofu for about five minutes and it's golden brown, add sauce and turn heat to low. Gently stir once or twice as sauce thickens, a minute or two. Serve peppers and tofu sauce over linguine.

Nutrients per 1½-cup serving: Calories: 357, Total Fat: 10 g, Sat. Fat: 1 g, Carbs: 52 g, Fiber: 10 g, Sugars: 5 g, Protein: 21 g, Sodium: 209 mg, Cholesterol: 0 mg

Keen on Quinoa

We love quinoa and you should too! Here's everything you need to know about this protein-packed ancient grain.

Tosca Reno, *Clean Eating* columnist and bestselling author of *The Eat-Clean Diet*® series, talks about why you should make sure to keep this quick-cooking superfood in your pantry. Best part? Kids love it!

What is quinoa?

Quinoa (keen-wa) is not really a grain but the seed of the Chenopodium or goosefoot plant. When the plant blooms and turns to seed, the quinoa can be harvested. Thanks to its cooking characteristics, quinoa is then used in much the same way that grains are. It cooks in little time and yields a grain-like dish.

Quinoa seeds look very much like millet and come in many colors, such as red, pink, brown, black and beige. Interestingly, quinoa has its own way of telling you when it is properly cooked: The seed splits open and sends the germ spiraling around each grain. When it comes to cooking quinoa, it is difficult to get it wrong.

Quinoa cooks much like couscous: You boil it briefly to allow the grains to soak up water and then let the cooked mixture stand covered for a few minutes; then you fluff it with a fork and serve. If you are really keen, you can eat the leaves of the quinoa plant as well (steamed or in a salad)!

Why do you recommend quinoa as a good source of protein for vegetarians?

Quinoa contains substantially more protein than any other grain. That is one reason why the United Nations refers to it as a "super crop." Some varieties of quinoa contain as much as 20 percent protein. Compare that with other grains, such as rice, which contains only seven-and-a-half percent.

Additionally, the protein in quinoa is complete. That means that every amino acid – there are 20 in all – appears in quinoa's nutritional profile, with particularly high concentrations of methionine and cysteine. I also like to combine quinoa with other grains such as oats and amaranth to increase the protein value.

The quinoa seed is also high in calcium and iron and is a relatively good source of vitamin E and several of the B vitamins.

I made quinoa but it had a bitter flavor. Did I do something wrong?

The bitter coating on the surface of quinoa is called saponin. Washing or soaking the seeds before using them can easily remove saponin. Simply place the dry, uncooked seeds in a fine mesh sieve and rinse well under cold running water. The presence of saponin will cause soapy bubbles to appear at first, but keep rinsing and soon the bubbles will disappear as the saponin coating is washed away. Then cook as directed.

How do I cook and use quinoa?

Quinoa can be used in stews, soups, pilafs, casseroles, stir-frys and salads (my favorite). It can also be used as a hot breakfast cereal – for those of you who are gluten intolerant, this is a godsend because quinoa is gluten-free. Quinoa seeds cook very quickly, much like couscous. Toast the seeds before cooking for a nuttier flavor. If you toast them long enough in a nonstick pan, the seeds will pop open and, voilà!, you have a dry breakfast cereal. Quinoa can also be ground to make quinoa flour, which can then be added to your baking.

Whole Grains in the Fast Lane

A recent analysis of 15 independent studies published in *Public Health Nutrition* found that people who eat three daily servings of whole grains average one-inch smaller waists. Help lower your weight while reducing your risk of heart disease and diabetes with these four tasty whole grains that cook in 15 minutes or less.

Quinoa

Gluten-free and protein-rich, quinoa "cooks like pasta in 11 to 12 minutes," says Lorna Sass, author of *Whole Grains for Busy People* (Clarkson Potter, 2008). "Toss it with black beans, salsa and chopped avocados."

Whole-Wheat Couscous

This five-minute side provides selenium, magnesium and fiber. For a burst of flavor and vitamin C, replace half the cooking water with 100 percent tomato or orange juice.

Bulgur

"Delicious with sliced apples and dates," says Robin Asbell, author of *The New Whole Grains Cookbook* (Chronicle Books, 2007), medium-grind bulgur steams in 10 minutes and has 10 grams of fiber per quarter-cup.

Teff

Each quarter-cup of this grain has over 20 percent of your daily iron, magnesium and copper. Simmer with low-fat milk for a hot cereal or use the flour for naturally sweet pancakes.

Penne with Creamy
Wild Mushroom Sauce, p. 87

Budget-Priced Meals

Whoever said eating healthy food has to be expensive never met our readers and recipe developers! Month after month, we offer you tasty, wholesome dishes with both your waistline and pocketbook in mind. From dinners for four for under $10 to single servings for $2 or less, clean eating has never been more budget friendly. By using pantry staples such as heart-healthy oils, spices and herbs, you save money (and time) at the grocery store. Go exotic with our Beef & Broccoli Orange Stir-Fry or aim for comfort with our Fish & Chips. Healthy, homemade and economical may sound too good to be true, but we've made it happen!

Tilapia Citrus Couscous Salad

*Serves 6. **Hands-on time:** 20 minutes. **Total time:** 25 minutes.*

Come Friday, you want a meal that is refreshing and refreshingly easy. Our Tilapia Citrus Couscous Salad fits the bill on both counts. The tang of lemon and lime juices will refresh and revitalize your dish, while the couscous and tilapia will fill your family's hungry bellies without overstuffing them.

INGREDIENTS:

- 1 cup dry whole-grain couscous
- Olive oil cooking spray
- ½ lb tilapia fillets (4 small or 2 large), skin and bones removed
- 2 large carrots, peeled and diced
- 1 stalk celery, ends trimmed and finely diced
- 1 medium yellow onion, finely diced
- ½ red bell pepper, cored, seeded and diced
- Zest and juice of 1 lime
- Zest and juice of ½ lemon
- 1 tsp Dijon mustard
- 1 Tbsp extra-virgin olive oil
- 1 clove garlic, minced
- 2 tsp dried parsley
- Sea salt and fresh ground black pepper, to taste

INSTRUCTIONS:

ONE: Cook couscous according to package directions.

TWO: Heat a large nonstick or cast-iron skillet over high heat for one minute. Spritz with cooking spray and reduce heat to medium-high. Place tilapia in skillet and cook for two minutes per side. Remove tilapia and let cool for five minutes before flaking with a fork.

THREE: In a large bowl, combine couscous, tilapia, carrots, celery, onion and bell pepper.

FOUR: In a medium bowl, whisk together lime zest and juice, lemon zest and juice, Dijon mustard, oil, garlic and parsley. Season with salt and black pepper. Pour dressing over tilapia-couscous mixture and stir until well combined. Garnish with additional parsley, if desired. Serve immediately or chill in refrigerator, covered, for up to one day.

Nutrients per 1-cup serving: Calories: 154, Total Fat: 3.5 g, Sat. Fat: 0.5 g, Carbs: 21 g, Fiber: 4 g, Sugars: 3 g, Protein: 11 g, Sodium: 88 mg, Cholesterol: 19 mg

Nutritional Bonus:
Not only are lemons and limes rich in vitamin C, they also contain the antioxidant limonin. The USDA has discovered that limonin may help lower cholesterol levels. Initial studies suggest that the citrus antioxidant may prevent your liver from producing a protein needed in the creation of cholesterol molecules.

Tilapia Citrus Couscous Salad

Nutritional Bonus:
Almonds add more than just crunch and flavor to meals – they're also host to a bevy of healthy minerals, including magnesium and potassium. Magnesium may improve the flow of oxygen and nutrients in the blood throughout the body, while potassium helps you maintain normal blood pressure.

68

Chicken Almondine

Chicken Almondine
WITH LEMON GREEN BEANS

Serves 4. **Hands-on time:** *30 minutes.* **Total time:** *30 minutes.*

Quick and simple, our Chicken Almondine is perfect to whip up on a frenzied weeknight yet elegant enough to serve your company. With savory, nutty almonds accentuating the natural sweetness of the chicken, this versatile dish could easily become a favorite in your household.

INGREDIENTS:

- ¼ cup slivered unsalted almonds, toasted, divided
- 1 Tbsp whole-wheat flour
- ¼ tsp Spanish paprika
- Sea salt and fresh ground black pepper, to taste
- 4 boneless, skinless chicken breasts (1 lb total), pounded to ½-inch thickness
- Olive oil cooking spray
- 1 lb fresh green beans
- Zest of 1 lemon (about 2 to 3 tsp)
- Juice of ½ lemon (about 1 Tbsp)

INSTRUCTIONS:

ONE: Grind half of the almonds to a powder using a food processor fitted with a standard blade or a spice grinder. In a medium bowl, combine ground almonds, flour and paprika. Season with salt and pepper. Dredge chicken breasts in almond-flour mixture and set aside.

TWO: Set a large nonstick or cast-iron skillet over high heat for one minute. Mist with cooking spray and heat for one more minute. Reduce heat to medium-high and sauté chicken for three minutes per side or until golden brown with no pink remaining. Remove from heat.

THREE: Bring a medium pot of water to boil. Add beans and blanch for one minute. Remove beans from water. In a large bowl, toss beans with lemon zest and juice, and season with salt and pepper.

FOUR: To serve, sprinkle remaining eighth-cup almonds over top of chicken, dividing evenly. Serve each chicken breast with three-quarters cup beans.

Nutrients per serving (1 chicken breast, about ½ Tbsp nuts, ¾ cup green beans): *Calories: 220, Total Fat: 6 g, Sat. Fat: 0.75 g, Carbs: 12 g, Fiber: 5 g, Sugars: 2 g, Protein: 30 g, Sodium: 111 mg, Cholesterol: 66 mg*

NOTE: To toast your almonds, add them to a small dry skillet over medium heat (no oil or cooking spray is required). When the skillet is hot, toast almonds for two to five minutes, until browned, stirring frequently and being careful not to burn them. Remove from heat immediately.

Fish & Chips

Serves: 4. **Hands-on time:** *30 minutes.* **Total time:** *45 minutes.*

Our healthy, whole-grain breaded fish and baked chips are so crunchy and delicious that you won't want to return to your previous greasy fish-frying ways. Plus, at under $2 and just 300 calories per serving, these fish and chips beat out any famous fast-food variety.

INGREDIENTS:

- 2 cups cubed multigrain bread
- 1 extra large sweet potato, peeled
- 4 (3- to 4-oz) white fish fillets (such as Alaskan pollock)
- ½ tsp Cajun seasoning or paprika
- Sea salt and fresh ground black pepper, to taste
- 2 egg whites

INSTRUCTIONS:

ONE: Preheat oven to 350°F. Bake bread cubes on a baking sheet for 10 minutes or until toasted. Leave oven on and at the same temperature after they are done.

TWO: Using a food processor fitted with a standard blade, grind bread cubes into about one-and-a-half cups breadcrumbs, about three minutes.

THREE: Using a mandolin, slice sweet potato into paper-thin slices. (If you don't have a mandolin, slice thinly with knife.)

FOUR: Lay sweet potato slices on baking sheets lined with parchment paper or aluminum foil. Bake in preheated oven at 350°F for about eight minutes. Reduce oven to 250°F and continue baking for four to five minutes or until slightly browned and crisp. Makes about four cups chips.

FIVE: Preheat oven to 425°F.

SIX: Sprinkle fillets with seasoning, salt and pepper. Place egg whites in one bowl and breadcrumbs in another. Dip fillets into egg white, then roll in breadcrumbs and place into shallow cooking pan. Bake for six minutes. Serve each fillet with one cup of chips.

Nutrients per serving (1 fillet and 1 cup chips): *Calories: 300, Total Fat: 5 g, Sat. Fat: 1 g, Carbs: 44 g, Fiber: 4 g, Sugars: 5 g, Protein: 14 g, Sodium: 640 mg, Cholesterol: 80 mg*

Ginger Tofu Stir-Fry Rice Bowl

*Serves 6. **Hands-on time:** 30 minutes. **Total time:** 45 minutes.*

Our Ginger Tofu Stir-Fry sings with fresh vegetables and is spiked with crispy, savory tofu cubes for protein. And each serving provides only one gram of saturated fat!

INGREDIENTS:

- 1½ cups brown rice
- 4 Tbsp whole-wheat flour
- 1½ tsp onion powder
- 1 tsp garlic powder
- ⅛ tsp cayenne pepper
- 2 tsp ginger powder, divided
- 14 oz firm low-fat tofu, cut into cubes
- Olive oil cooking spray
- ½ red bell pepper, cored, seeded and julienned
- 1 carrot, peeled and julienned
- 1 stalk celery, chopped
- 1 yellow onion, diced
- 6 oz frozen snow peas
- 2 Tbsp low-sodium tamari soy sauce
- 1 Tbsp rice or apple cider vinegar

INSTRUCTIONS:

ONE: Cook brown rice according to package directions.

TWO: Meanwhile, in a small bowl, stir together flour, onion powder, garlic powder, cayenne and one teaspoon ginger powder. Dredge each tofu cube in flour mixture and set aside.

THREE: Set large nonstick or cast-iron skillet over high heat for one minute. Mist with cooking spray and heat for one more minute. Reduce heat to medium-high and sauté tofu for about three to five minutes, flipping halfway through, until lightly browned. Remove tofu from skillet and set aside.

FOUR: Mist same pan with cooking spray. Sauté bell pepper, carrot, celery, onion and pea pods until cooked, about three to four minutes. (TIP: The pea pods and other veggies are cooked when they turn a brighter shade.)

FIVE: In another small bowl, whisk together remaining teaspoon ginger powder, soy sauce and vinegar. Reduce heat of skillet with vegetables to medium-low and pour soy sauce mixture on top of vegetables. Add tofu to vegetables and cook for about two minutes. Remove from heat. Serve one cup vegetable-tofu mixture over a half-cup rice in individual bowls.

Nutrients per serving (1 cup vegetable-tofu mixture and ½ cup cooked rice): *Calories: 284, Total Fat: 5 g, Sat. Fat: 1 g, Carbs: 48 g, Fiber: 4 g, Sugars: 4 g, Protein: 12 g, Sodium: 357 mg, Cholesterol: 0 mg*

Nutritional Bonus:
Ginger has long been used as a digestive aid, but recent research has shown its effects are much greater than that. Studies at the University of Michigan and the University of Minnesota have found ginger induces cell death in ovarian cancer cells and slows the growth of colorectal cancer cells. Many studies have confirmed its value as an anti-inflammatory agent.

Lean Tofu Pad Thai

*Serves: 8. **Hands-on time:** 30 minutes. **Total time:** 30 minutes.*

Pad Thai is perhaps the most well-known Thai dish outside of Thailand, and its name literally means "Thai-style frying." Our lean and budget-conscious version includes brown rice noodles and additional vegetables for a fiber and antioxidant boost.

INGREDIENTS:

- 8 oz brown rice noodles
- 4 Tbsp unsalted tomato paste
- 4 Tbsp apple cider vinegar
- 3 Tbsp honey
- 2 Tbsp Thai fish sauce
- 1 Tbsp fresh lime juice
- ⅛ tsp cayenne pepper
- Olive oil cooking spray
- 1 egg white, whisked
- 2 cups chopped green cabbage
- 1 cup bean sprouts
- 2 green onions, julienned or thinly sliced lengthwise
- 1 large carrot, peeled and julienned or cut into thin matchstick pieces
- 12 oz firm tofu, cubed
- ¼ cup minced cilantro
- 2 Tbsp crushed unsalted peanuts
- Lime wedges and additional cilantro, for garnish (optional)

INSTRUCTIONS:

ONE: Cook brown rice noodles according to package directions. Drain and set aside.

TWO: In a small bowl, whisk together tomato paste, vinegar, honey, fish sauce, lime juice and cayenne. Set aside.

THREE: Heat a large cast-iron or nonstick pan or wok over medium-high heat for one minute. Mist with cooking spray. Add egg white and sauté until cooked, about two minutes. Remove egg white from heat and dice into small pieces.

FOUR: In the same pan, misted again with cooking spray, sauté cabbage, bean sprouts, onions and carrot over medium-high heat for two minutes. Add tofu and cook for another two minutes. Add cooked egg white and cilantro, sautéing for another two minutes. Then stir in tomato paste mixture. Add cooked noodles. Stir until completely combined and thoroughly heated, about three to four more minutes.

FIVE: Remove from heat and toss with peanuts before serving. Garnish with lime wedges and additional cilantro, if desired.

Nutrients per 1-cup serving: Calories: 220, Total Fat: 4 g, Sat. Fat: 0 g, Carbs: 38 g, Fiber: 4 g, Sugars: 11 g, Protein: 11 g, Sodium: 510 mg, Cholesterol: 0 mg

NOTE: Traditional Pad Thai uses tamarind paste and rice vinegar, which can both be found at Asian markets. Since tamarind paste is not as readily available at many grocery stores, we've come up with a tomato-paste mixture that will give our version of this Asian classic the perfect sweet-and-sour balance. And, to keep grocery costs down, we've opted to use a pantry staple such as apple cider vinegar instead of authentic rice vinegar. Don't worry, no one will notice the difference!

Chicken Pomodoro Angel Hair Pasta

Serves 4. **Hands-on time:** *30 minutes.* **Total time:** *30 minutes.*

Pomodoro literally means tomato in Italian and that's what this dish is all about: ripe, red tomatoes bursting with flavor and nutrients. The addition of carrots to our sauce helps enhance the sweetness of the tomatoes.

INGREDIENTS:

- 12 oz whole-wheat angel hair pasta
- 3 carrots, peeled and roughly chopped
- Olive oil cooking spray
- 4 boneless, skinless chicken breasts (about 4 oz each), pounded thin
- 1 medium yellow onion, finely diced
- 3 cloves garlic, minced
- 2 lb fresh tomatoes, preferably Roma, seeded and coarsely chopped
- 1 tsp Italian seasoning
- 2 Tbsp dried basil
- Sea salt and fresh ground black pepper, to taste
- 2 oz low-fat feta cheese, crumbled
- 4 Tbsp minced Italian flat-leaf parsley

INSTRUCTIONS:

ONE: Cook pasta according to package directions. Drain and set aside but keep warm.

TWO: Bring a large pot of water to a boil. Place steamer basket in pot and steam carrots in basket for eight minutes or until tender. Remove carrots from steamer and set aside.

THREE: Set a large nonstick or cast-iron skillet over high heat for one minute. Mist with cooking spray and add chicken. Sauté for about three to four minutes per side or until browned on each side and cooked through until no longer pink. Remove chicken from heat and let rest for one minute before cutting into half-inch chunks.

FOUR: Heat same large nonstick or cast-iron skillet again over high heat for one minute. Reduce heat to medium, mist skillet with cooking spray and add onion and garlic. Sauté for about five minutes or until onion is translucent. Add tomatoes and cook for another five minutes. Remove from heat.

Nutritional Bonus:
Before digging deep into your wallet for that expensive anti-aging face cream, try stocking up on tomatoes. One single tomato contains 20 percent of your recommended daily amount of vitamin A, which helps form and maintain healthy skin, not to mention teeth and skeletal and soft tissue.

FIVE: In a food processor fitted with a standard blade, roughly purée carrots and onion-tomato mixture or pulse for about two to three minutes. Pour sauce into a medium-size pot and heat over medium heat. Stir in Italian seasoning and basil and season with salt and pepper. Add chicken and cook for another two minutes before removing from heat.

SIX: Divide pasta among four bowls or plates. Pour one cup chicken-tomato sauce over each portion of pasta. Sprinkle each with about two teaspoons of feta and garnish with one tablespoon of parsley.

Nutrients per serving (1 cup sauce and 4 oz pasta): Calories: 554, Total Fat: 6 g, Sat. Fat: 2 g, Carbs: 82 g, Fiber: 13 g, Sugars: 12 g, Protein: 43 g, Sodium: 362 mg, Cholesterol: 70 mg

Nutritional Bonus:
Munching on broccoli is a smart move to help strengthen your immunity, and it's not simply because of the vitamin C content. The super-green is also a good source of the water-soluble vitamin B6, which aids the immune system in producing antibodies.

Beef & Broccoli Orange Stir-Fry
OVER SOBA NOODLES

*Serves 6. **Hands-on time:** 45 minutes. **Total time:** 45 minutes.*

Fast and simple stir-frys can be a winning solution for time-crunched families. But emptying your wok or skillet over the usual brown rice gets a bit boring, so we've opted for buckwheat-rich soba noodles instead.

INGREDIENTS:

- 12 oz soba noodles
- Olive oil cooking spray
- 1 lb lean round steak, pounded to ¼-inch thickness and sliced into strips
- ½ cup diced white onion
- 2 cups fresh broccoli florets, separated into bite-size pieces
- ½ red bell pepper, julienne cut
- 3 Tbsp low-sodium tamari soy sauce
- Juice of 1 medium orange
- 1 Tbsp orange zest
- 2 cloves garlic, minced
- 2 tsp raw organic honey
- 2 tsp whole-wheat flour

INSTRUCTIONS:

ONE: Cook noodles according to package directions. Drain and set aside.

TWO: Heat large nonstick or cast-iron skillet over high heat for one minute. Reduce heat to medium-high, mist pan with cooking spray and sauté steak for about five minutes or until cooked through. (For medium doneness, the steak will still be slightly pink in the middle.) Remove steak, leaving juices in the pan.

THREE: Mist same pan again with cooking spray. Add onion, broccoli and pepper and sauté over medium-high heat for about five minutes or until cooked through.

FOUR: In a medium bowl, whisk together soy sauce, orange juice and zest, garlic and honey.

FIVE: Add steak back to vegetables in pan and pour in soy sauce mixture. Sauté steak and vegetables over medium-high heat for about two minutes, then whisk in flour to thicken, about two to three minutes. Add noodles to pan and cook until warmed, about three more minutes. Remove from heat and serve.

Nutrients per 1-cup serving: Calories: 270, Total Fat: 2 g, Sat. Fat: 0 g, Carbs: 51 g, Fiber: 4 g, Sugars: 6 g, Protein: 14 g, Sodium: 520 mg, Cholesterol: 10 mg

Whole-Wheat Oricchiette
WITH STEAK & VEGETABLES

*Serves 6. **Hands-on time:** 45 minutes. **Total time:** 45 minutes.*

Sometimes we crave comfort even when the temperature is high. But steer clear of comfort fare that overheats your kitchen. Our steak and pasta dish is the perfect answer: Lean steak and tasty summer squash and zucchini are accented by fresh basil and tomatoes.

INGREDIENTS:

- 12 oz whole-wheat oricchiette pasta
- Olive oil cooking spray
- 1 lb extra-lean round steak, thin cut
- 1 yellow onion, diced
- 3 cloves garlic, minced
- 2 zucchini, quartered lengthwise and sliced
- 2 yellow summer squash, halved lengthwise and sliced
- 1¼ lb Roma tomatoes, cored, seeded and julienne cut*
- 2 Tbsp chopped fresh basil

INSTRUCTIONS:

ONE: Cook pasta according to package directions.

TWO: Set a large nonstick or cast-iron skillet over high heat for one minute. Mist with cooking spray and heat for one more minute. Reduce heat to medium-high and sauté steak for about two minutes per side, until each side is browned to achieve medium doneness. Remove steak from pan and let cool for about five minutes before slicing into thin strips.

THREE: Mist same pan with cooking spray. Sauté onion for about three minutes. Then add garlic, zucchini and squash and sauté for five more minutes or until all vegetables are cooked. Stir in tomatoes, then add steak back to pan and warm for one to two minutes. Remove mixture from heat.

FOUR: In a large bowl, mix steak and vegetables with pasta. Stir in basil and serve. Garnish with additional chopped basil, if desired.

Nutrients per serving (1 cup steak-vegetable mixture and ¾ cup cooked pasta): *Calories: 330, Total Fat: 6 g, Sat. Fat: 1.5 g, Carbs: 46 g, Fiber: 11 g, Sugars: 5 g, Protein: 28 g, Sodium: 65 mg, Cholesterol: 33 mg*

*TECHNIQUE TIP: While you may often slice tomatoes horizontally, a vertical or julienne cut is an attractive alternative. To julienne tomatoes, first slice them in half, then scoop out the seeds and loose pulp. Then turn them over, skin-side-up, press down lightly on the skin to slightly flatten them and slice the tomatoes lengthwise.

Sancocho

*Serves 4. **Hands-on time:** 45 minutes. **Total time:** 1.5 hours.*

Sancocho is a traditional meat-and-potatoes soup in Latin and Spanish cuisine – it's excellent for keeping your family full and warm on a cold night.

INGREDIENTS:

BROTH

- 2 tsp olive oil
- 1 medium onion, chopped coarsely
- 3 garlic cloves, minced
- 1 carrot, chopped
- 2 cups reduced-sodium chicken broth
- 2 cups water
- 2 chicken breasts, bone in and skin removed

SOUP

- 1 tsp olive oil
- 1 onion, chopped
- ½ jalapeño pepper, ribs and seeds removed, finely chopped
- 1 clove garlic, minced
- 1 tsp whole cumin seeds
- 1 sweet potato, cut into ½-inch cubes
- 1 red pepper, seeded and chopped
- Chopped cilantro (optional)

INSTRUCTIONS:

BROTH

ONE: In a stockpot, heat oil over medium heat. Add onion and garlic; cook until onion is translucent, about five minutes, stirring often. Add carrot; cook for two to three more minutes.

TWO: Stir in chicken broth and water and increase heat to medium high. When the broth starts to boil, add chicken breasts; cover and reduce heat to a simmer. Cook for 15 to 20 minutes until the chicken breasts are cooked through. Turn off the heat; remove the chicken from the broth and set aside. Strain the broth into a bowl and place in the refrigerator while you prepare the meat. Discard the strained vegetables.

THREE: When the chicken is cool enough to handle, remove the meat from the bones with your fingers and break it up into bite-size pieces; discard bones. Refrigerate the chicken meat until you're ready to use it.

FOUR: Remove the broth from the refrigerator and, with a spoon, skim off any fat that has settled on the surface.

SOUP

ONE: In a clean stockpot, heat oil over medium heat. Add onion, jalapeño pepper, garlic and cumin seeds; cook until fragrant, about two or three minutes, stirring frequently. Add reserved broth and sweet potato; cook until sweet potato is just tender, about 15 minutes.

TWO: Remove one cup of soup and purée it in a blender. Stir the puréed mixture back into the soup.

THREE: Add red pepper; cook for an additional five minutes. Stir in reserved chicken until heated through, about five minutes.

FOUR: Serve in soup bowls and garnish with chopped cilantro (if desired).

Nutrients per 1½-cup serving: Calories: 118, Total Fat: 3 g, Sat. Fat: 0.5 g, Carbs: 12 g, Fiber: 2 g, Protein: 11 g, Sugars: 4 g, Sodium: 331 mg, Cholesterol: 21 mg

Chicken à la King Wrap

*Serves 4. **Hands-on time:** 30 minutes. **Total time:** 30 minutes.*

Traditional Chicken à la King drips with butter and cream. Our slimmed-down, clean version still reigns supreme with flavor, but skim milk and chicken stock are called upon to lessen the caloric and fatty load.

INGREDIENTS:

- Olive oil cooking spray
- ½ lb boneless, skinless chicken breasts, cubed
- ¼ cup diced white onion
- 1 cup thinly sliced white mushrooms (about 4 oz)
- ½ cup fresh carrots, diced
- ½ cup frozen peas, thawed
- 2 Tbsp whole-wheat flour
- ½ cup low-sodium chicken stock
- ¾ cup skim milk
- Sea salt and fresh ground black pepper, to taste
- 4 whole-wheat tortillas (8 inches in diameter)
- 1 to 2 Tbsp chopped fresh flat-leaf parsley (for garnish)

INSTRUCTIONS:

ONE: Heat a large nonstick or cast-iron skillet over high heat for one minute. Reduce heat to medium-high, mist pan with cooking spray and sauté chicken for about five minutes or until cooked through and no longer pink. Remove chicken from pan.

TWO: Mist same pan again with cooking spray. Add onion, mushrooms and carrots and sauté until cooked through, about five minutes. Add peas and sauté until cooked, about three minutes.

THREE: Add chicken back to pan and stir in flour. Add stock and milk, one-quarter cup at a time. Stir constantly until sauce is thickened, about four minutes. Season with salt and pepper.

FOUR: To serve, ladle half- to three-quarters of a cup chicken-vegetable mixture into each tortilla. Sprinkle with parsley. Roll up tortilla.

Nutrients per serving (1 tortilla and ⅔ cup chicken-vegetable mixture): Calories: 270, Total Fat: 5 g, Sat. Fat: 0.5 g, Carbs: 34 g, Fiber: 4 g, Sugars: 5 g, Protein: 20 g, Sodium: 310 mg, Cholesterol: 30 mg

Windy City Pie

DEEP-DISH PIZZA

Serves 12 (1 pizza). **Hands-on time:** 30 minutes.
Total time: 60 minutes.

The Chicago-style deep-dish pizza contains layers of toppings in a deep pan with the crust pulled up around the sides to form a makeshift bowl. But don't let our version's low-fat mozzarella, turkey sausage, heaps of vegetables and whole-wheat crust fool you – it's just as gooey and savory as the original. Knife and fork required!

INGREDIENTS:

- 8 oz fresh, all-natural, extra-lean turkey sausage
- 2 Tbsp olive oil, divided
- 1 medium yellow onion, thinly sliced
- 1 each small red and green sweet bell pepper, thinly sliced
- 1½ cups thinly sliced button mushrooms
- ⅛ tsp each sea salt and fresh ground black pepper
- 2 tsp cornmeal (if pkg specifies a grind, opt for fine, not coarse)
- 1 (1-lb) ball CE's Whole-Wheat Pizza Dough (see recipe, right) or 1 (1-lb) pkg store-bought whole-wheat pizza dough
- 6 oz low-fat mozzarella cheese, shredded, divided
- 1 cup Simple Tomato Sauce (see recipe, right) or your favorite jarred natural tomato sauce
- 1 Tbsp coarsely chopped fresh oregano sprigs

EQUIPMENT:

- 12-inch deep-dish pizza pan or nonstick cake pan

INSTRUCTIONS:

ONE: Preheat oven to 450°F. Cut a slit along the length of the sausage(s), remove and discard casing, place sausage meat into a small bowl and refrigerate until needed.

TWO: In a medium sauté pan, heat one tablespoon oil over medium-high heat. Add onion and sauté for two minutes, until tender. Add bell peppers and mushrooms and cook for an additional three minutes. Season with salt and pepper and transfer vegetable mixture to a bowl. Set aside.

THREE: Return pan to burner over medium-high heat. Add sausage meat and cook, breaking up meat with a wooden spoon, until meat is fully cooked, about four minutes. Place sausage meat in a paper-towel-lined bowl to drain excess fat.

FOUR: Brush inside of pizza pan with remaining tablespoon oil and sprinkle with cornmeal. Roll out dough to about 14 inches in diameter. Place rolled dough directly into pan (diameter of dough should be wider than the bottom of pan) and press into the bottom and sides of pan gently, carefully stretching the dough about one-and-a-half inches up the sides of the pan.

FIVE: Sprinkle half of mozzarella over bottom of crust. Evenly layer sausage meat, then sautéed vegetables onto crust. Pour tomato sauce evenly over top and sprinkle with remaining mozzarella.

SIX: Bake for 20 to 25 minutes or until crust is golden brown, cheese is bubbling and filling is hot throughout. Remove from oven and let rest for five minutes to allow filling to set. Cut into 12 wedges. Sprinkle each slice with a quarter-teaspoon oregano and serve immediately.

Nutrients per slice: Calories: 186, Total Fat: 9 g, Sat. Fat: 2 g, Carbs: 17 g, Fiber: 3 g, Sugars: 3 g, Protein: 10 g, Sodium: 329 mg, Cholesterol: 16 mg

Web Bonus!

Visit **cleaneatingmag.com/pizzadough** for a step-by-step guide on how to roll the perfect pizza dough!

Nutritional Bonus:

Tomatoes contain large amounts of the antioxidant lycopene, which is more easily absorbed by the body when tomatoes are cooked than when eaten raw. Lycopene clings tightly to vegetable fibers, which are broken down during processing.

CE's Whole-Wheat Pizza Dough

Makes 2 (1-lb) dough balls. **Hands-on time:** 30 minutes.
Total time: 2 hours.

INGREDIENTS:

- 1 Tbsp raw organic honey
- 1 cup less 1½ Tbsp lukewarm water (105°F to 110°F), divided
- 1 pkg active dry yeast (¼ oz or 2½ tsp)
- 2½ cups whole-wheat flour, divided
- 4 tsp vital wheat gluten (Try: Bob's Red Mill)
- 1 tsp sea salt
- 3 Tbsp olive oil, divided

INSTRUCTIONS:

ONE: In a large bowl, mix together honey and one-third cup water. Sprinkle in yeast and allow to proof, undisturbed (do not stir or move bowl), for 10 minutes or until yeast is foamy. (NOTE: If yeast does not foam, it is dead and your dough will not rise. Discard and start again with fresh ingredients.)

TWO: While yeast is proofing, mix together two cups flour, wheat gluten and salt in another large bowl.

THREE: Once yeast is foamy, add remaining water and two tablespoons of oil to yeast mixture. Pour in flour mixture and gently fold in until just combined. Mixture will form a very wet ball. Coat the bottom of another large bowl with remaining oil. Transfer dough to bowl, rolling ball just to coat with oil. Cover bowl tightly with plastic wrap and set aside at room temperature to rise for one hour. Dough will be very soft and sticky.

FOUR: Lightly dust counter with flour. Transfer dough to floured surface and roll lightly in flour, dusting your hands with additional remaining flour as needed. Gently knead dough, using remaining flour as needed, for about one minute. Form dough into a ball and place back into bowl. Cover again tightly with plastic wrap and set aside at room temperature to rise for 30 minutes.

FIVE: Transfer dough back to floured surface, adding more flour if needed, and cut dough in half to form two balls. Lightly knead each for about 30 seconds and reform into balls. Dough is now ready to use or freeze. To store, wrap each ball individually in plastic wrap. Dough can be kept refrigerated for 24 hours or frozen for up to one month.

TO USE FROM REFRIGERATOR: Remove dough from fridge and allow to warm a little at room temperature, about 10 minutes, before forming pizza crust.

TO USE FROM FROZEN: Transfer dough from freezer to fridge and allow to defrost overnight before following "Use From Refrigerator" steps above.

Nutrients per serving (⅛ of each dough ball):
Calories: 96, Total Fat: 3 g, Sat. Fat: 0.5 g, Carbs: 15 g, Fiber: 2 g, Sugars: 1 g, Protein: 3 g, Sodium: 121 mg, Cholesterol: 0 mg

To Make Whole-Wheat Pizza Dough Gluten Free:

- Swap whole-wheat flour for an all-purpose gluten-free baking flour mix. (One to try: Bob's Red Mill)
- Remove vital wheat gluten from recipe.
- Increase yeast to two packages.
- Add one teaspoon baking powder to flour mixture.
- Reduce water to one-third cup.
- Add one-third cup egg whites in Step Three when adding flour to proofed yeast.
- Have a bit of extra water on hand in case mixture is dry.
- Add four teaspoons xanthan gum (available at health food stores) to dry ingredients.
- Add two teaspoons apple cider vinegar after combining yeast and dry ingredients.

Simple Tomato Sauce

Makes about 2 cups. **Hands-on time:** 25 minutes.
Total time: 1 hour, 25 minutes.

INGREDIENTS:

- 8 medium Roma tomatoes
- 1 Tbsp olive oil
- 1 medium white onion, diced
- 3 cloves garlic, chopped
- 1 Tbsp tomato paste
- 8 large basil leaves
- 2 tsp raw organic honey
- Sea salt and fresh ground black pepper, to taste

OPTION: Add your favorite herbs and spices to the mix to customize our sauce and change it up from pizza to pasta.

INSTRUCTIONS:

ONE: Bring a pot of water to a boil over high heat. While water is boiling, use a small knife to remove each tomato core and cut a tiny X into the bottom of each tomato.

TWO: Prepare an ice bath in a large bowl. Immerse tomatoes into boiling water for one to two minutes or until skin begins to come off. Remove tomatoes with a slotted spoon and immerse into ice bath for about one minute. Once cooled, remove tomatoes from water and remove skin by peeling it back from the X in the bottom. Slice tomatoes in half, scoop out and discard seeds. Coarsely chop tomatoes and place into a bowl.

THREE: In a medium saucepan, heat oil over medium-high heat. Add onion and garlic and sauté until onion becomes translucent. Add tomatoes, tomato paste and basil and cook, stirring frequently, until sauce comes to a boil. Reduce heat to medium-low and simmer for 45 minutes to one hour, stirring frequently.

FOUR: Remove from heat and purée with a hand blender until smooth. Add honey, season with salt and pepper and mix well. Ladle sauce into resealable containers, let cool to room temperature, cover and refrigerate until needed. Sauce can be kept refrigerated for up to five days or frozen for up to two months.

TIP: Freeze sauce in one-cup containers for easy portioning and defrosting.

Nutrients per 1-cup serving: Calories: 160, Total Fat: 8 g, Sat. Fat: 1 g, Carbs: 22 g, Fiber: 4 g, Sugars: 14 g, Protein: 3 g, Sodium: 140 mg, Cholesterol: 0 mg

Sausage, Kale & Purple Potato Frittata

Sausage, Kale & Purple Potato Frittata

Serves 8. **Hands-on time:** *30 minutes.* **Total time:** *45 minutes.*

Perfect for or breakfast or dinner, frittatas are vehicles for almost any meats, vegetables and cheeses you have on hand. Best of all, they make great leftovers – take a wedge to work for tomorrow's brown-bag lunch!

INGREDIENTS:

- 6 small purple potatoes
- 1 (3-oz) fresh chicken sausage link, cut into ¼-inch slices
- 1 bunch fresh kale, ribs removed and chopped roughly
- 8 eggs
- 4 oz reduced-fat goat cheese, broken into small chunks

INSTRUCTIONS:

ONE: Preheat oven to 350°F. Bring a medium pot of water to a boil; cook potatoes until a fork goes through them cleanly, about 20 minutes. Drain in a colander and run cold water over them to cool. Slice into quarter-inch rounds and set aside.

TWO: In a medium-size ovenproof frying pan over medium heat, fry sausage slices until they're slightly browned; remove sausage from the pan. Increase heat to medium high and stir-fry kale, stirring constantly; remove pan from heat and set kale aside.

THREE: In a medium bowl, whisk eggs together until combined.

FOUR: Spread potato slices over bottom of frying pan and top with sausage. Stir kale into egg mixture and pour eggs over potatoes and sausage. Top frittata with chunks of goat cheese.

FIVE: Over medium-low heat, cook frittata until top just starts to set and cheese looks soft. Place frying pan in oven; bake for 10 to 12 minutes or until cheese is bubbling and eggs are firmly set. Let rest for 10 minutes before cutting into eighths.

Nutrients per serving: Calories: 159, Total Fat: 7 g, Sat. Fat: 2 g, Carbs: 13g, Fiber: 2 g, Protein: 12 g, Sugars: 1 g, Sodium: 204 mg, Cholesterol: 225 mg

Steak & Farfalle Pasta
WITH CREAMY TOMATO SAUCE

Serves 8. **Hands-on time:** *30 minutes.*
Total time: *1 hour, 30 minutes (includes 1 hour for marinating).*

While most creamy sauces are so laden with butter and oil that you can actually see the fat glistening off the pasta, we've chosen to keep it light with a tomato-based sauce smoothed with low-fat sour cream. Top that off with lean steak and lesser-known whole-wheat farfalle pasta and you've got yourself a deliciously clean dinner sure to please any pasta lover in your family.

INGREDIENTS:

- 5 cloves garlic, finely minced, divided
- ¼ cup red wine vinegar
- 1 tsp Dijon mustard
- ½ tsp ground cinnamon
- ½ tsp fresh ground black pepper
- 1 lb lean eye round steak, cubed
- 16 oz whole-wheat farfalle pasta
- Olive oil cooking spray
- 1 medium yellow onion, finely diced
- 1 (28-oz) jar no-salt-added crushed tomatoes
- 1½ tsp Italian seasoning
- 1 tsp dried basil
- 8 oz low-fat sour cream

INSTRUCTIONS:

ONE: Prepare marinade: In a bowl, whisk together three cloves garlic, vinegar, mustard, cinnamon and pepper. Pour marinade over steak cubes in another container, cover and refrigerate for at least one hour. (You can also leave steak to marinate overnight.)

TWO: Cook farfalle according to package directions. Drain and set aside.

THREE: Drain steak cubes and discard marinade. Heat a large cast-iron or nonstick skillet over high heat for one minute. Reduce heat to medium-high, mist with cooking spray and sauté steak until browned on each side, about four minutes total. Remove steak from pan and set aside.

FOUR: Mist same pan with cooking spray again, add onion and remaining two cloves garlic and sauté until brown, about two to three minutes. Add tomatoes and reduce heat to medium low. Add seasoning, basil and sour cream and combine. Cook for an additional two to three minutes, then mix in reserved steak and cook for two more minutes, until meat and sauce are completely warmed.

FIVE: Serve one cup farfalle with three-quarters of a cup of steak sauce. Garnish with an additional sprinkling of Italian seasoning, if desired.

Nutrients per serving (1 cup pasta and ¾ cup steak sauce): Calories: 380, Total Fat: 7 g, Sat. Fat: 3 g, Carbs: 52 g, Fiber: 4 g, Sugars: 9 g, Protein: 28 g, Sodium: 350 mg, Cholesterol: 45 mg

Salmon Melts

Serves 6. **Hands-on time:** 30 minutes. **Total time:** 30 minutes.

Tuna melts are a classic deli item, but we've upped the taste factor by substituting fresh salmon for canned tuna and adding dill, lemon and paprika for a punch of flavor.

INGREDIENTS:

- Olive oil cooking spray
- 1 large wild-caught salmon fillet (about ½ lb), boneless and skin intact
- 1 large carrot, peeled and shredded
- 2 stalks celery, ends trimmed and finely diced
- 1 medium yellow onion, finely diced
- 6 oz nonfat plain Greek-style yogurt
- 2 tsp Dijon mustard
- ¾ tsp dried dill, plus additional for garnish (optional)
- Zest of ½ lemon (about 1 tsp)
- Juice of ½ lemon (about 1 Tbsp)
- ¼ tsp Spanish paprika
- Sea salt and fresh ground black pepper, to taste
- 12 slices low-sodium whole-wheat bread (about 1 oz each)
- 2 Roma tomatoes, sliced
- 6 slices low-fat provolone cheese (about ¾ oz each)

INSTRUCTIONS:

ONE: Heat a large nonstick or cast-iron skillet over high heat for one minute. Spritz with cooking spray and reduce heat to medium-high. Place salmon fillet, meat side down, in skillet and cook for two minutes. Then flip and cook for two minutes, skin side down. Remove fillet from skillet and, using a fork and knife, remove skin from salmon and discard. Let fillet cool for five minutes.

TWO: In a large bowl, use a fork to flake salmon. Add carrot, celery and onion to salmon. Stir to combine.

THREE: In a medium bowl, whisk together yogurt, mustard, dill, lemon zest and juice and paprika. Season with salt and pepper. Pour yogurt mixture over salmon-vegetable mixture and stir until well-combined.

FOUR: Toast bread in toaster. Preheat broiler to high.

FIVE: Arrange six slices of toast on a baking sheet. Divide tomato slices evenly among toast. Top each with half-cup salmon-vegetable mixture. Place cheese slices on top of salmon-vegetable mixture, dividing evenly. Broil on high for three minutes. Remove from heat, top with six remaining slices of toast and serve immediately. Garnish with additional dill before topping with remaining slices of toast, if desired.

Nutrients per sandwich: Calories: 305, Total Fat: 8 g, Sat. Fat: 2.5 g, Carbs: 36 g, Fiber: 7 g, Sugars: 3 g, Protein: 24 g, Sodium: 257 mg, Cholesterol: 31 mg

TIP:
According to Seafood Watch, a program run by the Monterey Bay Aquarium to help consumers choose seafood based on sustainability and health safety, you should eat salmon caught wild in the North Pacific only. Most salmon farming practices are detrimental to both health and the environment. Avoid eating Atlantic salmon and wild salmon caught south of Cape Falcon, Oregon.

Salmon Patties
WITH SAUTÉED SQUASH & ZUCCHINI

*Serves: 4. **Hands-on time:** 30 minutes. **Total time:** 30 minutes.*

During many periods of financial hardship, salmon loaves and patties were popular sources of low-cost family fare. We've updated this time-honored recipe by adding fresh cilantro and grated carrots for a boost of flavor and added texture, and we've made it even better for you by using protein-rich egg whites and whole-wheat bread crumbs in lieu of the white version. The result is a delicious meal that will feed your family for less than $5 – that's just more than a buck per person!

INGREDIENTS:

- 1 medium yellow onion, half diced and half thinly sliced, divided
- 1 (6-oz) can salmon packed in water, without bones or skin, drained
- 2 egg whites, whisked
- 1 tsp Dijon mustard
- ½ cup whole-wheat bread crumbs
- 1 medium carrot, peeled and grated
- 2 Tbsp minced fresh cilantro, divided
- Olive oil cooking spray
- 2 medium yellow summer squash, thinly sliced, or 12 baby patty pan squash, cut in half
- 1 medium zucchini, thinly sliced
- Sea salt and fresh ground black pepper, to taste
- Additional fresh herbs, chopped, or green onion curls, for garnish (optional)

INSTRUCTIONS:

ONE: In a large bowl, mix together diced onion, salmon, egg whites, mustard, bread crumbs, carrot and one tablespoon cilantro. Using your hands, form mixture into four large patties, each about four to five inches in diameter.

TWO: Heat a large nonstick or cast-iron pan over medium-high heat for one minute. Mist with cooking spray. Place all four patties in pan and cook for two to three minutes on each side or until lightly browned. Remove patties from pan and set aside.

THREE: Wipe out same large nonstick or cast-iron pan with paper towel; then heat over medium-high heat for one minute. Mist with cooking spray again. Add squash, zucchini and thinly sliced onion. Sauté for about two minutes, then add one tablespoon water. (The water will help steam vegetables and cook them more thoroughly.) Cook for another five minutes or until squash and zucchini are tender and onion is translucent. When vegetables are just finished cooking, add remaining tablespoon cilantro and mix. Remove from heat. Season with salt and pepper.

FOUR: Serve one patty with three-quarters of a cup vegetables. Garnish with additional herbs, if desired.

Nutrients per serving (1 patty and ¾ cup vegetables): Calories: 210, Total Fat: 4.5 g, Sat. Fat: 0.5 g, Carbs: 30 g, Fiber: 6 g, Sugars: 6 g, Protein: 16 g, Sodium: 340 mg, Cholesterol: 25 mg

FRUITY TWIST: Eat these delicious patties unadorned, or dress them up with a simple fruit sauce. Combine one-quarter cup no-sugar-added fruit preserves (strawberry or raspberry works best) with one-quarter cup water. Cook preserves in a small saucepan over medium heat, stirring until thickened and warm. Remove from heat and drizzle over patties.

Individual Chicken "Pot Pies"

Individual Chicken "Pot Pies"

*Serves 4. **Hands-on time:** 30 minutes. **Total time:** 40 minutes.*

Chicken pot pie is the ultimate taste of comfort. Unfortunately, most pot pies rely on lard or butter-laden crusts, which are far from comforting if you're trying to live a clean lifestyle. We've transformed this traditional recipe by topping the "pies" with tasty whole-wheat biscuits, slimming the eats without sacrificing the taste.

INGREDIENTS:

FILLING

- Olive oil cooking spray
- 1 lb boneless, skinless chicken breast, diced
- 1 large yellow onion, diced
- 2 large carrots, peeled and diced
- 1 cup frozen peas
- 2 cups low-sodium chicken broth
- 4 tsp minced fresh thyme
- 2 Tbsp whole-wheat flour
- Fresh ground black pepper, to taste

BISCUITS

- ¾ cup skim milk
- 2¼ tsp apple cider vinegar
- 2 cups plus 2 Tbsp whole-wheat pastry flour, divided
- 1 Tbsp baking powder
- 1 tsp baking soda
- ⅛ tsp sea salt (optional)
- 1 Tbsp safflower or olive oil

INSTRUCTIONS:

ONE: Preheat oven to 450°F.

TWO: Prepare filling: Heat a large cast-iron or ovenproof nonstick pan over medium-high heat for one minute. Mist with cooking spray. Sauté chicken until no longer pink, about three minutes.

THREE: Add onion and carrots. Sauté until onion is slightly browned, about five minutes. Add peas and sauté for one minute or until thawed.

FOUR: Stir in broth and thyme and cook until broth is warmed, about two minutes. Stir in two tablespoons of flour and reduce heat to medium. Stir constantly until broth is thickened, about two minutes. Season with pepper and turn off heat, but do not remove pan from element.

FIVE: Begin preparing biscuits: Pour milk in a cup, then add vinegar to milk. Let stand for two minutes.

SIX: In a large mixing bowl, blend two cups whole-wheat pastry flour, baking powder, baking soda and salt, if desired. Stir in milk-vinegar mixture, a quarter-cup at a time, add oil, and then add remaining two tablespoons whole-wheat pastry flour. (The dough will be slightly sticky. If it is too sticky, add another tablespoon or two of flour.)

SEVEN: Using your hands, form 12 small biscuits about two inches in diameter. (You can dust your hands with a little bit of flour to make this easier.) Ladle chicken-vegetable mixture into four large ramekins, individual casserole dishes or soup tureens, about three-quarters of a cup per serving. Place three biscuits on top of each ramekin and place all ramekins onto a cookie sheet or baking pan lined with aluminum foil. (The biscuits will bake on top of chicken-vegetable mixture.) Place pan on rack in middle of oven. Bake for 10 minutes or until chicken-vegetable mixture is bubbling and biscuits are slightly browned on top. To serve, place ramekins on individual plates, as they will be too hot to handle.

NOTE: Adding apple cider vinegar to the skim milk slightly curdles it, which will give the biscuits a buttermilk flavor.

NOTE: Instead of using your hands to form the biscuits, you can also roll out dough and use a small cookie cutter to cut out 12 biscuits.

Nutrients per individual pot pie (¾ cup chicken-vegetable mixture and 3 small biscuits): Calories: 565, Total Fat: 10 g, Sat. Fat: 2 g, Carbs: 70 g, Fiber: 13 g, Sugars: 8 g, Protein: 49 g, Sodium: 518 mg, Cholesterol: 97 mg.

83

BUDGET-PRICED MEALS

TIP:
Cutting out your favorite comfort foods is not the way to stick with clean eating. If you feel deprived you are more likely to revert to unhealthy habits. A better choice is to make cleaner versions of those comfort foods, so you can continue to enjoy them for a very long and healthy lifetime.

Stuffed Chicken
WITH VEGETABLES & LEMON BASIL PASTA

*Serves: 4. **Hands-on time:** 20 minutes. **Total time:** 1 hour.*

Many stuffed chicken and pasta dishes can be heavy and calorie dense, but our chicken and whole-wheat pasta are light on all accounts. Lemon and basil add a zip of freshness to the spaghetti, while the chicken breasts are stuffed with flavorful yet filling low-cal vegetables and fiber-rich multigrain breadcrumbs.

INGREDIENTS:

- Olive oil cooking spray
- ½ cup chopped onion
- 1 cup chopped, loosely packed spinach
- 3 cloves garlic, minced, divided
- 3 Roma tomatoes, seeded, cored and diced, divided
- 2 Tbsp multigrain breadcrumbs
- ½ pkg whole-wheat spaghetti (about ½ lb)
- 4 (4-oz) boneless, skinless chicken breasts, pounded thin
- 4 Tbsp finely minced fresh basil
- 1 Tbsp extra-virgin olive oil
- Juice and zest of 1 lemon
- 1½ Tbsp parmesan cheese, grated (optional)

INSTRUCTIONS:

ONE: Heat a large nonstick or cast-iron skillet over medium-high heat for two minutes. Mist with cooking spray and add onion, spinach, one clove garlic and one tomato. Sauté for five minutes or until just cooked. Remove from heat and mix in breadcrumbs. Set aside.

TWO: Bring a large pot of water to a boil over high heat and cook spaghetti according to package directions.

THREE: To stuff chicken, place about two tablespoons of vegetable-breadcrumb mixture in the middle of each piece of chicken. Fold chicken piece over filling and secure with toothpicks.

FOUR: Heat a large nonstick or cast iron skillet over medium-high heat for two minutes. Mist with cooking spray. Place stuffed chicken into pan and cook until golden brown (about three to four minutes per side).

FIVE: Drain pasta when finished cooking, then put back into pot and toss with basil, oil, lemon juice and zest, and remaining two cloves garlic.

SIX: To serve, divide pasta among four plates, top with stuffed chicken breast and garnish each with a tablespoon or two of remaining tomatoes and parmesan, if desired.

Nutrients per serving (1 stuffed chicken breast and ½ cup pasta): Calories: 450, Total Fat: 9 g, Sat. Fat: 2 g, Carbs: 49 g, Fiber: 9 g, Sugars: 4 g, Protein: 45 g, Sodium: 105 mg, Cholesterol: 95 mg

Pasta Roll-Ups
WITH TURKEY & SPINACH

*Serves 8. **Hands-on time:** 45 minutes. **Total time:** 1.5 hours.*

Here's a good way to sneak some greens into your kids' diets – and time into your schedule! These lasagna-style roll-ups can be made ahead of time and reheated for a quick, easy weeknight meal.

INGREDIENTS:

- 1 tsp extra-virgin olive oil
- 1 small onion, finely chopped
- 1 clove garlic, minced
- 1 lb extra-lean ground turkey breast
- ¾ tsp ground cinnamon
- ¼ tsp ground nutmeg
- 1 (28-oz) jar tomatoes in juice
- 1 tsp sea salt
- 8 sheets dried high-protein or whole-wheat lasagna noodles
- 1 (10-oz) box frozen chopped spinach, thawed
- 1 (15-oz) container low-fat ricotta cheese
- 1 egg
- ¾ cup shredded reduced-fat mozzarella cheese

INSTRUCTIONS:

ONE: In a large skillet, heat olive oil over medium heat. Add onion and cook until softened, about five minutes. Add garlic and cook another minute. Turn heat to medium-high and add ground turkey, breaking it up with a spatula. Cook until meat shows no sign of pink. Stir in cinnamon and nutmeg, then add tomatoes, their juice and salt. Reduce heat to medium-low, stir, cover and let simmer for 20 minutes, occasionally stirring and breaking up tomatoes with a wooden spoon.

TWO: Meanwhile, bring a large pot of water to boil. Cook pasta according to package directions. Drain, rinse and allow to cool in a colander.

THREE: Preheat oven to 400°F. Squeeze all moisture possible from thawed spinach and place in a large bowl. Add ricotta cheese, egg and a quarter-cup mozzarella cheese. Stir until combined.

FOUR: Spread one cup of cooked tomato sauce into bottom of a 9 x 10-inch casserole dish. Lay a cooked lasagna noodle flat in front of you. Use your fingers to spread one-eighth of ricotta mixture across the noodle and roll it up. Place rolled pasta, seam side down, into the casserole dish. Repeat with remaining noodles. Spread remaining tomato sauce over roll-ups, then top with remaining half-cup mozzarella.

FIVE: Bake, covered with foil, for 20 minutes. Remove foil and broil for five minutes or until roll-ups are browned and bubbly.

Nutrients per serving: Calories: 234, Total Fat: 3 g, Sat. Fat: 0 g, Carbs: 27 g, Fiber: 5 g, Sugars: 7 g, Protein: 28 g, Sodium: 508 mg, Cholesterol: 76 mg

THE BEST OF CLEAN EATING

Nutritional Bonus:
Potatoes are not simply empty carbs. This nightshade family member (other members include tomatoes, eggplants, peppers and tomatillos) offers vitamins C and B6, potassium, manganese and fiber. Plus, the tubers contain the antioxidant chlorogenic acid, which may help limit and even reduce the oxidation of LDL cholesterol (a contributor to arterial plaque). Leave skins intact in order to reap the most antioxidant benefits.

French
Tuna
Salad

French Tuna Salad
WITH GREEN BEANS, POTATOES & CAPERS

Serves 4. **Makes** *¼ cup dressing.* **Hands-on time:** *30 minutes.* **Total time:** *30 minutes.*

This salad was made popular in North America by celebrated chef Julia Child, who threw lettuce leaves and potatoes into the mix. Complemented by garlicky Dijon mustard dressing, this hearty salad is perfect for a summer lunch or any time at all.

INGREDIENTS:

SALAD

- 4 eggs
- 4 Yukon gold potatoes, quartered
- Pinch sea salt
- 1 cup fresh green beans, ends trimmed
- 1 head red leaf lettuce, leaves torn
- 1 (4 or 5-oz) pouch solid white tuna
- 1 cup cherry tomatoes, halved
- 1 small bunch radishes, sliced
- ¼ red onion, thinly sliced
- ¼ cup chopped, pitted mixed olives
- 4 tsp drained capers

DRESSING

- 2 Tbsp red wine vinegar
- ½ tsp Dijon mustard
- ⅛ tsp anchovy paste, optional
- 1 tsp shallot, minced
- 1 garlic clove, minced
- 1 Tbsp chopped fresh Italian flat-leaf parsley
- Sea salt and fresh ground black pepper, to taste
- 2 Tbsp extra-virgin olive oil

INSTRUCTIONS:

ONE: Place eggs in a small saucepan of cold water over high heat. Bring to a boil, cover, remove from heat and let sit for 15 minutes. Drain, cover eggs in cold water and set aside three to four minutes. Drain, peel and rinse eggs to remove any traces of shell. Cut in half and discard yolks.

TWO: Fill small saucepan with cold water once again. Add potatoes and salt, then simmer over high heat until potatoes are tender when pierced with a fork, 10 to 15 minutes. Drain and set aside.

THREE: Bring small saucepan of water to a boil over high heat. Add beans and cook for one minute, until crisp-tender. Drain, plunge beans into an ice bath and drain again.

FOUR: In a bowl, whisk together all dressing ingredients except oil. Slowly add oil while whisking.

FIVE: Place one-fourth of lettuce, egg white, potato, beans, tuna, tomatoes, radishes, olives and capers each in separate piles in four large, shallow bowls. Drizzle one tablespoon dressing over each bowl, and serve.

Nutrients per salad with 1 Tbsp dressing: *Calories: 390, Total Fat: 15 g, Sat. Fat: 3.3 g, Carbs: 44 g, Fiber: 8.5 g, Sugars: 5 g, Protein: 22 g, Sodium: 536 mg, Cholesterol: 229 mg*

Penne
WITH CREAMY WILD MUSHROOM SAUCE

Serves 5. **Hands-on time:** *30 minutes.* **Total time:** *1 hour.*

Pasta dishes are a staple of many homes, but this one is far from ordinary! The combination of dried and fresh mushrooms along with ricotta cheese gives it a savory creaminess the whole family will rave about!

INGREDIENTS:

- 1 oz dried wild mushrooms
- 1 cup boiling water
- 2 tsp extra-virgin olive oil
- 1 (8 oz) package sliced mushrooms
- 1 Tbsp fresh thyme
- 1 clove garlic, minced
- 1 cup fat-free ricotta cheese
- 2 Tbsp grated Parmesan cheese
- 1 egg yolk
- 1 tsp kosher salt
- 1 (16 oz) package whole-grain or high-protein penne pasta

INSTRUCTIONS:

ONE: Place dried wild mushrooms in a medium bowl. Pour boiling water over them and let rehydrate for 20 minutes. Drain mushrooms and liquid into a measuring cup; set both wild mushrooms and liquid aside (there should be just over three-quarters cup liquid in the measuring cup).

TWO: Heat oil in a frying pan over medium heat. Sauté sliced mushrooms with thyme and garlic until soft and fragrant, about 10 minutes, stirring often. Add reserved wild mushrooms; cook for two to three more minutes.

THREE: While the mushrooms are cooking, combine ricotta cheese, Parmesan cheese, egg yolk, salt and three-quarters cup of the reserved wild mushroom liquid in a blender; purée.

FOUR: Bring a large pot of water to a boil. Cook penne according to the package directions; drain and set aside. Reserve one-quarter cup of the pasta water to thin the sauce, if necessary.

FIVE: Reduce the mushroom mixture to medium-low heat and slowly stir in the cheese mixture. Stir continuously for five to seven minutes until the sauce is thickened and coats the back of a spoon; remove from heat. Stir in cooked penne, adding some of the reserved pasta water if the sauce gets too thick, and serve.

Nutrients per 6-oz serving: *Calories: 363, Total Fat: 3 g, Sat. Fat: 1 g, Carbs: 75 g, Fiber: 11 g, Protein: 18 g, Sugars: 4 g, Sodium: 271 mg, Cholesterol: 44 mg*

For a photo of this recipe see p. 64.

Dilled Salmon Roll-Ups

Serves 4. **Hands-on time:** 15 minutes. **Total time:** 30 minutes.

This simple yet elegant dish combines the flavors of dill and salmon to create a wrap that's perfect for lunch. Slice your roll-ups in two-inch pieces for impressive appetizers.

INGREDIENTS:

- 6 oz raw salmon fillet
- ¼ cup Greek-style nonfat yogurt
- ½ clove garlic, minced
- ¼ tsp dried dill
- 1 stalk celery, chopped finely
- 2 (12-inch) whole-wheat lavash breads
- 1 medium tomato, sliced
- 2 leaves lettuce or cabbage

INSTRUCTIONS:

ONE: Over medium-high heat, set a steamer basket over one inch of water in a medium pot; bring water to a boil.

TWO: Place salmon in the steamer basket. Cover the pot and, depending on the thickness of the fish, cook for eight to ten minutes. It should flake easily with a fork when done. Place the cooked fish in a mixing bowl and seperate with a fork.

THREE: When the salmon has cooled slightly, add yogurt, garlic, dill and celery; stir to combine.

FOUR: Place lavash breads side by side on a cutting surface. Down the middle of each bread, spread the salmon mixture, leaving two inches uncovered at each end. Place sliced tomato over the salmon mixture and top with lettuce or cabbage leaf.

FIVE: Fold the two-inch uncovered ends toward each other and over the filling; then roll the bread up from the other direction. Cut each roll-up in half and serve.

Nutrients per ½ roll-up: Calories: 159, Total Fat: 6 g, Sat. Fat: 1 g, Carbs: 16 g, Fiber: 3 g, Protein: 13 g, Sugars: 3 g, Sodium: 76 mg, Cholesterol: 25 mg

Roasted Eggplant & Kale Penne
WITH TOASTED PINE NUTS & FETA

Serves 6. **Hands-on time:** 30 minutes. **Total time:** 30 minutes.

Eggplant is a common vegetable throughout the Southern Mediterranean, where it is often fried. Roasting is a simpler, not to mention healthier, method of preparing the nightshade veggie, bringing out its natural sweetness while removing any bitter edge.

INGREDIENTS:

- 2 Tbsp pine nuts
- 1 eggplant, cut into 1-inch chunks
- 1 Tbsp plus 1 tsp olive oil, divided
- Sea salt and fresh ground black pepper, to taste
- 8 oz whole-wheat penne
- 1 bunch kale, stalks removed
- ¼ tsp crushed red pepper flakes
- 2 cloves garlic, finely chopped
- 2 oz reduced-fat feta cheese
- 1 Tbsp torn fresh oregano leaves

INSTRUCTIONS:

ONE: Preheat oven to 400°F. Spread pine nuts on a baking sheet and bake until golden brown, careful not to burn, three minutes. Remove from baking sheet and set aside.

TWO: Drizzle eggplant with one tablespoon oil and season with salt and black pepper. Toss to combine. Spread eggplant out in a single layer. Roast in oven at 400°F, stirring once, until soft and starting to brown, about 15 minutes.

THREE: Meanwhile, cook penne according to package directions, until tender but firm. Reserve half-cup cooking water and drain pasta.

FOUR: Chop kale roughly. Heat remaining teaspoon oil in a large skillet over medium-high heat. Add crushed red pepper and garlic and cook for one minute. Using tongs, fold in kale and season with salt and black pepper. Add one tablespoon water and cook, stirring occasionally, until kale wilts and becomes soft, about three minutes.

FIVE: In a large serving bowl, combine penne, eggplant, kale, pine nuts and quarter-cup reserved cooking water, adding more if necessary. Top with feta and oregano and serve.

Nutrients per 2-oz serving: Calories: 215, Total Fat: 8 g, Sat. Fat: 1 g, Carbs: 34 g, Fiber: 7 g, Sugars: 2 g, Protein: 8 g, Sodium: 216 mg, Cholesterol: 1.7 mg

Roasted Eggplant & Kale

Nutritional Bonus:

Although still largely unknown to many people, kale is a leafy green that shouldn't be overlooked. Packed with vitamins A, C, and K and rich in calcium, this amazing vegetable also contains seven times more betacarotene than broccoli and 10 times more lutein, which helps maintain good vision.

10 ways to slash your grocery bill
(without sacrificing nutrition)

1 DON'T LEAVE HOME WITHOUT IT: Planning ahead and penning a grocery list helps avoid pricey (and often calorie-laden!) impulse buys. But remember, sticking to your list is just as vital and cost effective as drafting it in the first place!

2 SURF TO SAVE: Plan your weekly menu around your market's regular online ad. You'll save while injecting variety into your meal plan, too. Flyers are usually posted Tuesdays.

3 PICK YOUR PRODUCE WISELY: In-season fruits and vegetables usually cost less and last longer. Visit sustainabletable.org to find out what's at its peak right now in your area.

4 CUT SPENDING WITH THE RIGHT CUT OF MEAT: A rack of lamb can rack up the dollars. Opt for cheaper meats like extra-lean ground beef and bone-in chicken breast.

5 SKIP THE SNACK PACKS: One-hundred-calorie packs can cost two-and-a-half times more than regular boxes, not to mention the fact that they're usually laced with sugar, sodium, chemicals and preservatives. Pre-portion your own CE-approved snacks, such as nuts and seeds, into resealable bags and save.

6 CHECK THE EXPIRY DATE: Skim milk may be cheap, but not if turns sour before you finish the carton. Check the best-before date to avoid pouring your money down the drain.

7 LOOK BEYOND EYE LEVEL: Higher priced name brands are usually stocked right in your line of sight. Simply reach up or down for discounts and do a little math by comparing the unit prices of products for the best buy. (Put that calculator on your cell phone to good use!)

8 PICK LESS PRICEY PROTEIN: Once in a while, skip the meat section and go straight to inexpensive eggs and bargain-priced beans. And remember that dried beans are cheaper than canned.

9 USE COUPON COMMON SENSE: Coupons can help with the bottom line, but getting $1 off an item that's only going to sit in your fridge won't do your finances any favors.

10 BRING YOUR OWN BAGS: Some stores give you a discount for each grocery bag you bring along. Save pennies and the planet.

In-season fruits and vegetables usually cost less and last longer.

Herb Pairing Guide

Want to use herbs to lighten, brighten and dress up seasonal dishes? Our flavor-pairing guide shows you how to go beyond garnishing.

MINT: Brightens up savory recipes such as roasted vegetable salad and Middle Eastern dishes like grilled lamb. Try replacing half the amount of fresh parsley called for in a recipe with fresh mint. Finely chop just before adding to recipes, as mint tends to discolor quickly.

BASIL: Always at home on pizza or in tomato sauce-based Italian dishes, this herb adds zip to green salads and whole grains, too. To avoid bruising the tender leaves, tear basil by hand or slice thinly with a very sharp knife.

CILANTRO: A preeminent ingredient in Mexican cooking, this herb is also delicious with Asian flavors. Remove leaves from the stems, chop and add to fresh salsas or fish tacos; you can even use it to dress up purchased guacamole.

ROSEMARY: Native to the Mediterranean coast, rosemary is often used to flavor meats such as lamb, pork and chicken. Try it on mashed or baked potatoes, over top of vegetables or within your homemade vinaigrettes. Use sparingly, as the herb has a strong flavor. Remove leaves by sliding your thumb and index finger up the stem and chop very finely with a sharp knife.

THYME: Imparts a subtle lemony note to grilled chicken or fish. Makes a great addition to most marinades. Gently run your thumb and index finger up the stem to remove the tiny leaves – no chopping required!

CHIVES: Adds an onion-like flavor – without the aftertaste – to vegetables such as fresh corn, peas and baby potatoes. Tastes great with eggs, too. For a pretty presentation, arrange two long chives in the shape of an "X" over the plate for garnish. Or finely chop this versatile herb into quarter-inch pieces.

Five-Ingredient Meals

Grilled Shrimp, p. 110

How many weeknights have you rushed to the supermarket straight from work, thrown some random items into your cart and hurried home, only to find yourself without a clue when it comes to what's on the menu? Dinnertime disasters are a thing of the past with our simplest recipes – all satisfying and all containing five or fewer ingredients. We favor fresh, seasonal produce, high-quality proteins and smart flavor boosters, designed to come together in a tasty dish in less time than it takes to order a pizza. From our Healthy French Onion Soup to our savory Spinach & Chicken Sausage Pizza, from our hearty Black-Eyed Pea Stew to our Whole-Wheat Pancakes, you'll never face that mealtime mania again!

Healthy French Onion Soup
WITH CROUTONS

Serves: 12. **Hands-on time:** *15 minutes.* **Total time:** *45 minutes.*

The rich flavor of French onion soup comes from the caramelized onions, which are cooked slowly until their sugars melt and they begin to brown.

INGREDIENTS:

SOUP

- 2 cups finely diced red onion
- 1½ cups finely diced sweet, yellow onion
- ½ cup finely diced white onion
- 2 Tbsp unfiltered, fresh apple cider
- 1 Tbsp whole-wheat flour

CROUTONS

- 1 loaf multigrain French bread, sliced very thinly into a minimum of 24 pieces
- 12 oz fresh chèvre or low-fat Swiss or farmers' cheese, grated
- 1 to 2 Tbsp fresh thyme, for garnish (optional)

PANTRY STAPLES:

- 2 Tbsp extra-virgin olive oil
- 8 cups low-sodium chicken broth
- 1 tsp vanilla extract
- 1 tsp honey

INSTRUCTIONS:

ONE: Heat a large pot over medium-high heat for one minute. Add oil and heat for another minute. Reduce heat to medium-low and add onions. Sauté, stirring occasionally with lid half-covering pot, about 20 minutes. Onions will slowly caramelize.

TWO: Add apple cider and stir to deglaze. Add flour and stir to thicken. Add broth, vanilla and honey. Increase heat to medium-high and bring to a simmer, about 10 minutes. Reduce heat to low or turn off until ready to serve.

THREE: Preheat broiler to high. Lay bread slices on cookie sheet and broil for one to two minutes until lightly toasted.

TO SERVE

ONE: Preheat broiler to high. Ladle three quarters of a cup warm soup into ovenproof ceramic bowls or soup tureens.

TWO: If using chèvre, spread chèvre onto 24 croutons – each crouton should receive about a half-ounce cheese. If using grated Swiss or farmers' cheese, skip to step three.

THREE: Place two croutons into each soup bowl. If using grated cheese, sprinkle on top of croutons and soup. Sprinkle thyme on top of cheese, if desired.

FOUR: Place soup bowls under broiler. Broil for five to six minutes, until cheese is melted and slightly browned (chèvre will get more creamy). Remove and serve immediately.

Nutrients per serving (1 cup soup, 2 croutons): *Calories: 220, Total Fat: 10.5 g, Sat. Fat: 5 g, Carbs:16 g, Fiber: 1 g, Sugars: 3 g, Protein: 12 g, Sodium: 520 mg, Cholesterol: 35 mg*

Nutritional Bonus:
Onions are a good source of vitamin C – one medium onion supplies 20 percent of your daily needs. Onions also contain quite a bit of a flavonoid called quercetin, which studies have shown helps eliminate free radicals in the body.

Healthy French Onion Soup

Tilapia
WITH SOY SAUCE & PINEAPPLE SCALLION RICE

*Serves 4. **Hands-on time:** 18 minutes. **Total time:** 1 hour, 5 minutes.*

Ingredients that do double duty are the secret to pulling off a simple meal. Here, you'll use pineapple chunks in the rice, while the pineapple juice creates a sauce for the fish.

INGREDIENTS:

- 1 cup brown rice
- 4 (6-oz) tilapia fillets
- 2 Tbsp low-sodium tamari sauce
- 1 (8-oz) can no-sugar-added pineapple chunks, roughly chopped and juice reserved
- 6 scallions, white and light green parts, sliced (about ½ cup), divided

PANTRY STAPLES:

- Olive oil cooking spray
- Ground black pepper and sea salt, to taste

INSTRUCTIONS:

ONE: Preheat oven to 450°F. Bring two cups water to a boil in a small saucepan over high heat. Add rice, reduce heat to low, cover and simmer 50 minutes or until water is absorbed and rice is tender. Remove from heat and steam with lid on for 10 minutes.

TWO: Meanwhile, place tilapia fillets in a baking dish coated with cooking spray. In a small bowl, combine soy sauce with three tablespoons pineapple juice, then pour over tilapia. Season with pepper, to taste. Bake 15 to 20 minutes, or until cooked through.

THREE: Coat a skillet with cooking spray and heat on medium low. Reserve two tablespoons green-scallion pieces for garnish. Add remaining scallions to skillet and cook for two minutes. Add pineapple chunks and cook for 45 seconds. Fold scallion-pineapple mixture into steamed rice, and season with salt and pepper, to taste.

FOUR: Mound one cup rice onto each of four plates. Place a tilapia fillet off-center over each mound of rice. Drizzle pan juices over fillets, garnish with reserved scallions and serve.

Nutrients per serving (6 oz fillet, 1 cup rice): *Calories: 250, Total Fat: 3.5 g, Sat. Fat: 1.5 g, Carbs: 47 g, Fiber: 2 g, Sugars: 5 g, Protein: 37 g, Sodium: 460 mg, Cholesterol: 84 mg*

MAKE IT GLUTEN FREE: Look for wheat-free soy sauces (some varieties include wheat for flavoring and color). Try Eden Organic Tamari Soy Sauce. Tamari is a natural type of soy sauce with a delicate flavor, and can be found in natural food stores.

Nutritional Bonus:
The combination of fiber-rich whole-grain rice and protein-packed tilapia will provide sustained energy, keeping you full for hours.

Black-Eyed Pea Stew
WITH COLLARD GREENS & POTATOES

Serves 4. ***Hands-on time:*** *10 minutes.* ***Total time:*** *35 minutes.*

Hearty greens like collards require a slow simmer – perfect for a late winter stew. And by including beans and potatoes, you won't miss the meat in this comforting, low-fat dish.

INGREDIENTS:

- 4 cups low-sodium vegetable broth
- 8 oz collard greens, chopped (about 8 cups)
- 1 (14.5-oz) jar no-salt-added diced tomatoes
- 12 oz red potatoes, cut into ½-inch dice (about 2 cups)
- 1 (15.5-oz) can black-eyed peas, rinsed and drained

PANTRY STAPLES:

- Ground black pepper, to taste

INSTRUCTIONS:

ONE: Bring broth and two cups water to a boil in a large saucepan or Dutch oven over high heat. Add collard greens, cover and simmer for 15 minutes.

TWO: Add tomatoes and potatoes, and return to a simmer. Cover and cook until potatoes are tender, 10 to 12 minutes. Stir in peas and simmer until heated through, about two minutes. Season with pepper, to taste, and serve immediately.

Nutrients per 2¼-cup serving: Calories: 180, Total Fat: 1 g, Sat. Fat: 0 g, Carbs: 37 g, Fiber: 8 g, Sugars: 5 g, Protein: 10 g, Sodium: 710 mg, Cholesterol: 0 mg

FIVE-INGREDIENT MEALS

Nutritional Bonus:
One serving of this low-calorie soup provides nearly one third of your daily fiber needs and 21 percent of your iron requirements for the day.

Nutritional Bonus:
Beans are nutrient dense,
counting as both a protein and
a vegetable serving. In these
tacos, they also contribute
B-vitamins and bump up the
fiber count to seven grams per
serving – 29 percent of your
daily requirement!

Turkey Black
Bean Bean
Soft Tacos

Turkey Black Bean Soft Tacos

*Serves 6. **Hands-on time:** 10 minutes. **Total time:** 20 minutes.*

Ground turkey paired with black beans makes these tacos lean and filling. Corn tortillas are a whole-grain food, making them a tasty and wholesome alternative to white-flour tortillas.

INGREDIENTS:

- 12 corn tortillas
- 1¼ lbs extra-lean ground turkey
- 1 (15-oz) can low-sodium black beans, rinsed and drained
- 1 cup, plus 2 Tbsp chunky low-sodium salsa
- 2 cups chopped romaine lettuce (packed)

PANTRY STAPLES:

- Olive oil cooking spray
- Ground black pepper and sea salt, to taste

INSTRUCTIONS:

ONE: Preheat oven to 350°F. Loosely wrap tortillas in foil, making two packets of six tortillas each. Place packets on a baking sheet and bake for 10 to 15 minutes, or until hot.

TWO: Coat a skillet with cooking spray and heat on medium high. Add turkey and cook until lightly browned and cooked through, about six to eight minutes, breaking up meat as you go. Season with salt and pepper, to taste. Remove from heat and set aside.

THREE: Unwrap foil packets and place two tortillas on each of six plates. For each plate, distribute half-cup turkey, quarter-cup beans, three tablespoons salsa and one-third cup lettuce evenly between both tortillas. Serve immediately.

Nutrients per serving (2 corn tortillas, ½ cup turkey, ¼ cup beans, 3 Tbsp salsa, ⅓ cup lettuce): *Calories: 276, Total Fat: 2.5 g, Sat. Fat: 0 g, Carbs: 37 g, Fiber: 7 g, Sugars: 2 g, Protein: 28 g, Sodium: 343 mg, Cholesterol: 46 mg*

Rutabaga Purée
WITH GOAT CHEESE & CHIVES

*Serves 4. **Makes** about 2 cups. **Hands-on time:** 10 minutes. **Total time:** 20 minutes.*

It takes quite a bit of muscle to peel and cut the huge waxy rutabagas sold in most grocery stores. Instead, check your local farmers' market or organic produce section for sweet little unwaxed rutabagas. They're smaller than your fist, have a tapered oval appearance, are deliciously sweet and much easier to handle.

INGREDIENTS:

- 1 lb small rutabagas, trimmed, peeled and cut into quarters
- ½ tsp sea salt (optional), plus additional, to taste
- 2 Tbsp low-fat goat cheese*
- 2 Tbsp thinly sliced chives
- Fresh ground black pepper, to taste

*TIP: Most goat cheeses are naturally lower in fat than standard cow's milk cheese. The label will likely not state "low fat," so simply look for a milk-fat content of 20 percent or less.

INSTRUCTIONS:

ONE: Place rutabagas into a medium pot and cover with cold water. Bring to a boil over high heat, add half teaspoon salt, if desired, and cook until rutabaga is tender when pierced with a fork, about 15 minutes.

TWO: Remove from heat and drain water from rutabagas. In a food processor, purée rutabagas until smooth. Add cheese and purée until combined. Scrape purée into a bowl, stir in chives and season with salt and pepper. Serve immediately.

MAIN-DISH PAIRING: Sweet rutabaga is the perfect complement to any savory winter entrée such as roast turkey breast.

Nutrients per ½-cup serving: *Calories: 60, Total Fat: 1.5 g, Sat. Fat: 1 g, Carbs: 9 g, Fiber: 3 g, Sugars: 6 g, Protein: 2 g, Sodium: 270 mg, Cholesterol: 5 mg*

NUTRITIONAL BONUS: Rutabagas, often called Swedes, were originally a cross between cabbage and turnip. The often-overlooked starchy vegetable is an excellent source of vitamin C, which is great news during cold and flu season – the vitamin can act as a natural antihistamine, helping to reduce cold symptoms.

Smothered Steak Sandwiches

Serves 4. **Hands-on time:** *20 minutes.* **Total time:** *30 minutes.*

Flank steak is an affordable, lean cut, which benefits from quick cooking. Since it does not have extensive marbling, cooking to medium rare or medium, and slicing thinly against the grain, will result in the most tender texture.

INGREDIENTS:

- 2 green bell peppers, sliced (about 2 cups)
- 1 medium yellow onion, sliced into ½ circles (about 1 cup)
- 1 (14.5-oz) jar no-salt-added diced tomatoes
- 1 lb flank steak
- 1 whole-wheat baguette, cut crosswise into 4 pieces

PANTRY STAPLES:

- Olive oil cooking spray
- Ground black pepper and sea salt, to taste

INSTRUCTIONS:

ONE: Coat a large skillet with cooking spray and heat on medium high. Place bell peppers in skillet and cook for five minutes, stirring often; then add onion, cooking five minutes more or until vegetables are tender and lightly browned. Add tomatoes, bring to a simmer and cook until slightly thickened, five to eight minutes. Season with salt and black pepper, to taste, and remove from heat.

TWO: Meanwhile, coat another skillet with cooking spray and heat on medium high. Season steak on both sides with salt and pepper, to taste. Place in skillet and cook until browned, four to five minutes. Turn and cook opposite side four to five minutes more for medium rare. For medium doneness, cook each side for five to six minutes. Remove from skillet and rest on cutting board five to ten minutes. Thinly slice against the grain.

THREE: Cut each baguette section horizontally and fill with steak, then with vegetable mixture. Pierce with toothpicks to hold sandwiches together, if desired. Serve immediately.

Nutrients per serving (5½-inch piece of baguette, 4 oz steak, ¾ cup vegetables): *Calories: 330, Total Fat: 10 g, Sat. Fat: 4 g, Carbs: 24 g, Fiber: 4 g, Sugars: 6 g, Protein: 33 g, Sodium: 240 mg, Cholesterol: 50 mg*

Nutritional Bonus:

One three-ounce serving of lean beef contains only one more gram of saturated fat than the same amount of boneless, skinless chicken. Plus, lean beef offers a bevy of nutrients such as iron, zinc and B-vitamins like niacin, riboflavin, thiamin and vitamins B12 and B6.

Baked Chicken & Asparagus Casserole

Serves 4. ***Hands-on time:*** *5 minutes.* ***Total time:*** *45 minutes.*

The word casserole comes from the French word for "saucepan," a large, deep dish that's also used as a serving vessel. This dish requires very little prep so it's easy to whip up – you can spend time with your family while it cooks.

INGREDIENTS:

- 1 can Campbell's condensed 98% fat-free cream of broccoli soup
- 1¼ cups cooked wild rice
- 24 asparagus spears
- 4 (4-oz) boneless, skinless chicken breasts
- 4 oz low-fat Monterey Jack cheese, shredded

INSTRUCTIONS:

ONE: Preheat oven to 350°F. In a bowl, whisk together water and soup.

TWO: Spread rice in a 9 x 13-inch casserole dish. Arrange asparagus stalks lengthwise atop rice, then lay chicken breasts on top. Pour soup mixture over everything and sprinkle with cheese. Cover with aluminum foil and bake for 40 minutes or until chicken is cooked through.

Nutrients per 1½-cup serving: *Calories: 469, Total Fat: 10 g, Sat. Fat: 5 g, Carbs: 50 g, Fiber: 6 g, Sugars: 4 g, Protein: 45 g, Sodium: 795 mg, Cholesterol: 91 mg*

Portobello Mushroom Ragout

*Serves 6. **Hands-on time:** 15 minutes. **Total time:** 25 minutes.*

Portobellos are "meaty" mushrooms, often used in place of hamburger meat in vegetarian recipes, so they are a perfect choice for this pasta sauce.

INGREDIENTS:

- 1 medium red onion, diced
- 2 cloves peeled garlic, pressed or minced
- 2 (6-oz) pkgs portobello mushroom caps, cleaned, trimmed and diced
- ½ tsp dried thyme
- 1 (15-oz) jar chopped plum tomatoes or 2 cups chopped plum tomatoes in Tetra-pak box

PANTRY STAPLES:

- 2 Tbsp olive oil
- Sea salt and fresh ground black pepper, to taste

INSTRUCTIONS:

ONE: Heat olive oil in a large saucepan and sauté the onions until lightly browned, three to four minutes, stirring often.

TWO: Add garlic, sauté for one minute, then stir in mushrooms and thyme. Continue to cook over high heat until the mushrooms have softened and given off their juices, two to three minutes.

THREE: Add tomatoes and cook until the mixture is thick, about 10 minutes. Serve over wheatberry, bulgur wheat pilaf or soft cornmeal polenta. Ragout can be cooled and refrigerated for up to four days. Garnish with additional thyme, if desired.

Nutrients per ¾-cup serving: Calories: 92, Total Fat: 5 g, Sat. Fat: 1 g, Carbs: 10 g, Fiber: 3 g, Sugars: 5 g, Protein: 3 g, Sodium: 238 mg, Cholesterol: 1 g

NUTRITIONAL BONUS: One single serving of this Portobello Mushroom Ragout contains both soluble and insoluble fiber, which promote a feeling of fullness after eating and good intestinal health. Like other mushrooms, portobellos are virtually fat free and contain no cholesterol.

Turkey Jacket Potato

*Serves 4. **Hands-on time:** 14 minutes. **Total time:** 25 minutes.*

Extra-lean ground turkey breast is one of the top sources of lean protein—necessary fuel for your muscles and an important component in stabilizing blood sugar.

INGREDIENTS:

- 12 oz extra-lean ground turkey breast
- 4 large baking potatoes
- ½ cup salsa
- ½ cup low-fat sour cream
- Italian seasoning, to taste

INSTRUCTIONS:

ONE: Brown ground turkey in a medium skillet over medium-high heat until cooked through, about 10 to 12 minutes.

TWO: Pierce potatoes with a fork and place inside a clean, damp brown paper bag. Microwave on high for approximately five minutes. Turn over and cook another five minutes. Test potatoes by inserting a knife into each, and increase cooking time if needed. Once cooked through, let cool for about five minutes. Slice open potatoes. Scoop out center, leaving about a quarter-inch for stability.

THREE: Mash scooped-out potato with other ingredients, and then stuff ⅛ of mixture back into each potato half. Serve immediately, or microwave again for about one minute each to serve very hot.

Nutrients per serving: Calories: 430, Total Fat: 5 g, Sat. Fat: 2.5 g, Carbs: 67 g, Fiber: 7 g, Sugars: 3.5 g, Protein: 29 g, Sodium: 224 mg, Cholesterol: 51 mg

Turkey Jacket Potato

Nutritional Bonus:

A microwaved medium potato eaten with the skin provides half of your required daily value of vitamin C and more than four grams of dietary fiber.

Honey Mustard-Glazed Salmon
WITH LENTILS & KALE

*Serves 4. **Hands-on time:** 15 minutes. **Total time:** 45 minutes.*

Mixing up your own honey-mustard sauce is a snap and allows you to skip the processed versions. Brown lentils are a good choice for this dish because they tend to hold their shape when cooked and are easier to find than red or green varieties.

INGREDIENTS:

• 1 cup brown lentils, picked over and rinsed

• 8 oz kale, chopped (about 8 packed cups)

• 4 (6-oz) wild-caught salmon fillets

• 1 Tbsp honey

• 2 Tbsp Dijon mustard

PANTRY STAPLES:

• Ground black pepper and sea salt, to taste

• Olive oil cooking spray

INSTRUCTIONS:

ONE: Preheat oven to 450°F.

TWO: In a large saucepan over high heat, bring four cups water to a boil. Add lentils and kale. Cover and simmer over medium-low heat for 25 minutes, stirring occasionally. Remove lid and simmer five to ten minutes more or until lentils and kale are tender. Season with salt and pepper, to taste.

THREE: Meanwhile, place salmon fillets on a baking sheet lined with foil and coated with cooking spray. Season salmon with salt and pepper, to taste. Bake for 12 minutes.

FOUR: In a small bowl, stir together honey and mustard. When salmon is ready, remove fillets from oven and coat thoroughly with honey-mustard glaze. Return to oven and bake 10 to 15 minutes more or until cooked through.

FIVE: Divide lentil mixture among four plates. Top each with a salmon fillet and serve immediately.

Nutrients per serving (6 oz fillet, ¾ Tbsp glaze, 1¼ cups lentil mixture): *Calories: 471, Total Fat: 12 g, Sat. Fat: 1 g, Carbs: 39 g, Fiber: 16 g, Sugars: 6 g, Protein: 48 g, Sodium: 282 mg, Cholesterol: 93 mg*

Nutritional Bonus: Not only does this nutrient-rich dish provide over 100 percent of your daily needs for vitamins A and C, but it also offers nearly two-thirds of your fiber requirement and an impressive ratio of omega-3 fatty acids to omega-6s.

THE BEST OF CLEAN EATING

Grilled Stone Fruit
WITH CREAMY YOGURT

Serves 4. ***Hands-on time:*** *10 minutes.*
Total time: *1 hour, 10 minutes (includes yogurt straining).*

Stone fruits, such as peaches, apricots and plums, have pits in their center. Grilling these fruits gives them a smoky, slightly charred flavor that is a perfect match for their natural sweetness.

INGREDIENTS:

- 1 cup low-fat plain yogurt
- 2 tsp fresh-squeezed orange juice
- Zest of 1 orange
- 4 medium peaches or nectarines, unpeeled
- 3 Tbsp pure maple syrup

INSTRUCTIONS:

ONE: Line a strainer with two sheets of unbleached paper towel or cheesecloth and set over a medium bowl. Place yogurt in strainer and set aside in refrigerator for one hour, until yogurt is slightly thickened. Discard liquid that has drained out of yogurt and collected in bowl. In a small bowl, combine strained yogurt, orange juice and zest; set aside.

TWO: Preheat a grill pan over medium-high heat. (**NOTE:** A countertop grill can also be used.)

THREE: Cut peaches in half and remove pit.

FOUR: Grill peaches, cut-side-down, until softened, about five minutes (no flipping required).

FIVE: Divide peaches evenly among four plates (two halves per plate). Top each pair with quarter of yogurt mixture and two-and-a-quarter teaspoons maple syrup.

Nutrients per serving (2 peach halves, ¼ yogurt mixture, 2¼ tsp maple syrup):
Calories: 105, Total Fat: 0 g, Sat. Fat: 0 g, Carbs: 25 g, Fiber: 2 g, Sugars: 12 g, Protein: 4 g, Sodium: 35 mg, Cholesterol: 1.5 mg

Nutritional Bonus:
Two pancakes provide over six grams of dietary fiber. A high-fiber diet is associated with a reduced risk of developing Type II diabetes, and it's also essential for maintaining digestive health. The National Academy of Sciences' Institute of Medicine recommends that women under age 50 consume 25 grams of fiber every day.

Whole-Wheat Pancakes

Whole-Wheat Pancakes

Serves 4 (2 pancakes each). ***Hands-on time:*** *20 minutes.* ***Total time:*** *20 minutes.*

There is nothing better – aside from coffee – than the smell of fresh pancakes on a Saturday morning. Ours are made with whole-wheat flour and oats, making it easier than ever to get enough fiber.

INGREDIENTS:

- 1¼ cups oats (large flakes)
- 1¼ cups skim milk
- 1 large egg
- 1 cup whole-wheat baking flour
- 1 tsp low-sodium baking powder

PANTRY STAPLES:

- 1 Tbsp canola oil

INSTRUCTIONS:

ONE: In a medium bowl, mix oats with milk; let stand five minutes.

TWO: Add egg and oil to oats mixture, then stir to combine. Add dry ingredients and mix until just blended.

THREE: Spoon out quarter-cup of mixture onto hot skillet. Cook until golden brown. Flip and cook until other side is golden. Optional: For an antioxidant boost, add quarter-cup fresh blueberries to batter before cooking.

Nutrients per 2-pancake serving: *Calories: 272, Total Fat: 7 g, Sat. Fat: 1 g, Carbs: 43 g, Fiber: 6 g, Sugars: 4.5 g, Protein: 11 g, Sodium: 60 mg, Cholesterol: 54 mg*

Roasted Salmon

Serves 4. ***Hands-on time:*** *10 minutes.* ***Total time:*** *20 minutes.*

The American Heart Association recommends that we eat at least two servings of fish per week. Meeting that recommendation is a breeze with this delicious roasted salmon recipe – you'll have perfectly baked fish every time you make it.

INGREDIENTS:

- 4 (4-oz) salmon fillets, fresh from a reliable source, if possible
- Juice of 1 lemon
- 1 bunch of fresh green onions
- ¼ cup combined chopped fresh parsley, rosemary, thyme and chives

PANTRY STAPLES:

- 2 tsp best-quality olive oil
- Sea salt and fresh black pepper

INSTRUCTIONS:

ONE: Preheat oven to 450°F.

TWO: Prepare a baking dish with a light coating of cooking spray or olive oil. Place salmon fillets in the baking dish, skin side down. Brush a coat of olive oil on the salmon. Sprinkle each fillet with sea salt and black pepper. Squeeze the juice of the lemon over the salmon. Lay the green onions over the salmon.

THREE: Roast the fillets in the oven for about 10 minutes. Remove from heat. Remove the wilted green onions. Dust each fillet with a generous helping of the chopped herbs. Serve hot.

Nutrients per serving: *Calories: 263, Total Fat: 19 g, Sat. Fat: 5 g, Carbs: 3 g, Fiber: 0.5 g, Sugars: 0.5 g, Protein: 24 g, Sodium: 70 mg, Cholesterol: 60 mg*

Spinach & Chicken Sausage Pizza

Serves 6. Hands-on time: *15 minutes.* **Total time:** *25 minutes.*

When fresh tomatoes aren't in season, jarred tomatoes with no added salt are a healthy solution – and they taste sweet and flavorful all year round.

INGREDIENTS:

- 6 oz spinach leaves
- 1 (14.5-oz) jar, no-salt-added diced tomatoes, drained
- 1 whole-wheat thin pizza crust (such as Boboli 12" 100% Whole Wheat Thin Crust)
- 2 fully cooked, all-natural, deli chicken sausages, sliced into ¼-inch thick pieces
- 3 oz part-skim mozzarella cheese, grated (about ¾ cup)

PANTRY STAPLES:

- Olive oil cooking spray
- Ground black pepper, to taste

INSTRUCTIONS:

ONE: Preheat oven to 450°F.

TWO: Coat a skillet with cooking spray and heat on medium low. Add spinach and cook until wilted, about four minutes. Season with pepper, to taste. Remove from heat and set aside.

THREE: Place one cup tomatoes in a fine mesh strainer and press out as much liquid as possible. Spread tomatoes onto pizza crust. Top with spinach, sausage and mozzarella. Bake 10 minutes, or until sausage is lightly browned and cheese is melted. Rest pizza on a cutting board for five minutes, slice into six equal pieces and serve.

Nutrients per ⅙ of pizza: *Calories: 230, Total Fat: 8 g, Sat. Fat: 4 g, Carbs: 25 g, Fiber: 5 g, Sugars: 3 g, Protein: 12 g, Sodium: 205 mg, Cholesterol: 25 mg*

Web Bonus!

Get six more pizza pie combos!
cleaneatingmag.com/pizzacombos

Nutritional Bonus:

A serving of our clean pizza provides more than three quarters of your daily calcium need, but that's not all from the mozzarella cheese. Spinach is also a good source of calcium: one cooked cup offers about 245 milligrams of the bone-building mineral (that's a bit more than the calcium in three quarters of a cup of skim milk at 240 milligrams!).

Turkey & Chickpea Burger

*Serves 4. **Hands-on time:** 10 minutes. **Total time:** 25 minutes.*

This isn't your ordinary burger. Instead of ground beef, our patties are made with ground turkey breast and chickpeas, which cuts the fat nearly in half and ups the dietary fiber by about six grams.

INGREDIENTS:

- 1 (15-oz) can chickpeas, drained and rinsed
- ½ cup roughly chopped scallions
- 1 tsp ground cumin
- 2 Tbsp Worcestershire sauce
- ¾ lb ground turkey breast (12 oz), 99% fat free

PANTRY STAPLES:

- 1 tsp fresh ground black pepper
- ¼ tsp sea salt
- Olive oil cooking spray

INSTRUCTIONS:

ONE: In a food processor, combine chickpeas, scallions, cumin, pepper, salt and Worcestershire sauce. Pulse until smooth.

TWO: Transfer chickpea mixture to a large mixing bowl. Add turkey and mix by hand until combined.

THREE: Divide turkey-chickpea mixture into four equal portions, shaping each into a three-quarter-inch patty. Heat a large nonstick skillet over medium-high heat. Coat skillet with cooking spray and cook patties for four to six minutes on each side.

TRY THIS: **Serve on a whole-wheat bun, topped with spinach, tomatoes, onions and Dijon mustard.**

Nutrients per 6-oz patty: Calories: 190, Total Fat: 2.5 g, Sat. Fat: 0 g, Carbs: 16 g, Fiber: 4 g, Sugars: 4 g, Protein: 26 g, Sodium: 530 mg, Cholesterol: 35 mg

Nutrients per 6-oz patty with whole-wheat bun, spinach, tomatoes and Dijon mustard: Calories: 310, Total Fat: 4.5 g, Sat. Fat: 0 g, Carbs: 40 g, Fiber: 7 g, Sugars: 8 g, Protein: 30 g, Sodium: 910 mg, Cholesterol: 35 mg

TIP: **It's not only the meat that can make or break a burger, so ditch the usual toppings. Rather than slathering on ketchup and mayonnaise, pile the burger with spinach, tomatoes and onions, which add vitamins C, A and K, iron, potassium, lycopene and lutein.**

Nutritional Bonus:
With over 50 percent of your daily recommended intake of protein, treat yourself to this tasty burger after exercising to fuel your muscles.

Grilled Shrimp

*Serves 6. **Hands-on time:** 15 minutes. **Total time:** 30 minutes.*

Shrimp is quick-cooking, and it's usually the last item you'll place over the coals, so have the skewers soaked or the basket loaded before lighting the charcoal or gas fire. The quick yet flavorful marinade adds a splash of citrus tang touched by garlic – the perfect complement to any summer picnic.

INGREDIENTS:

- 1 Tbsp olive oil
- 3 Tbsp lemon juice (about ½ lemon)
- 2 garlic cloves, peeled and minced
- 1 lb fresh medium-sized shrimp, shells on

INSTRUCTIONS:

ONE: In a small bowl, stir together olive oil, lemon juice and minced garlic. Place shrimp in another bowl and pour marinade over top. Let sit for 15 to 20 minutes.

TWO: Thread shrimp onto 10-inch wooden skewers (previously soaked in water for 10 minutes) or put into grilling basket. Place over medium-high heat for four to five minutes, turning halfway through cooking time. Serve immediately.

Nutrients per 2 skewers: Calories: 103, Total Fat: 3.5 g, Sat. Fat: 0.5 g, Carbs: 2 g, Fiber: 0 g, Sugars: 0 g, Protein: 15 g, Sodium: 112 mg, Cholesterol: 115 mg

TIP: To keep lean protein and veggies from sticking to the barbecue grate, dab a wadded paper towel with olive oil, hold it in long-handled tongs, and rub it over the hot grate. A few minutes per side seals in juices and creates a crust, making it easier to turn food without breakage.

For a photo of this recipe, see p. 92.

Easy & Elegant Salmon
WITH FENNEL & CARROTS IN PARCHMENT

*Serves 4. **Hands-on time:** 15 minutes. **Total time:** 30 minutes.*

A julienne cut is when your produce is sliced into even, thin strips. This is easy to do, especially if you have a mandolin slicer. Learning this cutting technique adds a stylish flair to your dinner presentation, and it ensures your food will be cooked evenly throughout.

INGREDIENTS:

- 4 (5-oz) wild-caught salmon fillets, skin and bones removed
- 1 clove garlic, minced
- 1 fennel bulb, cored and thinly sliced
- 1 carrot, peeled and thinly sliced into matchsticks
- 1 lemon, thinly sliced

PANTRY STAPLES:

- 2 tsp extra-virgin olive oil, divided
- Sea salt and fresh ground black pepper, to taste

INSTRUCTIONS:

ONE: Preheat oven to 375°F.

TWO: Cut four 12 x 16-inch pieces of parchment. On each piece of parchment, place one salmon fillet. Drizzle each with a quarter-teaspoon oil and season with salt and pepper.

THREE: Top each fillet with garlic, fennel and carrot, dividing each evenly, then drizzle a quarter-teaspoon oil over each pile of vegetables. Season with salt and pepper, then finish each with two or three lemon slices.

FOUR: To close packet, bring long sides together and fold down toward fillet. Fold remaining two short sides of parchment under fillet. Packet should be securely closed without being too tight, so fish and vegetables can steam.

FIVE: Place four parchment packets on a baking sheet and bake for 15 to 20 minutes, until fish is opaque and gently flakes apart when carefully tested for doneness. Serve salmon and vegetables in packets for your guests to unwrap at the table!

Nutrients per serving (5 oz salmon, ⅓ cup vegetables): Calories: 253, Total Fat: 12 g, Sat. Fat: 1.7 g, Carbs: 9 g, Fiber: 3.6 g, Sugars: 1 g, Protein: 29 g, Sodium: 300 mg, Cholesterol: 78 mg

Easy & Elegant Salmon

Nutritional Bonus:

Aside from providing inflammatory-fighting, brain-boosting omega-3 fatty acids, salmon also provides a bevy of B vitamins – especially vitamin B12 which is essential for maintaining a healthy nervous system and forming red blood cells.

Lemon
Paprika
Prawns

Lemon Paprika Prawns
WITH ZUCCHINI & COUSCOUS

Serves 4. ***Hands-on time:*** *20 minutes.* ***Total time:*** *20 minutes.*

Paprika is a red spice made from dried bell peppers, used to both season and color foods. It can be part of a grilling rub, added to soups and stews, or sprinkled over the top of meat. Paprika and lemon give this prawn dish a sweet, citrus flavor that screams of summer. Best of all, you can have this dinner on the table in 20 minutes flat.

INGREDIENTS:

- 1 cup whole-wheat couscous
- 1 lemon, halved, divided
- 1 lb large wild prawns, peeled and deveined, tails on
- 1 tsp paprika
- 2 baby zucchini, halved lengthwise and thinly sliced into half moons

PANTRY STAPLES:

- 1 Tbsp olive oil
- Sea salt and ground black pepper, to taste

INSTRUCTIONS:

ONE: Cook couscous according to package directions, fluff with a fork, cover and set aside.

TWO: Thinly slice half of lemon and place in a plastic resealable bag. Add prawns, oil, paprika, salt and pepper to bag and shake to combine.

THREE: Bring a quarter-cup water to a boil in a medium saucepan over high heat, add zucchini and steam until tender, two minutes.

FOUR: Heat a large skillet over medium-high heat. Pour prawn mixture excluding lemon slices into skillet, spread in a single layer and cook for two minutes per side side until prawns start to curl. Add juice from remaining half of lemon and toss to combine.

FIVE: Mound couscous on a large serving platter, top with zucchini, prawns, lemon slices and any juices from pan. Serve immediately.

Nutrients per serving (4 oz prawns, ½ cup zucchini, ½ cup couscous): Calories: 324, Total Fat: 6 g, Sat. Fat: 0.8 g, Carbs: 38 g, Fiber: 7 g, Sugars: 3 g, Protein: 29.5 g, Sodium: 254 mg, Cholesterol: 172 mg

NUTRITIONAL BONUS: Not only is zucchini filled with vitamins A and C, this cylindrical shaped vegetable may lower elevated homocysteine levels, a problem that can lead to an increased risk of heart attack, stroke, blood clot formation and Alzheimer's disease.

Stuffed Squash
WITH BASMATI RICE, SHRIMP & SPINACH

Serves 6. ***Hands-on time:*** *25 minutes.* ***Total time:*** *1 hour, 30 minutes.*

The beautiful round shape of acorn squash makes it a natural for stuffing. Once you've enjoyed what's inside, don't forget to eat the "bowl" – it's a great source of vitamins A, B6 and C.

INGREDIENTS:

- 1 cup brown basmati rice
- 9 oz large raw peeled shrimp with tails off, cut into bite-size pieces
- 3 small acorn squash (about 1¼ lbs each), halved lengthwise and seeded
- 3 oz spinach (about 5 cups loosely packed), roughly chopped
- ⅓ cup whole-wheat bread crumbs

PANTRY STAPLES:

- Olive oil cooking spray
- 1 tsp fine sea salt, divided
- ¾ tsp fresh ground black pepper, divided
- 2 tsp dried thyme
- 2 tsp olive oil

INSTRUCTIONS:

ONE: Prepare rice according to package directions. When rice is about three minutes from being done, stir in shrimp. Continue to cook, covered, until rice is done and shrimp is cooked through. Remove from heat and let stand, covered.

TWO: While rice is cooking, preheat oven to 375°F. Coat a large rimmed baking sheet with cooking spray. Sprinkle inside of squash with half a teaspoon salt and half a teaspoon pepper, dividing evenly. Arrange squash cut-sides-down on prepared baking sheet and roast until easily pierced with a knife, about 30 minutes. Remove squash from oven, leaving oven on at same temperature.

THREE: In a large bowl, combine shrimp-rice mixture, spinach, thyme, remaining half teaspoon salt and quarter teaspoon pepper. Fill squash halves with mixture, dividing evenly. In a small bowl, combine bread crumbs and oil. Sprinkle bread-crumb mixture over stuffing, dividing evenly. Arrange squash on baking sheet stuffing-side-up and bake until stuffing is heated through and browned on top, about 20 minutes.

PROTEIN SWAP: Not in the mood for shrimp tonight? Try adding diced tofu or cooked chicken to your squash stuffing instead.

Nutrients per ½ stuffed squash (including squash "bowl"): Calories: 290, Total Fat: 4 g, Sat. Fat: 0 g, Carbs: 53 g, Fiber: 6 g, Sugars: 5 g, Protein: 15 g, Sodium: 430 mg, Cholesterol: 65 mg

Fish

Want to cook with fish but intimidated by what's involved? Fear not: We'll eliminate all the guesswork for you.

How many times have you cooked with fish, had a great meal and then had a few fillets left over in the fridge? A few days later, you remember the leftovers and think about finishing them off. But then you stop yourself and think, I cooked the fish on Sunday... today is Tuesday... is it still good? Then you call around and ask your girlfriend or mom if it's safe to eat. You both think about it and then, using your better judgment, toss it, thinking it's better to be safe than sorry.

Or how often have you cruised by the local fish market, thinking how nice it would be to have something fresh for dinner that night, but you're not sure what to look for and how to prepare it and you're too shy to ask the man behind the counter?

Now there's no need to wonder any longer. With the help of our expert, we'll teach you the ABCs of fish, so that it can become a regular part of your clean-eating menu.

Shop Around

According to Ruth Frechman, a registered dietitian and spokesperson for the American Dietetic Association in Los Angeles, you should look for freshness when buying fish. "Check the expiration date, if any," she says. "Look for firm, moist fish with a shiny skin and clear eyes. The most important thing to consider is the smell – it shouldn't smell fishy. Get the fish home immediately and refrigerate it."

When asked if it's better to buy fresh or frozen, Frechman says that fresh fish will taste better, but you can keep frozen fish in the freezer for six months. However, once fish is thawed, it has to be cooked within one or two days.

The Prep

If you're buying a whole fish, there's a lot to do before you can cook it. The prepwork varies, depending on how you want to cook it, but usually your first job is to remove the scales. Next, lose the tail and fins. Slice open the fish and gut it. Finally, cut off the head and rinse the fish in cold water. Feel around for any remaining bones. If you're squeamish about this or new to it, Frechman says that it's probably easier to just buy the fillet and skip all that.

HEALTH MATTERS

By now, we should all be up to date on the health concerns that come with dining on fish – most commonly, the mercury content. Keep in mind that the larger the fish, the higher the mercury.

For more information on mercury levels in fish visit **cfsan.fda.gov**.

Got 10 Minutes?

That's the most you'll need to cook your fish, whether you're baking, broiling or grilling. Here's your guide.

- Bake for six to eight minutes at 500°F for every half-inch of thickness.
- Steam for six to eight minutes.
- Grill for six to nine minutes over medium coals.
- Boil one-inch pieces for five minutes.
- Broil four inches from heat for five minutes; flip and cook for another five to seven minutes.
- You'll know it's fully cooked when fish flakes easily with a fork.

Instructions can be found in recipes from *Better Homes and Gardens New Dieter's Cookbook* (Meredith Books, 2003) edited by Kristi M. Thomas, RD.

Get Cooking

The great thing about fish is that there are so many options when it comes to cooking. Baked, broiled, grilled, or poached, take your pick. The cooking temperature depends on the cooking method. You'll know if it hasn't been cooked enough because it will look raw. When cooked fully, the fish should flake easily with a fork at the thickest part.

It's so important to make sure that fish is cooked thoroughly. "With undercooked fish, there's a chance of getting parasites," says Frechman. Pregnant and nursing women should not eat raw fish, including sushi. If there are leftovers, they should be refrigerated immediately and eaten within one or two days.

Oh yeah, and about those leftovers: If you're storing cooked fish in the fridge, make sure you eat it within three or four days and four to six months if you freeze it. If you haven't cooked it yet, it's good for only one or two days raw in the fridge and six months in your freezer.

CHECK THE FISH FOR CLEAR EYES.

LOOK FOR A FIRM, MOIST FISH WITH SHINY SKIN.

AVOID SEAFOOD THAT SMELLS FISHY.

CHECK FOR AN EXPIRATION DATE.

DATE OF EXPIRY
01/17/11

Seasonal Foods

Spice Roasted Root Vegetables, p. 136

What comes to mind when you think of seasonal foods? Fresh fruits and vegetables bursting with flavor? Vibrant, colorful produce just begging you to whip it up into something delicious? All Clean Eaters can agree upon our love for seasonal foods! We even plan our monthly recipes around foods in their seasonal peak. Think bright green spinach and sweet berries in the summer and plump pumpkins and winter squash in the fall. Take advantage of the bounty of the earth!

THE BEST OF CLEAN EATING

SEASONAL LEGEND

- Early Spring
- Late Spring
- Early Summer
- Late Summer
- Early Fall
- Late Fall
- Winter

Arugula Polenta ●
WITH CHICKEN

*Serves 6. **Hands-on time:** 15 minutes. **Total time:** 20 minutes.*

Also known as rocket, Italian cress, roquette and rucola, arugula is a leafy green with a hot and peppery taste. It can be eaten raw in salads or cooked – it is especially delicious sautéed in olive oil or steamed.

INGREDIENTS:

- 4 (6-oz) boneless, skinless chicken breasts
- ½ tsp fresh ground black pepper
- 3¾ cups low-sodium chicken broth
- ¼ tsp sea salt, divided
- 1⅓ cups polenta (or organic coarse cornmeal)
- 4 cups coarsely chopped arugula
- ½ cup nonfat Greek-style yogurt
- 1 medium tomato, cut into ¼-inch dice

INSTRUCTIONS:

ONE: Sprinkle both sides of chicken with pepper.

TWO: Heat a large skillet over medium heat. Add chicken and cook until well browned and cooked through, about six minutes per side. Transfer chicken to a plate, loosely cover with foil and let rest at least five minutes.

THREE: While chicken is cooking, bring broth and salt to a boil in a medium saucepan over medium-high heat. Add polenta in a thin stream, whisking constantly. Return to a boil, reduce to a simmer over low heat, cover and cook until polenta is tender, eight to ten minutes.

FOUR: If polenta seems too thick, add more broth, a few tablespoons at a time. Remove saucepan from heat and stir in arugula and yogurt.

FIVE: Cut chicken on a diagonal into half-inch slices. Divide polenta among shallow bowls. Top with chicken and tomato, dividing both evenly, and serve.

Nutrients per serving (²/₃ cup polenta, about 3½ oz chicken, 2 Tbsp tomato): *Calories: 280, Total Fat: 8 g, Sat. Fat: 2.5 g, Carbs: 31 g, Fiber: 3 g, Sugars: 3 g, Protein: 45 g, Sodium: 550 mg, Cholesterol: 100 mg*

FREEZE THIS RECIPE: Place single-serving portions of polenta, chicken and tomatoes in freezer containers and freeze for three to four months. To reheat, defrost in fridge overnight, then wrap in foil packets, place on a rimmed baking sheet and warm in oven at 325°F to 350°F.

Arugula
Polenta

Baked Apples & Figs ● ●

Serves *4 to 6.* **Hands-on time:** *5 minutes.* **Total time:** *45 minutes.*

Cozy up by that fire with this baked after-dinner treat. The natural sweetness of apples paired with figs, which are actually inverted flowers, is something to savor when you need a little winter warmth.

INGREDIENTS:

- 2 Tbsp honey (or 2 Tbsp agave syrup)
- 2 Tbsp brown sugar
- 2 tsp cinnamon
- 1 tsp nutmeg
- 1 tsp vanilla
- 4 apples, peeled and chopped
- 10 figs, stems removed, finely chopped
- ½ cup granola

INSTRUCTIONS:

ONE: Preheat oven to 350°F. Combine the first five ingredients in a bowl and mix thoroughly. Add apples and figs and mix until coated in sugar mixture.

TWO: Pour mixture into a greased 12 x 12-inch baking dish. Sprinkle granola on top. Cover with foil and bake for 25 minutes or until apples are tender.

THREE: Remove cover and bake for five minutes. Let stand for five to ten minutes before serving.

Nutrients per serving: Calories: 177, Total Fat: 3 g, Sat. Fat: 0.5 g, Carbs: 42.5 g, Fiber: 3.5 g, Protein: 1 g, Sugars: 33 g, Sodium: 7 mg, Cholesterol: 21 mg

Pumpkin Pasta Surprise ●

*Serves 6. **Hands-on time:** 33 minutes. **Total time:** 35 minutes.*

Pumpkin is sweet, bright in color and full of flavor. To make your own purée, cut a pumpkin in half, scoop out the seeds, and bake face down in a roasting pan with a cup of water for 90 minutes at 350°F. When it's done, simply scoop out the insides and process until blended.

INGREDIENTS:

• 1 (13-oz) pkg whole-grain pasta or brown rice pasta

• 1 lb lean ground turkey or chicken

• 1 small onion, finely chopped

• 1 clove garlic, finely chopped

• 1 large carrot, finely shredded

• 1 Roma tomato, chopped into small chunks

• 1 small zucchini, finely chopped (peel left on)

• 1 roasted red pepper, chopped

• 1¾ cups pumpkin purée

• 1 (10-oz) jar pasta sauce

• 1 Tbsp low-fat plain cream cheese

INSTRUCTIONS:

ONE: Cook pasta according to package directions (undercook it slightly as it will continue to cook a bit in the sauce).

TWO: Meanwhile, in a skillet over medium heat, brown turkey for seven to ten minutes or until no pink remains. Drain any fat, return pan with turkey to stove and add onion and garlic. Sauté turkey mixture until onions are translucent. Add carrot, tomato and zucchini and sauté for about three to five minutes, until tender.

THREE: Add red pepper, pumpkin purée and pasta sauce (if mixture is too thick, add a bit of water). Cover and simmer for seven to ten minutes, until zucchini is soft. Add cream cheese, then turn off heat and let cream cheese melt.

FOUR: Add pasta and mix, cover and let stand for two minutes. Enjoy!

TIP: **Roast several peppers at once and freeze them so they are handy.**

Nutrients per 1-cup serving: Calories: 402, Total Fat: 3.5 g, Sat. Fat: 0.5 g, Carbs: 62 g, Fiber: 6 g, Sugars: 7 g, Protein: 25 g, Sodium: 72 mg, Cholesterol: 38 mg

Spinach, Chicken & Mushroom Dinner Crepes ○

*Serves 4. **Hands-on time:** 25 minutes. **Total time:** 1 hour, 45 minutes (includes chilling time).*

Zucchini is also known as summer squash. Enjoy this dish full of nutritious summer fare when you're in the mood for something unique.

INGREDIENTS:

• 1 large egg

• 2 large egg whites

• ¾ cup whole-wheat pastry flour

• 1 cup skim milk

• Olive oil cooking spray

• 1 cup chopped onions

• 4 oz cremini or white mushrooms, sliced

• 10 oz boneless, skinless chicken breast, chopped (2 cups)

• 2 Tbsp dry white wine

• 4 cups spinach

• 1 tsp dried tarragon

• 3 oz Neufchâtel cheese or soft goat cheese (chèvre)

• 1 oz low-fat Swiss cheese, finely shredded

• 2 medium Roma tomatoes, chopped

INSTRUCTIONS:

ONE: Prepare crepes: In a blender, combine egg and egg whites, flour and milk. Process until well mixed, then chill for one hour. Put blender jar back on base; pulse to re-mix batter. Heat an 8-inch nonstick crepe pan or small sauté pan over medium-high heat. Mist with cooking spray. Add a quarter cup batter, then swirl to coat pan. Cook until crepe is set, about one minute. Run a spatula around edges and flip, cooking for just a few seconds after flipping. Invert pan over a cutting board to drop crepe onto the board and allow crepe to cool. Repeat until you have eight crepes.

TWO: Mist a cast-iron or nonstick skillet with cooking spray and sauté onions over medium heat. When onions start to soften and brown, about five minutes, add mushrooms and chicken and stir. Over medium-high heat, sear chicken undisturbed for a few minutes. Once browned, stir occasionally until chicken is cooked through and mushrooms are tender, about five minutes. Add wine and cook, stirring, until wine reduces by half. Add spinach and tarragon and stir, turning leaves until they are wilted and bright green. Move contents of pan to one side and add Neufchâtel cheese to the other side. Mash Neufchâtel cheese with your spatula to melt, then stir into chicken mixture. Remove skillet from heat and allow mixture to cool slightly.

THREE: Preheat oven to 375°F. Assemble crepes: Measure quarter-cup portions of chicken mixture into the center of each crepe, then roll up and place on a baking pan or casserole. Top with Swiss cheese, dividing evenly, and bake for 20 minutes. Garnish with tomatoes and serve.

Nutrients per 2-crepe serving: Calories: 324, Total Fat: 8 g, Sat. Fat: 4 g, Carbs: 30 mg, Fiber: 5 g, Sugars: 6.5 g, Protein: 30 g, Sodium: 270 mg, Cholesterol: 114 mg

Zucchini & Shrimp Stir-Fry ● ○
WITH TOFU & SNOW PEAS OVER BARLEY

Serves 4. ***Hands-on time:*** *20 minutes.* ***Total time:*** *25 minutes.*

Zucchini seems to pop up everywhere in the summer: in friends' gardens, farm stands and city farmers' markets. So it's time to add this noble vegetable to your easy-to-prepare favorites such as stir-fries.

INGREDIENTS:

• ½ cup barley, rinsed thoroughly

• 1 cup low-sodium vegetable broth

• 2 Tbsp peanut oil

• 1 large onion, sliced

• 3 scallions, white and green portions, chopped

• 1 lb frozen or fresh shrimp with tails on, peeled and deveined, rinsed well

• 2 Tbsp low-sodium soy sauce

• 1 large zucchini squash, washed, scored and cut into matchstick pieces

• 1 large red bell pepper, sliced

• 8 oz extra-firm tofu, drained and cut into 1-inch cubes

• 2 cups fresh sugar snap peas

INSTRUCTIONS:

ONE: In a medium saucepot, bring one cup water to a rapid boil. Add barley. Stir in vegetable broth. Reduce heat to a simmer and cook for approximately 20 minutes or until barley is tender. Remove from heat. Drain. Set aside and cool.

TWO: Meanwhile, heat a wok or a deep-frying pan over medium heat until a drop of water sizzles. Add oil, swish around pan and quickly add onion, scallions, shrimp and soy sauce. Stir gently. Add zucchini, pepper and tofu and continue to stir. Add peas and stir until they are tender.

THREE: Carefully plate shrimp-vegetable stir-fry over barley. Serve piping hot.

Nutrients per serving (1 cup barley and vegetables, 5 shrimp): *Calories: 420, Total Fat: 13 g, Sat. Fat: 2 g, Carbs: 37 g, Fiber: 9 g, Sugars: 9 g, Protein: 35 g, Sodium: 530 mg, Cholesterol: 170 mg*

Eggplant Parmesan ● ●
WITH BULGUR & PINE NUTS

Serves 6. ***Hands-on time:*** *25 minutes.* ***Total time:*** *40 minutes.*

Baking instead of frying the eggplant and coating it in whole-wheat bread crumbs turns this usually heavy meal into a low-fat, healthy dish that's easy to make and delicious to eat.

INGREDIENTS:

• Olive oil cooking spray

• 3 large egg whites, lightly beaten

• ¾ cup whole-wheat panko or bread crumbs

• 6 Tbsp grated low-fat Parmesan cheese

• 1½ tsp dried oregano

• 1 tsp garlic powder

• ¼ tsp sea salt

• 2 globe eggplants (about 2¼ lbs total)

• 1⅓ cup low-sodium chicken broth

• 1 cup bulgur

• 2 medium tomatoes (about 14 oz), cut into large chunks

• 1 Tbsp no-salt-added tomato paste

• 2 cloves garlic

• 12 large basil leaves, divided

• 1 cup shredded part-skim, low-moisture mozzarella cheese

• 2 Tbsp pine nuts, toasted

INSTRUCTIONS:

ONE: Preheat oven to 425°F. Coat two rimmed baking sheets with cooking spray. Set aside.

TWO: Place egg whites in a shallow bowl. In another shallow bowl, combine panko, Parmesan, oregano, garlic powder and salt. Trim ends off eggplants and cut each eggplant crosswise into three-quarter-inch slices. One at a time, dip eggplant slices in egg whites, then panko mixture, arranging coated slices on prepared baking sheets. Bake until eggplant is tender and golden brown, about 25 minutes.

THREE: Meanwhile, in a medium saucepan over high heat, bring chicken broth to a boil. Stir in bulgur, cover, turn off heat and set aside for 30 minutes.

FOUR: While eggplant is cooking and bulgur is softening, combine tomatoes, tomato paste, garlic and eight basil leaves in a food processor and pulse to make a chunky sauce. Transfer to a small saucepan over medium heat. Bring to a boil, reduce to a simmer and cook, stirring occasionally, until sauce has thickened slightly, eight to ten minutes.

FIVE: Remove eggplant from oven and preheat broiler. Arrange an oven rack about eight inches from heating element.

Continued ▶

SIX: Spoon tomato sauce over eggplant slices, dividing it evenly. Sprinkle mozzarella over tomato sauce, dividing it evenly. Use a spatula to place six eggplant slices on top of six others, making six two-slice stacks on one baking sheet. Broil until mozzarella is browning on top and melted in the middle, about three minutes.

SEVEN: Meanwhile, chop or thinly slice remaining four basil leaves. Stir basil and pine nuts into bulgur. Serve alongside Eggplant Parmesan.

Nutrients per 1 Eggplant Parmesan stack and ½ cup bulgur mixture: *Calories: 340, Total Fat: 13 g, Sat. Fat: 2.5 g, Carbs: 54 g, Fiber: 15 g, Sugars: 7 g, Protein: 19 g, Sodium: 410 mg, Cholesterol: 10 mg*

FREEZE THIS RECIPE: Store Eggplant Parmesan stacks apart from bulgur – in resealable bags or freezer containers – then freeze both for three to four months. Ideally, leave basil out of any bulgur you'll be freezing, but it's not critical. To reheat, defrost in fridge overnight, then wrap Eggplant Parmesan in foil packets, place packets on a rimmed baking sheet and rewarm in oven at 325°F to 350°F until heated through. Bulgur can be rewarmed in a saucepan over medium-low heat with a little water.

Eggplant Parmesan

Summer Fun:
Sloppy Joes are the perfect treat for backyard summer parties. Make it fun by including your kids in the process. Have them chop up the veggies. Then set up an assembly station to prepare the Sloppy Joes. Summertime cooking fun is for everyone when you include your kids in the process. Don't forget the napkins!

Tex Mex
Turkey
Sloppy Joes

Tex Mex Turkey Sloppy Joes ● ●

WITH CORN & PEPPERS

*Serves 6. **Hands-on time:** 35 minutes. **Total time:** 60 minutes.*

Sloppy Joes are chock full of the most delicious summer veggies. Fresh corn, bell peppers, onions and tomatoes are brimming from gardens around the country at this time of year. Stock up at your local farm stand or harvest them from your own home garden.

INGREDIENTS:

- 1 ear fresh corn, shucked
- 8 oz extra-lean ground turkey breast
- 1 red bell pepper, cut into ½-inch dice
- 1 yellow bell pepper, cut into ½-inch dice
- 1 large red onion, cut into ½-inch dice
- 4 tsp chile powder
- 1 tsp garlic powder
- ¼ tsp sea salt
- 2 medium tomatoes (about 14 oz), cut into ¼-inch dice (about 1¾ cups)
- 1 cup low-sodium chicken broth
- 1 Tbsp no-salt-added tomato paste
- 2 tsp low-sodium soy sauce
- 3 whole-wheat hamburger buns
- 1 Tbsp arrowroot dissolved in 2 Tbsp cold water
- ½ cup shredded low-fat Monterey Jack cheese

INSTRUCTIONS:

ONE: Use a small, sharp knife to cut kernels off corn (you should have about one cup). Set kernels aside.

TWO: In a large nonstick skillet over medium-high heat, cook turkey, breaking it up with a spatula or spoon, until it begins to brown, three to four minutes. Add red and yellow peppers and cook, stirring occasionally, for two minutes. Add onion and cook, stirring occasionally, for four minutes. Add chile powder, garlic powder and salt and cook, stirring occasionally, for one minute. Stir in tomatoes, corn, broth, tomato paste and soy sauce, increase heat to high and bring to a boil. Reduce to a simmer, cover and cook for 20 minutes.

THREE: Meanwhile, preheat broiler. Position a broiler pan three to four inches from heating element. Split buns and place open-faced on broiler pan. Toast buns until lightly browned, two to three minutes.

FOUR: Add arrowroot mixture to Sloppy Joe mixture, stirring until sauce thickens, 30 to 60 seconds.

FIVE: To serve, place a bun half on each plate, open-faced. Top buns with Sloppy Joe mixture, dividing evenly. Sprinkle with cheese, dividing evenly, and serve.

Nutrients per Sloppy Joe (¾ cup Sloppy Joe mixture, ½ bun, 4 tsp cheese): Calories: 190, Total Fat: 4 g, Sat. Fat: 1.5 g, Carbs: 25 g, Fiber: 4 g, Sugars: 6 g, Protein: 16 g, Sodium: 290 mg, Cholesterol: 25 mg

Grilled Chicken ◐ ○

IN MELON BOWLS

*Serves 4. **Hands-on time:** 25 minutes. **Total time:** 25 minutes.*

The juicy freshness of melon just screams summertime. There is something so fun about eating your meal out of an edible bowl, especially one that gushes sweetness. Serve this dish at your next summer party – it's sure to be a big hit!

INGREDIENTS:

- 2 large cantaloupes, washed, scrubbed, cut in half and seeded
- 1 lb boneless, skinless chicken breast, thinly sliced
- 1 Tbsp olive oil
- 1 cup cooked green fava beans or lima beans, chilled
- 1 cup shredded Romaine lettuce
- 2 oz unsalted cashews
- 1 cup 100% orange juice
- Juice of 1 lime
- 3 oz fresh blueberries
- 1 cup nonfat Greek-style yogurt (optional)
- Mint leaves for garnish

INSTRUCTIONS:

ONE: With a melon baller, scoop out each cantaloupe half. Set aside melon balls. Drain remaining liquid from melon and keep in reserve. Set aside melon halves and keep chilled until ready to use.

TWO: Coat chicken in oil. Heat a grill pan over medium heat and add chicken. Cook for approximately 10 to 15 minutes, turning at least once, making sure breasts are browned. Remove from pan and set aside. When cool, cut into small bite-size pieces. Chill in refrigerator.

THREE: Place chilled chicken in a large mixing bowl. Add beans and lettuce; toss gently. Add melon balls, cashews, orange juice, lime juice and reserved cantaloupe liquid. Toss gently again. Divide mixture evenly among four cantaloupe bowls. Top with blueberries and a dollop of yogurt, if desired. Garnish with mint.

FOUR: Keep well chilled in refrigerator, covered with plastic wrap, until ready to serve.

Nutrients per serving (4 oz chicken and 3 oz melon mix): Calories: 510, Total Fat: 15 g, Sat. Fat: 3.5 g, Carbs: 63 g, Fiber: 8 g, Sugars: 43 g, Protein: 36 g, Sodium: 180 mg, Cholesterol: 65 mg

Mini Blueberry Buckwheat Ricotta Dessert Pancakes ○

Makes about 2 dozen silver-dollar-size pancakes.
Hands-on time: 35 minutes. Total time: 35 minutes.

Blueberry bushes are brimming with these delicious blue orbs in summertime. Make it a fun afternoon by picking your own at a local farm. You'll feel great when eating these pancakes knowing they're full of nutritious, in-season berries.

INGREDIENTS:

- ½ cup buckwheat flour
- 1 cup whole-wheat pastry flour
- 1 tsp baking powder
- ½ tsp baking soda
- ¼ tsp sea salt
- 1 whole large egg plus 1 egg white, beaten together
- ½ cup low-fat ricotta cheese, drained
- ½ cup 100% orange juice
- 1 tsp almond extract
- 1 tsp pure vanilla extract
- ½ tsp orange extract
- 1 cup fresh blueberries
- 1 Tbsp olive oil
- Agave nectar for garnish (optional)

INSTRUCTIONS:

ONE: In a large bowl, whisk together buckwheat and pastry flours, baking powder, baking soda and salt. Set aside. In another bowl, whisk together eggs, cheese, orange juice and all extracts. Carefully pour wet ingredients into dry ingredients. Stir gently. Add blueberries. Do not over-beat; batter should be a bit lumpy.

TWO: Heat oil in a large skillet over medium heat. Using a tablespoon, place small amounts of batter on skillet. Flatten each pancake with the back of a spoon. Turn each pancake over once with a spatula, in approximately two to three minutes. When bottom browns, use a spatula to slide each pancake to a serving dish. Drizzle with agave nectar, if desired. Serve hot.

NOTE: Extra pancake batter can be frozen in a covered container and saved for a later date.

Nutrients per 4 pancakes: Calories: 190, Total Fat: 5 g, Sat. Fat: 1 g, Carbs: 28 g, Fiber: 5 g, Sugars: 5 g, Protein: 8 g, Sodium: 230 mg, Cholesterol: 35 mg

Papaya Salsa ●

Serves 6. Makes about 2 cups. Hands-on time: 5 minutes. Total time: 5 minutes.

Papayas are tropical fruits that appeal to most palates, making them a perfect addition to this summer salsa.

INGREDIENTS:

- 2 ripe papayas, peeled, seeded and diced
- ½ cup diced red bell pepper
- ½ cup diced red onion
- 1 jalapeño pepper, seeded and minced
- 1 clove garlic, minced
- Juice of 1 fresh lime
- ½ cup chopped cilantro
- 1 tsp ground cumin
- ½ tsp red pepper flakes
- Salt and pepper to taste
- 1 can black beans, rinsed and drained (optional)

INSTRUCTIONS:

In a large mixing bowl, combine all the ingredients and mix together. Cover and refrigerate until served. Serve with tortilla chips or over grilled fish or chicken.

Nutrients per ⅓-cup serving: Calories: 56, Total Fat: 2 g, Sat. Fat: 0 g, Carbs: 13.5 g, Fiber: 2.5 g, Protein: 1.25 g, Sugars: 7 g, Sodium: 6.5 mg, Cholesterol: 0 mg

Slow-Cooker Chestnut Stew ● ●

Serves 8. Hands-on time: 20 minutes. Total time: 6 hours, 20 minutes.
From Tosca Reno's Eat-Clean Diet® Cookbook

This savory stew is perfect for a cozy winter evening. Best of all, throw it together in the morning and it will be ready and waiting for you at the end of the day.

INGREDIENTS:

- ⅓ cup amaranth flour or flour of your choice
- ½ tsp sea salt
- ½ tsp ground black pepper
- 1 Tbsp crumbled dried oregano
- 1 Tbsp crumbled dried basil
- 3 lbs lean, boneless bison or beef, cut into 1-inch chunks
- 3 Tbsp extra-virgin olive oil
- 1 large sweet onion, peeled and chopped finely
- 4 cloves garlic, passed through a garlic press
- 2 thick carrots, peeled and chopped
- 4 stalks celery, trimmed and chopped

Continued ▶

- 2 sweet potatoes, peeled and cut into 1-inch chunks
- 1 cup steamed chestnuts, chopped
- 1 Tbsp tomato paste
- 3 cups water or beef or vegetable stock, low-sodium (gluten-free)

INSTRUCTIONS:

ONE: In a container with a lid, place flour, sea salt, pepper, oregano and basil. Put the lid on the container and shake. Now add bison or beef to the flour and shake again to coat each piece. Set aside.

TWO: Heat one-and-a-half tablespoons olive oil in a large skillet and set over medium heat. Remove the meat cubes from the flour mixture one at a time and place in skillet. You may have to brown them in batches. Once the meat is nicely browned, remove from the skillet. Place the meat in the bowl of a slow-cooker. Add all remaining ingredients to the slow-cooker, mix gently and set to high. Cook covered for six hours. Serve hot!

Nutrients per 2-cup serving: *Calories: 358, Total Fat: 10.5 g, Sat. Fat: 3 g, Carbs: 26.5 g, Fiber: 3 g, Protein: 37 g, Sugars: 5.5 g, Sodium: 454 mg, Cholesterol: 99 mg*

Slow-Cooker Chestnut Stew

Arugula, Asparagus & Salmon

THE BEST OF CLEAN EATING

Arugula, Asparagus & Salmon ●●○
WITH BLACKBERRY GLAZE

Serves 4. **Hands-on time:** *15 minutes.* **Total time:** *30 minutes.*

Blackberries make for the perfect seasonal addition to this light summer meal. The purple juice complements the bright pink salmon on a background of deep green vegetables that will satisfy the eye as well as the appetite.

INGREDIENTS:

- 12 oz wild-caught salmon fillet, skin and bones removed
- Olive oil cooking spray
- 2 cups asparagus tips
- 2 cups blackberries, divided
- 2 tsp raw honey
- 4 tsp low-sodium soy sauce
- 2 tsp dark sesame oil
- ¼ cup fresh orange juice
- 6 cups arugula
- 4 large scallions, thinly sliced on the diagonal

INSTRUCTIONS:

ONE: Preheat oven to 400°F. Divide salmon into eight equal-sized pieces. Mist a baking sheet with cooking spray. Place salmon on baking sheet and bake for about 18 minutes. (When done, salmon will flake but still stay together.) Remove from oven and let cool.

TWO: Set a steamer basket over a pot of boiling water and steam asparagus for two minutes, until tender-crisp. Rinse with cool water and chill in refrigerator. (If you are preparing asparagus more than one hour ahead of time, cover and chill.)

THREE: Take 16 blackberries and put them in a small bowl; set remaining blackberries aside. Mash 16 blackberries, then add honey, soy sauce, oil and orange juice. Stir to combine (berries will remain chunky).

FOUR: On each of four salad plates, arrange quarter of arugula, then top with quarter of asparagus, quarter of scallions, two pieces of salmon and quarter of reserved blackberries. Drizzle with blackberry-soy dressing, dividing evenly, and serve. If desired, garnish salad with orange zest.

Nutrients per 2½-cup serving: Calories: 220, Total Fat: 9 g, Sat. Fat: 1 g, Carbs: 17 g, Fiber: 6 g, Sugars: 10 g, Protein: 21 g, Sodium: 180 mg, Cholesterol: 47 mg

Scallops in Blackberry Chipotle Sauce ●
OVER COUSCOUS

Serves 4. **Hands-on time:** *25 minutes.* **Total time:** *25 minutes.*

Blackberries and smoky chipotles might sound like an odd pairing, but the combination works. (Trust us!) Sweet and tangy berries with a hint of spice and fire are infinitely more complex, plus the duo creates a ton of flavor with very little effort. Scallops are also low-labor fare – just pull off the little piece of tough muscle on one edge and pat them dry before cooking.

INGREDIENTS:

- 4 cups blackberries
- 2 tsp lemon zest
- ¼ cup fresh lemon juice
- 2 Tbsp raw honey
- 3 tsp chopped chipotle chiles in adobo sauce
- 1 cup whole-wheat couscous
- 2 tsp olive oil
- 20 oz large scallops, tough muscle removed and patted dry with paper towel
- Fresh cracked black pepper, to taste
- Fresh parsley, chopped, for garnish

INSTRUCTIONS:

ONE: In a small bowl, combine blackberries, lemon zest and juice, honey and chipotle chiles; set aside. In a small saucepan with a lid, bring one-and-a-half cups water to a boil, then add couscous. Cover tightly, remove from heat and let stand for five minutes.

TWO: Preheat a cast-iron skillet over high heat before drizzling in oil. Season scallops with pepper and sear them in skillet for two minutes per side. When scallop edges start to split, remove scallops and keep warm.

THREE: Add blackberry mixture to hot skillet and stir rapidly. When bubbling, reduce heat to low, and stir until berries start to break down and are heated through, about four minutes.

FOUR: Divide couscous evenly among four plates, spoon over top all but four tablespoons blackberry sauce, then top with seared scallops and drizzle with remaining blackberry sauce. Garnish with parsley.

Nutrients per serving (½ cup plus 2 Tbsp couscous, quarter of sauce, quarter of scallops): Calories: 461, Total Fat: 5 g, Sat. Fat: 0.5 g, Carbs: 56 g, Fiber: 11 g, Sugars: 16 g, Protein: 52 g, Sodium: 541 mg, Cholesterol: 110 mg

Curried Butternut Squash & Apple Soup ○

*Serves 4. **Hands-on time:** 30 minutes. **Total time:** 1 hour, 30 minutes.*

Butternut squash is the ultimate winter gourd. It's packed with nutritional benefit and boasts a bright orange color to complement any winter meal. Pair it with apples for a simple soup that's rich in flavor.

INGREDIENTS:

- 1 medium butternut squash
- 1 Tbsp canola oil
- 1 small onion, chopped
- 2 tsp curry powder
- 1 tsp ground cinnamon
- 4 cups water
- 1 apple, peeled, cored and chopped

INSTRUCTIONS:

ONE: Preheat oven to 425°F. Line a rimmed baking sheet with foil.

TWO: Cut squash in half lengthwise. Scrape the seeds and strings out from the center. Place the squash, cut side down, on the prepared baking sheet. Roast for 30 to 45 minutes or until the squash is softened. Remove the squash from the oven and let cool slightly.

THREE: When the squash can be safely handled, scrape the flesh into a bowl. Discard the peel.

FOUR: In a stockpot, heat oil over medium heat. Add onion; cook until translucent, about five minutes. Stir in curry powder and cinnamon; cook until fragrant. Add water, reserved squash and apple; cook for 10 minutes. Remove from heat and let soup cool for 10 to 15 minutes.

FIVE: Using a blender, purée the soup until it's smooth. For added smoothness, strain the soup through a fine-mesh strainer.

Nutrients per 2-cup serving: Calories: 116, Total Fat: 4 g, Sat. Fat: 0.3 g, Carbs: 22 g, Fiber: 4 g, Protein: 2 g, Sugars: 7 g, Sodium: 6 mg, Cholesterol: 0 mg

Noodles & Tofu ● ●
WITH BASIL & MINT DRESSING

*Serves 4. **Hands-on time:** 20 minutes. **Total time:** 35 minutes.*

Summer is the perfect time for herb gardens bursting with flavorful meal additions. This yummy meal boasts basil and spearmint, two herbs rich in flavor and color. Both your eyes and taste buds will be left satisfied!

INGREDIENTS:

- 16 oz extra-firm water-packed tofu (not silken)
- 12 oz whole-wheat angel hair pasta
- 4 tsp minced fresh ginger
- 4 tsp raw honey
- 2 tsp dark sesame oil
- 1½ tsp low-sodium soy sauce
- 2 Tbsp shredded fresh basil leaves
- 2 Tbsp shredded fresh spearmint
- ½ cup sliced red bell pepper

INSTRUCTIONS:

ONE: Drain tofu, then wrap in a kitchen towel. Put on a cutting board, place a weight on top, such as a heavy pot, and let drain for 30 minutes.

TWO: Meanwhile, cook pasta according to package directions; drain well.

THREE: Cut tofu into half-inch cubes. In a medium bowl, mix ginger, honey, oil, soy sauce, basil and spearmint. Add tofu and pepper, tossing to coat.

FOUR: Add pasta to bowl with tofu mixture and toss gently to coat pasta with dressing. Serve at room temperature or cover and chill in refrigerator for up to two days.

Nutrients per 2-cup serving: Calories: 471, Total Fat: 10 g, Sat. Fat: 0.25 g, Carbs: 74 g, Fiber: 10 g, Sugars: 10 g, Protein: 21 g, Sodium: 66 mg, Cholesterol: 0 mg

Low-Carb Spaghetti Squash • •
WITH SPINACH, GARLIC & PINE NUTS

*Serves 2. **Hands-on time:** 15 minutes. **Total time:** 1 hour.*

Substituting spaghetti squash for pasta is a great way to cut down on carb calories – and it's delicious layered with many traditional and not-so-traditional pasta toppings.

INGREDIENTS:

- Olive oil cooking spray
- ½ (3-lb) spaghetti squash, seeds scooped out
- 1 Tbsp olive oil, divided
- 4 cloves garlic, minced
- ⅓ cup low-sodium vegetable or chicken broth
- ¼ tsp fine sea salt, divided
- Pinch crushed red pepper (optional)
- 1 (10-oz) bag spinach
- 1½ tsp pine nuts, toasted, for garnish

INSTRUCTIONS:

ONE: Preheat oven to 375°F.

TWO: Coat a rimmed baking sheet with cooking spray. Place squash, flesh down, on sheet and bake until easily pierced with a fork, 50 to 60 minutes.

THREE: When squash is about 10 minutes from being done, warm half tablespoon oil in a large skillet over medium heat. Add garlic and cook for one minute. Stir in broth, one-eighth teaspoon salt and red pepper, if desired. Add spinach, handfuls at a time, stirring until it's all in the skillet and wilted. Cover to keep warm.

FOUR: When squash is done, use a fork to separate strands into a medium bowl. Add remaining oil and salt, and toss gently.

FIVE: Transfer "spaghetti" to plates or a platter, top with spinach mixture, garnish with pine nuts and serve.

Nutrients per serving (1¼ cups squash, 1 cup spinach mixture and ¾ tsp pine nuts): *Calories: 230, Total Fat: 10 g, Sat. Fat: 1.5 g, Carbs: 37 g, Fiber: 11 g, Sugars: 8 g, Protein: 7 g, Sodium: 530 mg, Cholesterol: 0 mg*

Nutritional Bonus:
Carrots are not only high in Vitamin A, which helps improve vision (particularly night vision), they are also high in fiber, low in sodium, and cholesterol and fat free.

Curried Carrot Soup

Curried Carrot Soup ● ● ●
WITH COCONUT MILK

*Serves 6. **Hands-on time:** 15 minutes. **Total time:** 35 minutes.*

Soup is the ultimate comfort food especially when a chill hits the air. Nutrition-laden carrots add that extra punch of color and sweetness to make this soup a fragrant bowl of nourishment that's simply magical for the soul. You'll warm up from the inside out.

INGREDIENTS:

- 1 Tbsp olive oil
- 2 leeks, white and light green parts only, roughly chopped
- 4 large carrots, peeled and chopped
- 2 Tbsp finely chopped fresh ginger
- 1 tsp curry powder
- 1 tsp ground cumin
- ¼ tsp cayenne pepper
- Sea salt and fresh ground black pepper, to taste
- 3 cloves garlic, chopped
- 4 cups low-sodium vegetable broth
- ½ cup low-fat coconut milk
- Fresh cilantro for garnish

INSTRUCTIONS:

ONE: Heat oil in a large soup pot over medium heat. Add leeks, carrots, ginger, curry powder, cumin, cayenne, salt and black pepper. Cook until vegetables are soft but not browned, about five minutes. Add garlic and cook for one minute over same heat.

TWO: Add broth and bring to a boil. Cover, reduce heat to low and simmer for 20 minutes, until vegetables are tender and flavors meld.

THREE: Remove soup from heat, add coconut milk and carefully blend with an immersion blender, stand blender or food processor until smooth, working in batches, if necessary. To serve, divide soup evenly among six bowls, garnishing with cilantro.

Nutrients per 1-cup serving: Calories: 93, Total Fat: 4 g, Sat. Fat: 1 g, Carbs: 13 g, Fiber: 3 g, Sugars: 4.3 g, Protein: 1.5 g, Sodium: 267 mg, Cholesterol: 0 mg

Grilled Salmon ●
WITH TUSCANY BEANS & HEIRLOOM TOMATOES

*Serves 4. **Hands-on time:** 20 minutes. **Total time:** 50 minutes.*

Distinct in flavor and often produced from seeds that have been passed down from generation to generation, heirloom tomatoes are considered to be the most flavorful variety of this fruit. They are perfectly paired with hearty beans as a side to your salmon.

INGREDIENTS:

- 1 (15-oz) can white kidney, great northern or cannellini beans, well drained and rinsed
- ½ onion, thinly sliced
- 1 large red bell pepper, chopped
- 4 (4- to 6-oz) wild-caught salmon fillets
- ¼ cup minced dried dill weed or 1 bunch fresh dill weed
- Olive oil cooking spray
- 2 large heirloom tomatoes, diced

MARINADE:

- ¼ cup extra-virgin olive oil
- ¼ cup balsamic vinegar
- 2 shallots, minced
- 4 cloves garlic, minced
- 2 oz capers, drained and rinsed well

INSTRUCTIONS:

ONE: Prepare marinade: In measuring cup, whisk together oil, vinegar, shallots, garlic and capers. Set aside.

TWO: In a bowl, toss beans, onion and pepper with half of marinade. Set aside. Pour remaining marinade over salmon and sprinkle with dill. Let marinate for at least 30 minutes or up to one day, covered, in the refrigerator.

THREE: Mist grill pan with cooking spray and heat over medium-high. Arrange salmon in pan in a single layer, discarding any remaining marinade. Cook, turning once, until golden on both sides and salmon flakes easily with a fork, about seven minutes per side (time will depend on thickness of fish).

FOUR: Toss tomatoes with bean salad and serve with salmon.

Nutrients per serving (4 oz salmon and 1 cup vegetable mix): Calories: 360, Total Fat: 17 g, Sat. Fat: 2.5 g, Carbs: 22 g, Fiber: 5 g, Sugars: 6 g, Protein: 29 g, Sodium: 390 mg, Cholesterol: 60 mg

Planked Scallops ○
WITH BLUEBERRY TARRAGON SAUCE

Serves 4 (main course) or 8 (appetizer). *Hands-on time:* 15 minutes.
Total time: 3 hours, 15 minutes.

Blueberries and scallops make for a delectable late summer pairing. Blueberries are ripe for the picking at this time of year and act as the perfect mate to plump, juicy scallops. This light and fresh dish will leave you nourished for enjoying a late summer sunset.

EQUIPMENT:

• Cedar plank

INGREDIENTS:

SCALLOPS

• 16 large scallops
• 2 Tbsp low-sodium soy sauce
• 2 Tbsp honey or pure maple syrup
• 1 Tbsp olive oil

SAUCE

• 2 large shallots, finely chopped
• 2 garlic cloves, minced
• 1 cup low-sodium, low-fat chicken or vegetable broth
• 2 cups fresh blueberries
• 1 tsp arrowroot
• 1 Tbsp water
• 2 Tbsp chopped fresh tarragon

INSTRUCTIONS:

ONE: Submerge plank in water for at least three hours. (Weigh down with cans so it doesn't float.) Toss scallops with soy sauce, honey and oil. When ready to cook, heat one side of barbecue to high and the other to medium. Place plank (without scallops) on medium-heat side and close lid. Heat for five minutes to release aromatic steam. Place scallops on hot plank and cook until firm to the touch, 10 to 12 minutes.

TWO: For the sauce, place shallots, garlic and half-cup broth in a small saucepan. Boil until almost all liquid is absorbed. Stir in blueberries and remaining half-cup broth. Reduce heat and simmer until berries start to break down. In a small bowl, dissolve arrowroot with water (or use more stock), then stir into berry mixture. Boil for one minute, then remove from heat and stir in tarragon.

Nutrients per main-course serving: Calories: 226, Total Fat: 4 g, Sat. Fat: 0.5 g, Carbs: 28 g, Fiber: 2 g, Sugars: 16 g, Protein: 20 g, Sodium: 623 mg, Cholesterol: 43 mg

One main course consists of 4 scallops and ¼ sauce.

TIP: To reduce the sugar in this entrée, simply cut the amount of honey in half – it'll lower the sugar to 12 grams. And, if you're watching your salt intake, try tossing scallops with only one tablespoon of soy sauce. You'll still get a bit of salty flavor while nixing 150 milligrams of sodium.

Farro Risotto ●
WITH WILD MORELS, ASPARAGUS & TRUFFLE OIL

Serves 4. *Hands-on time:* 45 minutes. *Total time:* 45 minutes.

Asparagus is a green spear of springtime perfection! It boasts a pop of colour and a nutritional laundry list that makes for the perfect farro pairing. The chewy texture of this ancient grain along with the crisp snap of asparagus is worth the wait (and the sore arm muscles!).

INGREDIENTS:

• 4 cups low-sodium broth (chicken, mushroom or vegetable)
• 1 Tbsp olive oil
• 1 cup halved wild morel mushrooms
• 2 cups sliced cremini mushrooms
• 3 Tbsp finely chopped shallots,
• 2 cloves garlic, minced
• 1 Tbsp finely chopped fresh thyme,
• Sea salt and fresh ground black pepper, to taste
• 1 cup whole-grain farro
• 1 small bunch baby asparagus, trimmed and cut diagonally into 1-inch pieces
• 3 Tbsp grated Parmigiano-Reggiano cheese
• 1 tsp white truffle infused olive oil

NOTE: If you can't find fresh wild morel mushrooms, go for dried (morel, oyster or shiitake) instead. When re-hydrating mushrooms, follow package instructions on re-hydration, save remaining liquid and add to stock to use in risotto.

INSTRUCTIONS:

ONE: In a medium saucepan, heat broth over medium-high heat until it comes to a simmer, then reduce heat to low.

TWO: Meanwhile, heat olive oil in a large skillet over medium-high heat. Add mushrooms and cook until softened and starting to brown, about three minutes. Stir in shallots, garlic and thyme and cook for two more minutes. Season with salt and pepper.

THREE: Stir farro into mushroom mixture and cook for three to four minutes. Reduce heat to low, add half-cup simmering broth, stir and cook until liquid is almost completely absorbed, about two minutes. Continue stirring in broth in half-cup increments, allowing liquid to absorb before adding more, until farro is tender but still slightly chewy, 30 to 35 minutes.

FOUR: Bring a small pot of water to a boil over high heat. Add asparagus and cook until tender, one minute. Drain, plunge asparagus into an ice bath for a few seconds and drain again. Add asparagus to risotto and stir.

FIVE: Add cheese to risotto and stir; season with salt and pepper. Divide risotto among four shallow bowls and top each with a quarter teaspoon truffle oil. Serve immediately.

Nutrients per 1-cup serving: Calories: 147, Total Fat: 8 g, Sat. Fat: 1.8 g, Carbs: 22 g, Fiber: 4 g, Sugars: 3 g, Protein: 5.5 g, Sodium: 398 mg, Cholesterol: 3 mg

Nutritional Bonus:

The humble and healthy mushroom boasts copper, vitamins B and D, and antioxidants such as selenium, which helps guard against the cell damage that may contribute to cancer and heart disease. Plus, mushrooms are great sources of potassium, with nearly 300 milligrams in each serving. And all of this comes for the price of only 20 calories per cup!

Farro Risotto

Spice Roasted Root Vegetables ● ●
WITH SAGE & ROSEMARY

Serves 4. ***Hands-on time:*** *10 minutes.* ***Total time:*** *45 minutes.*

You've chosen the perfect side dish to warm up your late fall or winter spread. Parsnips, rutabaga and yams are harvested gems that add a cornucopia of health to your meal. Turn anyone into a veggie lover with these root treats that go from ordinary to extraordinary with a few simple spices. Mmmm… don't they smell good!

INGREDIENTS:

- 1 parsnip, peeled and cut into 1-inch chunks
- 1 rutabaga, peeled and cut into 1-inch chunks
- 1 yam or sweet potato, peeled and cut into 1-inch chunks
- 2 Tbsp olive oil
- 1 tsp ground cumin
- ¼ tsp ground cinnamon
- 2 tsp finely chopped fresh sage
- 1 tsp finely chopped fresh rosemary
- Sea salt and fresh ground black pepper, to taste

INSTRUCTIONS:

ONE: Preheat oven to 425°F. Combine all ingredients in a large bowl and toss to combine. Transfer mixture to a large baking sheet in a single layer and roast until soft and lightly browned, stirring once or twice, 35 to 40 minutes. Serve warm.

Nutrients per 1½-cup serving: *Calories: 149, Total Fat: 7 g, Sat. Fat: 1 g, Carbs: 21 g, Fiber: 5 g, Sugars: 8 g, Protein: 2 g, Sodium: 261 mg, Cholesterol: 0 mg*

Nutritional Bonus:

Like the common potato, sweet potatoes boast natural anti-inflammatory properties, due largely to the presence of beta-carotene, vitamin C and magnesium. They are also extremely effective at regulating blood sugar, making them the ideal carbohydrate for those trying to stay slim.

GINGER: While essential to your holiday gingerbread cookies, this spice is also known for its medicinal properties, such as soothing upset stomachs and nausea and easing inflammation. Make a rub for pork tenderloin with ground ginger, fennel seeds and orange zest. Sauté fresh ginger with garlic to create a flavorful base for black bean or carrot soup.

NUTMEG: Often paired with cinnamon in baking, this woodsy spice stands on its own in savory dishes. Try adding a pinch to cooked greens, such as sautéed spinach or braised collards. And, the next time you make mashed cauliflower or celery root, add nutmeg, to taste, for surprising depth of flavor.

Seasonal Spices

Certain flavors are crucial to your autumn table. Our handy guide helps you enjoy them now and in the colder months ahead.

STAR ANISE: One of the ingredients in Chinese five-spice powder, this star-shaped seed is usually sold whole. You can add three to six seeds when making marinades for grilled meat or glazes for holiday ham. Plus, perk up your homemade chicken soup with fennel-like flavor by adding star anise along with whole black peppercorns.

CINNAMON: Made from the bark of the cinnamon tree, one teaspoon has as much antioxidant power as a half-cup of blueberries. A favorite for clean cookies, apple crisps and other sweets, you may also pair it with cumin and chile powder to season lamb kabobs or beef stew.

CLOVES: Best known as a flavoring for glazed ham, this potent spice is derived from a plant in the evergreen family. Use it to add a rich, sweet kick to dishes like baked beans, slow-roasted pork or turkey meatloaf.

ALLSPICE:
Though often mistaken for a seasoning blend, allspice is actually derived from the berries of a tree indigenous to Jamaica. Add its clove-like flavor to braised lamb shanks or beef stew along with other dry spices, or sprinkle onto butternut or acorn squash and roast for a deep, savory twist.

CARDAMOM: Aromatic and vaguely sweet, this spice is found in chai tea, coconut-based curries and traditional yeast breads, such as *pulla* from Finland. Perk up a pot of coffee by adding one-half to one full teaspoon to the grounds before brewing. Sprinkle on low-fat plain yogurt or add a pinch to your morning oatmeal along with a half-teaspoon of pure vanilla extract for an exotic morning treat.

Top 5 Spring Vegetables

Antioxidant Superstar ★

These selections made the top 15 list in the *Journal of Agricultural and Food Chemistry*'s top 100 foods for total antioxidant content. Cooked artichoke hearts, placing at number seven overall, are the highest-ranking vegetable. Strawberries place at number 11 overall.

Nutrient Superstar ★

An individual serving of this fruit or vegetable provides more than 15 percent of your total recommended daily allowance (RDA) for four or more different vitamins and minerals.

Asparagus ★

1 CUP: Calories: 27, Total Fat: 0 g, Carbs: 5 g, Fiber: 3 g, Protein: 3 g

GOOD SOURCE: Vitamins A, C, E and K, thiamine, riboflavin, folate, iron, potassium, manganese

LOOK FOR: Firm, bright-green stalks and compact tips. Store it in the fridge bundled tightly, upright in a tall jar with one inch of water for two to four days.

TRY IT: Blanched in a crudité platter or lightly tossed with olive oil, sea salt and pepper and roasted whole for 15 minutes at 375°F.

ARTICHOKES are considered a liver-cleansing food. They're packed with fiber, magnesium, potassium and eye-friendly carotenoids (lutein and zeaxanthin).

Artichokes ★ ★

1 MEDIUM: Calories: 60, Total Fat: 0 g, Carbs: 13.5 g, Fiber: 7 g, Protein: 4 g

GOOD SOURCE: Vitamins C and K, folate, iron, magnesium, phosphorus, potassium, manganese

LOOK FOR: A firm, heavy artichoke with compact center leaves, medium green.

TRY IT: Steamed, thorny leaf tips trimmed, in a steamer basket with water spiced with a few peppercorns, half teaspoon oregano, a splash of red wine and lemon wedge until you can pull off leaves easily (30 to 45 minutes). To eat, pull off leaves, dip in balsamic vinegar and drag base ends through your teeth, scraping off the tender pulp and discarding the tougher parts of the leaves. When leaves are gone, scoop out thistly fibers (choke) and enjoy tender "heart" (base) and stem.

Dandelion Greens

1 CUP: Calories: 25, Total Fat: 0 g, Carbs: 5 g, Fiber: 2 g, Protein: 1.5 g

GOOD SOURCE: Vitamins A, C, E and K, riboflavin, calcium, iron, manganese

LOOK FOR: Young, crisp and fresh green leaves; no yellowing. Store wrapped in a damp paper towel in the crisper for up to five days.

TRY THEM: Raw, whole, dipped in hummus or chopped (raw or steamed) in a salad with a zippy homemade low-fat Caesar dressing with lots of garlic.

Fava Beans

1 CUP (WHOLE, IN POD): Calories: 111, Total Fat: 1 g, Carbs: 22 g, Fiber: 37 g, Protein: 10 g

GOOD SOURCE: Thiamine, riboflavin, niacin, folate, iron, magnesium, phosphorus, potassium, manganese

LOOK FOR: Seven- to nine-inch pods, crisp with a medium-green colour and without many markings. Avoid shriveled or yellowing husks. One pound of pods yields about a half-cup of beans. Store whole pods in the refrigerator. Best used within a few days of purchase.

TRY THEM: Shell the beans like pea pods and cook them in lightly sea-salted boiling water for about two minutes. No need to remove bean skins if very young and fresh. Add to salads or toss with whole-wheat pasta, shaved low-fat Romano cheese, thin slivers of low-fat ham, a drizzle of olive oil and sea salt/pepper to taste.

Fiddlehead Ferns ★

200 GRAMS (JUST UNDER 1 CUP): Calories: 68, Total Fat: 1 g, Carbs: 11 g, Fiber: 3 g, Protein: 3 g

GOOD SOURCE: Vitamins A and C, riboflavin, niacin, iron, magnesium, phosphorus, potassium, zinc, manganese

LOOK FOR: Tightly coiled, rich green ferns about one inch in diameter with only one inch of stem extending beyond the coil. They taste best if eaten right after harvest. Fiddleheads do not keep very well, but if you have to store them, keep them tightly wrapped in plastic (to prevent drying) in the fridge for no more than a couple of days.

TRY THEM: Rinsed several times in cold water (rubbing them gently to remove any remaining chaff), steamed for 20 minutes, and added last to salads or sauces. They're great in a vegetable stir-fry with a light teriyaki sauce or in a lemon-butter sauté with morels or other wild mushrooms.

Steam FIDDLEHEAD FERNS for 20 minutes to eliminate potential toxins.

Top 5 Spring Fruits

Pineapple

1 CUP: Calories: 82, Total Fat: 0 g, Carbs: 22 g, Fiber: 2 g, Protein: 1 g

GOOD SOURCE: Vitamins B6 and C, thiamine, manganese

LOOK FOR: A ripe fruit (pineapple doesn't ripen after picking) with fresh green leaves, the "eyes" on the skin plump. It should be firm and give off a mild, sweet smell. Nosh on the pineapple right away for optimum flavor. But if you can't, refrigerate it for two to four days. And, if you want to hang on to cut pieces, pop them into a tightly sealed container in the fridge for up to a couple of days.

TRY IT: Peeled and cut into chunks for a fruit salad, or grilled in thick rings for two minutes per side with a sprinkling of cayenne pepper.

Avocados ★

1 CUP (SLICED): Calories: 234, Total Fat: 21 g (14 g monounsaturated), Carbs: 12.5 g, Fiber: 10 g, Protein: 3 g

GOOD SOURCE: Vitamins B6, C, E and K, riboflavin, niacin, folate, pantothenic acid, magnesium, potassium, manganese

LOOK FOR: Firm fruit that yields slightly to the touch, no dents or cuts. Avoid overripe, mushy pieces. If the avocado is hard, store at room temperature until fully ripe, then refrigerate up to three days if necessary.

TRY IT: Peeled, raw in a smoothie, or add half of a peeled, pitted avocado to two cups raw baby spinach and half an apple, and process well in a blender for raw soup.

Mangos

1 CUP (SLICED): Calories: 107, Total Fat: 0.5 g, Carbs: 28 g, Fiber: 3 g, Protein: 1 g

GOOD SOURCE: Vitamins A, B6 and C

LOOK FOR: Deep orange, red, yellow or pink skin. Should smell sweet and yield slightly to pressure; no fragrance means it's unripe. Opinions differ on how long you can refrigerate the fruit once ripe. Some say only two to three days, while other experts vow that mangos will keep for up to a week.

TRY IT: Peeled and cubed (two cups) with one-third of a cup chopped green onion, a quarter-cup chopped fresh cilantro, two tablespoons lime juice, one teaspoon agave nectar or raw honey, and one tablespoon minced fresh ginger for a seafood salsa.

> **Just two little APRICOTS boast two grams of fiber and 1,348 IU of vitamin A. They're also famous for being packed with carotenoids and antioxidants which are said to reduce the risk of many types of cancers.**

Apricots

1 CUP (HALVES): Calories: 74, Total Fat: 0.6 g, Carbs: 17 g, Fiber: 3 g, Protein: 2 g

GOOD SOURCE: Vitamins A and C, potassium

LOOK FOR: Plump fruit with orange or reddish translucent skin, no bruising. Should yield slightly to pressure and smell sweet. When ripe, store in a bag and stick in the fridge for up to a couple of days.

TRY IT: Pitted and eaten whole as a snack, or halved and baked with chicken.

Strawberries ⭐

1 CUP (WHOLE): Calories: 46, Total Fat: 0 g, Carbs: 11 g, Fiber: 3 g, Protein: 1 g

GOOD SOURCE: Vitamin C, folate, manganese

LOOK FOR: Plump and fragrant, bright-red berries with fresh green leaves; avoid bruised fruit. Store unwashed and uncovered in the fridge for up to four days. But remember to gently wash before use!

TRY THEM: In an energy drink using one-and-a-half cups berries blended with one-third of a cup pasteurized raw egg whites and a drop of raw honey or agave syrup, or two cups berries blended with two cups cold water, one-third of a cup dry white wine, a quarter-cup of raw honey and half a cup plain yogurt for a cold dessert soup.

Healthy Snacks

Black Bean Tostadas, p. 147

Three meals a day is so passé. Clean eating is a lifestyle that includes snacking between meals – two or three times a day! Snacking not only keeps your hunger at bay (preventing you from overeating at your next meal), it also keeps your body burning fuel all day long and gives you tons of energy, allowing you to go about the rest of your busy day without worrying about your growling stomach. From our Honey Almond Sunflower Loaf to our Crustless Broccoli & Cheese Mini Quiches, we've got something for everyone. Pair our Yummy Hummus with our Clean Eating Tortilla Chips, and you've got a nutritious snack that will satisfy the pickiest of picky eaters.

Banana Protein Muffins

Serves 12. **Hands-on time:** 10 minutes. **Total time:** 40 minutes.

These muffins are low in fat and sodium, and contain both fiber and protein. They're perfect for a midmorning or mid-afternoon boost. Best of all, they're so low in calories you can eat two!

INGREDIENTS:

- 12 egg whites
- ⅔ cup uncooked oatmeal
- ⅔ cup high-fiber cereal
- 2 fresh bananas
- 6 Tbsp low- or no-sugar jam
- Dash vanilla extract
- Cinnamon
- 1 tsp baking soda
- 1 tsp baking powder
- 6 pkgs SteviaPlus Fiber Packets or 8 to 12 drops SteviaClear Liquid Stevia
- Olive oil cooking spray
- 1 oz raw chopped pecans

INSTRUCTIONS:

ONE: Preheat oven to 350°F. In a blender, mix everything but the cereal. Fold the cereal into the batter.

TWO: Line muffin tins with aluminum cupcake liners (this affects the consistency) and spray with Pam.

THREE: Pour the mixture evenly into the liners and top with chopped pecans. Bake for 30 minutes.

TIP: These freeze well, but be sure to let them cool before freezing.

Nutrients per serving (1 muffin): Calories: 85, Total Fat: 2 g, Sat. Fat: 0 g, Carbs: 13 g, Fiber: 2 g, Sugars: 5.5 g, Protein: 5 g, Sodium: 166 mg, Cholesterol: 0 mg

Banana
Protein
Muffins

Quick & Easy
Sunflower
Seed Granola

Quick & Easy
Sunflower Seed Granola

Serves 12. **Hands-on time:** *5 minutes.* **Total time:** *45 minutes.*

Making your own granola is so much better for you than purchasing the store-bought kind. It's lower in fat, fresher and tailored to your own tastes – a winning combination.

INGREDIENTS:

- ¾ cup sunflower seeds
- 1½ cups uncooked oatmeal
- ¼ cup ground flaxseed
- ½ cup dried cranberries
- ½ cup slivered almonds
- ½ cup shredded unsweetened coconut
- 3 Tbsp natural peanut butter
- ½ tsp salt
- ⅓ cup agave syrup
- ½ tsp vanilla

INSTRUCTIONS:

ONE: Preheat oven to 300°F. Combine ingredients in a bowl and mix until evenly blended.

TWO: Press mixture in a baking pan and bake for 40 minutes.

Nutrients per serving: Calories: 234, Total Fat: 13 g, Sat. Fat: 3 g, Carbs: 25.5 g, Fiber: 9 g, Protein: 7.5 g, Sugars: 12.5 g, Sodium: 52 mg, Cholesterol: 0 mg

Black Bean Tostadas
WITH CHIPOTLES & CORN

Serves 1. **Hands-on time:** *15 minutes.* **Total time:** *15 minutes.*

Since lush legumes are staples in Mexican cuisine, we've opted for black beans. They boost the fiber content of this "sandwich" even further, while harmonizing with the flavors of lime and chipotle for a fiesta in your mouth!

INGREDIENTS:

- 1 cup cooked black beans
- 1 tsp minced chipotle pepper
- ½ tsp ground cumin
- ½ tsp chile powder
- 2 tsp fresh lime juice, divided
- ½ cup frozen corn kernels, thawed
- 1 multigrain sandwich thin or round (both halves), toasted
- 1 oz low-fat cheddar cheese, grated
- 1 cup frisée, washed, dried and torn
- 1 cup halved cherry tomatoes

INSTRUCTIONS:

ONE: In a food processor or medium bowl, purée or mash beans. Add chipotle, cumin, chile powder and one teaspoon lime juice, and mix well. Add bean mixture to a small pan and warm gently, stirring, over medium-low heat.

TWO: Warm corn in another small pan over medium-low heat.

THREE: Divide bean mixture between two halves of sandwich thin, spreading evenly. Place halves, bean-side-up, on a plate. Top with cheese and corn, dividing evenly. Sprinkle remaining one teaspoon lime juice over frisée, then scatter evenly over halves. Garnish with tomatoes and serve immediately.

Nutrients per 2 open-faced sandwiches: Calories 467, Total Fat: 4 g, Sat. Fat: 2 g, Carbs: 82 g, Fiber: 25 g, Sugars: 9 g, Protein: 31 g, Sodium: 399 mg, Cholesterol: 6 mg

NUTRITIONAL BONUS: While they may be full of the same incredibly healthy fiber and protein as all beans, black beans have something their relatives don't: Their black skins contain at least eight different kinds of antioxidants! For example, their anthocyanin content is comparable to that of grapes and cranberries. Rule of thumb: The darker the color of a bean, the more antioxidants it contains.

For a photo of this recipe, see p. 142.

Eggplant Dip
MELAZANOSALATA

*Makes 2 cups. **Hands-on time:** 10 minutes. **Total time:** 40 minutes.*

Eggplant is a common vegetable throughout the Southern Mediterranean, where it is often fried. Roasting is a simpler, not to mention healthier, method of preparing the nightshade veggie, bringing out its natural sweetness while removing any bitter edge.

INGREDIENTS:

- 1 large eggplant (about 2 lbs), washed and halved lengthwise
- ½ tsp plus 1 Tbsp olive oil, divided
- 2 cloves garlic, coarsely chopped
- ½ cup roughly chopped sweet onion (such as Vidalia)
- Olive oil cooking spray
- ¼ cup loosely packed fresh basil, roughly chopped
- ⅛ tsp ground black pepper
- ¼ tsp sea salt

INSTRUCTIONS:

ONE: Preheat oven to 400°F. Brush cut sides of eggplant with a half-teaspoon oil, reserving a bit of oil for garlic and onion. Toss reserved bit of oil with garlic and onion. Place eggplant cut-sides-down in a large roasting pan misted with cooking spray. Arrange garlic and onion around eggplant. Roast in oven for 30 minutes. Set aside.

TWO: When eggplant is cool enough to handle, remove seeds (they will come out in strips) and scoop out meat with spoon. Place eggplant meat, garlic, onion, basil, remaining one tablespoon oil, pepper and salt in the bowl of a food processor fitted with a standard blade. Pulse about eight to ten times or until smooth but still chunky. Serve immediately or chill for one hour. Dip will keep for up to two days in refrigerator.

Nutrients per ¼-cup serving: *Calories: 40, Total Fat: 2 g, Sat. Fat: 0 g, Carbs: 5 g, Fiber: 3 g, Sugars: 2 g, Protein: 1 g, Sodium: 60 mg, Cholesterol: 0 mg*

NUTRITIONAL BONUS: Largely due to the eggplant, our Melazanosalata, or Eggplant Dip, offers as much fiber as a medium apple and more than half a cup of cooked long-grain brown rice.

"Raw" Beanless Zucchini Hummus

*Serves 4 to 6. **Hands-on time:** 5 minutes. **Total time:** 5 minutes.*

Have you ever tried adding zucchini to your dip? Its spring-like flavor is fresh and crisp, plus you get an added punch of folate, potassium and vitamin A.

INGREDIENTS:

- 3 zucchinis, peeled and chopped
- 6 Tbsp lemon juice
- 4 cloves garlic
- 2 tsp paprika
- 2 tsp sea salt
- ½ tsp cumin
- 1 tsp turmeric
- 2 pinches cayenne pepper
- ½ cup raw tahini
- 1 cup sesame or sunflower seeds, soaked
- Extra-virgin olive oil, for drizzle
- Fresh parsley, minced for garnish

INSTRUCTIONS:

ONE: Place all ingredients, except oil and parsley, into a blender or food processor and blend until smooth or to desired consistency. Drizzle with oil and garnish with parsley. Complement it with crudités, raw flax crackers or whole-grain pita bread. You can also spread it on sandwiches or mix it with salads.

Nutrients per 3-oz serving: *Calories: 140, Total Fat: 11 g, Sat. Fat: 1.5 g, Carbs: 8 g, Fiber: 2 g, Sugars: 1 g, Protein: 5 g, Sodium: 330 mg, Cholesterol: 0 mg*

Roasted Sweet Potato Fries

*Serves 4. **Hands-on time:** 15 minutes. **Total time:** 45 minutes.*

Chili powder brings life to any dish. It also is said to raise your metabolism slightly – perfect for those who are trying to stay slim.

INGREDIENTS:

- 2 large sweet potatoes, peeled
- 1 Tbsp canola oil
- 1 tsp chili powder

INSTRUCTIONS:

ONE: Preheat oven to 425°F. Line a rimmed baking sheet with aluminum foil.

TWO: Cut sweet potatoes in half lengthwise. Cut each half into three or four wedges.

THREE: In a mixing bowl, combine sweet potato wedges with oil. Sprinkle chili powder over sweet potatoes and stir again. Place sweet potato wedges on prepared baking sheet. Bake for 30 minutes, turning wedges several times during roasting so that they cook evenly.

Nutrients per serving: *Calories: 66, Total Fat: 1 g, Sat. Fat: 0 g, Carbs: 13 g, Fiber: 2 g, Protein: 1 g, Sugars: 3 g, Sodium: 36 mg, Cholesterol: 0 mg*

THE BEST OF CLEAN EATING

Tempting
Trail Mix

Tempting Trail Mix

Makes 16 servings. **Hands-on time:** 5 minutes. **Total time:** 5 minutes.

Next time you think about buying a snack from the convenience store or coffee truck, remember this trail mix. It's quick, easy and cost-effective too!

INGREDIENTS:

- 1 cup toasted oats cereal
- 1 cup raisins
- ½ cup dried cranberries
- ½ cup fiber cereal
- 1 cup roasted soy nuts (look for 10 grams of fat per ¼ cup)

INSTRUCTIONS:

ONE: Mix all ingredients in a large container with a lid. Close and shake.

TWO: Put quarter-cup portions into snack-sized bags for on-the-go eating.

Nutrients per ¼-cup serving: Calories: 103, Fat: 3 g, Sat. Fat: 0.5 g, Carbs: 18 g, Fiber: 2 g, Sugars: 9.25 g, Protein: 5 g, Sodium: 206 mg, Cholesterol: 0 mg

Everybody's Favorite Power Juice

Serves 1. **Hands-on time:** 5 minutes. **Total time:** 5 minutes.

Juicing your vegetables is an easy way to make sure you're getting proper vitamins and minerals in your daily diet. The ginger in this juice gives it a spicy kick.

INGREDIENTS:

- 3 cups spinach
- 2 to 3 carrots
- 1 apple
- 1 beet
- 1-inch square peeled chunk of fresh ginger (or more if you like it hot)

INSTRUCTIONS:

ONE: Wash spinach and apple, and scrub carrots and beet, but do not peel.

TWO: Peel ginger.

THREE: Juice everything, stir gently and enjoy.

Nutrients per serving: Calories: 212, Total Fat: 0.75 g, Sat. Fat: 0 g, Carbs: 53 g, Fiber: 14 g, Sugars: 30 g, Protein: 5 g, Sodium: 266 mg, Cholesterol: 0 mg

NUTRITIONAL BONUS: **The spinach provides lutein and zeaxanthin, two important carotenoids for eye health.**

Lotus Root Crisps & Avocado Salsa

Serves 4. **Hands-on time:** 15 minutes. **Total time:** 30 minutes.

A substitute for potato chips, our cholesterol-free crisps deliver crunch without the calories.

INGREDIENTS:

CRISPS

- 3 medium lotus roots, peeled and sliced into ⅛-inch discs
- 1 Tbsp fresh lemon juice, plus a few additional drops
- 1 Tbsp olive oil
- Pinch sea salt

SALSA

- 1 avocado, peeled and diced
- 1 Roma tomato, seeded and diced
- ½ cup cooked black beans
- 2 Tbsp diced red onion
- 2 Tbsp fresh lime juice
- 3 Tbsp chopped fresh cilantro
- ¼ tsp ground cayenne pepper
- Pinch sea salt

INSTRUCTIONS:

ONE: Prepare crisps: Submerge lotus discs in water with a few drops of lemon juice to prevent discoloration. Steam for six minutes.

TWO: Preheat oven to 450°F. Toss discs with one tablespoon lemon juice, oil and salt until evenly coated. Place discs onto a baking sheet and bake in oven for 20 minutes, flipping discs after 10 minutes.

THREE: Prepare salsa: In a medium bowl, combine all salsa ingredients and gently stir. Serve salsa immediately or prepare ahead of time and refrigerate for up to four hours. Serve crisps either hot or at room temperature with salsa.

Nutrients per serving (12 to 15 crisps and ½ cup salsa): Calories: 210, Total Fat: 10.5 g, Sat. Fat: 1.5 g, Carbs: 30 g, Fiber: 9 g, Sugars: 2 g, Protein: 5 g, Sodium: 230 mg, Cholesterol: 0 mg

Honey Almond Sunflower Loaf

(ALMOND MEAL; BUCKWHEAT & QUINOA FLOURS)

*Makes 1 loaf. **Hands-on time:** 10 minutes. **Total time:** 50 to 55 minutes.*

Gluten free without the fuss of added binders, this bread has a cake-like, soft crumb. Served with a bowl of stew or made into a nut butter sandwich for lunch, our loaf complements both sweet and savory flavors.

INGREDIENTS:

- 1 cup almond meal
- ¾ cup buckwheat flour
- 1¼ cups quinoa flour
- 3 tsp baking powder
- 1 egg
- 2 egg whites
- 1 cup unsweetened soy milk (or skim milk or unsweetened almond or rice milk)
- ⅓ cup olive oil
- 2 Tbsp raw organic honey
- ¼ cup plus 1 Tbsp unsalted sunflower seeds (raw or toasted), divided
- Olive oil cooking spray

INSTRUCTIONS:

ONE: Preheat oven to 350°F. In a medium bowl, whisk together meal, flours and baking powder.

TWO: In a small bowl, whisk together egg, egg whites, milk, oil, honey and a quarter cup seeds.

THREE: Add wet ingredients to dry ingredients and combine. Do not over-mix.

FOUR: Mist a 9- or 10-inch loaf pan with cooking spray. Pour batter into pan and sprinkle remaining one tablespoon sunflower seeds over top of loaf. Bake 40 to 45 minutes or until a toothpick inserted in the middle comes out clean. Cool bread before slicing.

OPTION: Loaded with heart-healthy monounsaturated fat, fiber, vitamins and protein, this bread can also be made into muffins for an on-the-go nutritious snack. Simply reduce baking time to 15 to 20 minutes for a standard muffin pan.

Nutrients per ½-inch slice: Calories: 150, Total Fat: 9 g, Sat. Fat: 1 g, Carbs: 13 g, Fiber: 3 g, Sugars: 2 g, Protein: 5 g, Sodium: 25 mg, Cholesterol: 10 mg

NUTRITIONAL BONUS: Pseudo-grains buckwheat and quinoa (technically seeds yet commonly referred to as grains) are both very high in lysine, an essential amino acid that aids the body in tissue growth and repair.

Power Yogurt for One

*Serves 1. **Hands-on time:** 2 minutes. **Total time:** 2 minutes.*

Easy to make, this protein-packed snack is perfect for when you need something to eat in a hurry. Mixing up the fruits will alter the flavor and keep this dish interesting each time you make it.

INGREDIENTS:

- ½ cup plain low-fat yogurt
- 1 scoop whey protein powder, flavor of choice
- ⅓ cup sliced strawberries
- 1 tsp flaxseed oil
- ½ tsp cinnamon

INSTRUCTIONS:

ONE: Place all ingredients in a bowl or take-away container and mix until protein powder is thoroughly blended in.

Nutrients per serving: Calories: 240, Total Fat: 7.5 g, Sat. Fat: 2 g, Carbs: 19 g, Fiber: 2 g, Sugars: 11 g, Protein: 27 g, Sodium: 86 mg, Cholesterol: 7 mg

Coconut Balls

*Makes 10 balls. **Hands-on time:** 10 minutes. **Total time:** 10 minutes.*

These yummy balls are sweet without any added sugar. The sweetness comes from the dried fruits – they are nature's candy!

INGREDIENTS:

- ½ cup raisins
- ¾ cup walnuts
- ½ cup dried pitted dates
- ½ cup dried apricots
- 2 Tbsp orange juice
- 1 tsp orange zest
- 1 small bag unsweetened shredded coconut

INSTRUCTIONS:

ONE: In a food processor, pulverize raisins, walnuts, dates and apricots for one to two minutes or until finely chopped. Add juice and zest. Blend for one to two minutes more or until mixture clumps together.

TWO: Place about a half-cup of coconut on a plate. Dampen hands with water, then form mixture into one-inch balls and roll them in coconut. Store balls in refrigerator.

Nutrients per coconut ball: Calories: 142, Total Fat: 8 g, Sat. Fat: 2 g, Carbs: 18 g, Fiber: 2 g, Sugars: 14 g, Protein: 2 g, Sodium: 3 mg, Cholesterol: 0 mg

NUTRITIONAL BONUS: Walnuts have the most heart-healthy omega-3 fatty acids of any nut. Apricots are loaded with vitamin A, which helps keep your eyes in fine working order.

Nutritional Bonus:

Whey is a terrific source of protein, making this creamy snack a perfect choice to recharge your muscles after a workout. Strawberries are anti-oxidant powerhouses with more vitamin C than any other berry. Just one cup has more of the immunity-boosting vitamin than a medium orange!

Power Yogurt for One

Sweet Potato Spread

Makes 2 cups. **Hands-on time:** 20 minutes. **Total time:** 40 minutes.

You've tried baking them whole, roasting them and turning them into fries. Now it's time to turn this versatile vegetable into a spread (it also works as a dip!).

INGREDIENTS:

- 2 medium sweet potatoes
- 1 carrot
- 1 onion
- ½ cup water
- 1 Tbsp tahini or natural unsalted almond butter
- ¼ tsp curry powder
- ¼ tsp ground cumin

INSTRUCTIONS:

ONE: In a saucepan, cover sweet potatoes with water and bring to a boil. Simmer over medium heat until potatoes are soft when pierced with a knife (about 30 minutes). Remove from saucepan. When cool, remove skin.

TWO: While potatoes are cooking, peel carrot and onion, and chop into small pieces. Place in another saucepan and cover with a half cup of water. Simmer until soft, about eight minutes.

THREE: Purée sweet potato in a food processor along with tahini or almond butter, curry powder and ground cumin until just combined. Add carrot-onion mixture and purée until smooth.

TIP: Serve with vegetable crudités or whole-wheat crackers.

Nutrients per 2-Tbsp serving: Calories: 21, Total Fat: 0.5 g, Sat. Fat: 0 g, Carbs: 4 g, Fiber: 1 g, Sugars: 1.5 g, Protein: 0.5 g, Sodium: 7 mg, Cholesterol: 0 mg

Garlic Bruschetta

Serves 6. **Hands-on time:** *10 minutes.* **Total time:** *15 minutes.*

The mild, almost chestnut-like taste of roasted garlic will turn your regular old bruschetta into something supreme. It will also improve your cardiovascular health – a win-win situation!

INGREDIENTS:

- ¾ cup seeded and diced vine-ripened tomatoes
- ¾ cup seeded and diced yellow or green tomatoes, preferably vine ripened
- 2 cloves roasted garlic, diced
- 1 Tbsp drained and chopped capers
- ¼ cup basil, chiffonade*
- 1 Tbsp extra-virgin olive oil
- Sea salt and fresh cracked pepper, to taste
- 6 slices bread, fresh Italian or French whole-grain baguette

INSTRUCTIONS:

ONE: In a bowl, combine tomatoes, garlic, capers, basil, oil, salt and pepper.

TWO: Toast both sides of bread in broiler for about 30 seconds each or until browned.

THREE: Spoon one ounce of bruschetta mix onto toasted bread.

Nutrients per 2 slices baguette, 2-oz bruschetta mix: Calories: 165, Total Fat: 3 g, Sat. Fat: 1.5 g, Carbs: 29 g, Fiber: 3 g, Sugars: 1 g, Protein: 0 g, Sodium: 305 mg, Cholesterol: 0 mg

***CHIFFONADE, French for "made of rags," is a technique used to thinly slice herbs and leafy vegetables into long strips. To chiffonade, stack a few leaves, roll and thinly slice.**

Nutritional Bonus:

For centuries garlic has been considered important for health, and numerous published studies have demonstrated why. Garlic inhibits coronary artery calcification, and has a demonstrated ability to decrease free radicals. Experts recommend eating up to two whole bulbs a day.

STEP-BY-STEP TO ROASTING A HEAD OF GARLIC:

ONE: Preheat oven to 400°F. Peel the outside layer of skin but leave enough to keep individual cloves bound together. (You can wear gloves to avoid smelly hands.)

TWO: With a kitchen knife, cut a quarter- to half-inch off the head, exposing the cloves.

THREE: Put into a baking dish or muffin tin. Using your fingers, spread olive oil thoroughly over the head of the garlic. Make sure it's coated all over, otherwise the edges will burn.

FOUR: Cover with tinfoil and bake for 30 minutes. To tell if it's done, poke with a toothpick. The toothpick should go through but feel slight resistance. You want it soft, not mushy.

Chicken Caesar Salad

WITH HOMEMADE CAESAR DRESSING

*Serves 4. **Makes** 1½ cups dressing. **Hands-on time:** 20 minutes.
Total time: 2 hours, 20 minutes (including marinating time).*

Once you make the dressing, this is a fast and easy Chicken Caesar Salad for days when you need a light lunch or dinner in a snap.

INGREDIENTS:

SALAD

- ⅔ cup Homemade Caesar Dressing (recipe below)
- 3 Tbsp Dijon mustard
- 1 tsp lemon juice, freshly squeezed
- ¾ lb boneless chicken breast
- 1 bunch Romaine lettuce, washed and torn into bite-sized pieces (about 10 cups)
- 14 cherry tomatoes, halved
- 4 slices whole grain bread

DRESSING

- 1 (300-g) pkg soft tofu
- 2 to 3 cloves garlic, minced
- ¼ cup freshly squeezed lemon juice
- 3 Tbsp extra-virgin olive oil
- 1 Tbsp Dijon mustard
- ½ tsp sea salt

INSTRUCTIONS:

ONE: Whirl all dressing ingredients in a food processor or blender until combined.

TWO: Preheat broiler. In a small bowl, combine salad dressing, mustard and lemon juice. In a separate bowl, reserve half the dressing mixture.

THREE: Place chicken and remaining dressing in a large plastic zipper bag, seal bag and shake to coat chicken with dressing, and marinate for two hours in the refrigerator.

FOUR: Lightly mist a broiler pan with nonstick spray. Place skinless, boneless chicken on prepared pan and broil for about 10 minutes, turning once. Let cool for five minutes. Meanwhile, in a large bowl, combine lettuce and tomatoes. When chicken is ready, cut it into strips on a diagonal. Add chicken and the rest of the dressing to your salad, and toss. Serve with whole grain bread.

Nutrients per serving (1½ cups salad, 1 Tbsp dressing): Calories: 300, Total Fat: 10.5 g, Sat. Fat: 3.5 g, Carbs: 27 g, Fiber: 5 g, Sugars: 5 g, Protein: 26 g, Sodium: 980 mg, Cholesterol: 45 mg

Breakfast Bars

*Makes 24. **Hands-on time:** 15 minutes. **Total time:** 35 minutes.*

Instead of visiting your local coffee house for a triple caramel latte and a scone for an on-the-go breakfast, reach for one of our Breakfast Bars before heading out the door. The grab-and-go meal offers heart-healthy monounsaturated fats from nuts, filling fiber thanks to rolled oats, impressive meat-free protein à la egg whites, and natural sweetness with dried fruit and maple syrup or honey.

INGREDIENTS:

- Olive oil cooking spray
- 1 cup unsalted pecans, chopped
- 1 cup unsalted roasted almonds, chopped
- ½ cup dried unsweetened apricots
- 1 cup dried unsweetened figs
- 1½ cups rolled oats
- ½ cup unsweetened golden raisins
- 1½ cups unsweetened brown rice cereal
- 3 egg whites
- ¼ cup pure maple syrup or raw organic honey
- ¼ tsp ground cinnamon
- ¼ tsp sea salt
- 1 tsp pure vanilla extract

INSTRUCTIONS:

ONE: Preheat oven to 350°F. Lightly mist a 13 x 9-inch baking pan with cooking spray.

TWO: Combine pecans, almonds, apricots and figs in a food processor. Lightly pulse until chopped. Transfer pecan mixture to a large mixing bowl; add oats, raisins and cereal.

THREE: In a separate bowl, combine egg whites, syrup or honey, cinnamon, salt and vanilla, stirring well. Add to pecan mixture, mixing well.

FOUR: Spread mixture into prepared pan, pressing down gently. Bake 20 to 25 minutes or until lightly browned. Allow to cool 15 to 30 minutes before slicing into three-inch bars.

FREEZING TIP: Breakfast Bars can be stored in an airtight container and refrigerated for up to two weeks or frozen for up to two months.

Nutrients per 3 x 3-inch bar: Calories: 201, Total Fat: 11 g, Sat. Fat: 1 g, Carbs: 25 g, Fiber: 4 g, Sugars: 6 g, Protein: 4 g, Sodium: 38 mg, Cholesterol: 0 mg

Web Bonus!

Get nine more quick and easy breakfast ideas!
cleaneatingmag.com/breakfastonthego

Peach Melba Yogurt Smoothie

*Serves 2. **Hands-on time:** 5 minutes. **Total time:** 5 minutes.*

Invented in the late 19th century by French chef August Escoffier to honor Australian soprano Dame Nellie Melba, this classic combination combines two of our favorite summer fruits: peaches and raspberries. Try plunging your peaches in boiling water then directly into an ice bath – it makes peeling them a breeze.

INGREDIENTS:

- 1 cup low-fat plain yogurt
- 1 cup fresh peach slices, peeled
- ½ cup raspberries, fresh or thawed if frozen
- 1 Tbsp raw honey
- 1 tsp fresh lemon juice
- ¼ tsp pure vanilla extract
- 2 Tbsp low-fat milk

INSTRUCTIONS:

ONE: Add all ingredients to a blender and purée until smooth. Divide mixture among two glasses and enjoy!

Nutrients per 1-cup (8 oz) serving:
Calories: 164, Total Fat: 2 g, Sat. Fat: 1 g, Carbs: 30 g, Fiber: 5 g, Sugars: 26 g, Protein: 7 g, Sodium: 92 mg, Cholesterol: 8 mg

Nutritional Bonus:

An excellent source of protein, yogurt also contains more calcium than a simple glass of milk. If you have a family history of osteoporosis, have at least one serving of nonfat or low-fat yogurt per day.

Nutritional Bonus:

Red peppers contain lycopene, a carotenoid that has been linked to a reduced risk of cardiovascular disease and macular degeneration, and protection from damaging UV rays.

Roasted Red Pepper & Cucumber Tea Sandwiches

Roasted Red Pepper & Cucumber Tea Sandwiches
ON PUMPERNICKEL

Serves 1. ***Hands-on time:*** *5 minutes.* ***Total time:*** *5 minutes.*

Perfect as a party appetizer or a summer snack, these simple sandwiches are packed with flavor and nutrients.

INGREDIENTS:

• 1 Tbsp Neufchâtel cheese (or low-fat plain cream cheese)
• 1 slice whole-grain pumpernickel rye bread (1 oz)
• 6 thin English cucumber slices
• ¼ cup roasted red peppers
• 4 small sprigs fresh dill
• 1 thin slice of lemon, quartered

INSTRUCTIONS:

ONE: Drain peppers and pat dry using a tea or paper towel, then cut into strips.

TWO: Spread cheese on bread. Top with cucumber slices and pepper strips.

THREE: Cut topped bread twice diagonally to create four triangles.

FOUR: Top each triangular with a sprig of dill and serve with slices of lemon for garnish.

Nutrients per open-faced sandwich: Calories: 138, Total Fat: 7 g, Sat. Fat: 1 g, Carbs: 17 g, Fiber: 3 g, Sugars: 2.5 g, Protein: 3 g, Sodium: 252 mg, Cholesterol: 0 mg

Clean Eating Tortilla Chips

Serves as little or as many as you like! ***Hands-on time:*** *5 minutes.* ***Total time:*** *20 minutes.*

Crunchy corn chips are the perfect companion to our hearty Mexican 5-Layer Dip. But many store-bought brands contain high amounts of unhealthy fats and oils. A simple solution? Make your own baked tortilla chips.

INGREDIENTS:

• 6-inch unsalted corn tortillas
• Olive oil cooking spray
• Cayenne pepper or mild chile powder, to taste

INSTRUCTIONS:

ONE: Preheat oven to 400ºF. Cut tortillas into quarters, lightly mist both sides with cooking spray and arrange in a single layer on two baking sheets. Dust tops with cayenne pepper, if you like a little spice, or chile powder for a more subtle flavor.

TWO: Bake in oven for five to six minutes per side or until crisp and lightly browned. Chips will continue to crisp slightly as they cool. Serve immediately or cool completely and store in an airtight container for up to eight hours.

Nutrients per 8 chips (2 6-inch tortillas): Calories: 125, Total Fat: 2 g, Sat. Fat: 0.25 g, Carbs: 24 g, Fiber: 3 g, Sugars: 0 g, Protein: 3 g, Sodium: 6 mg, Cholesterol: 0 mg

Mexican 5-Layer Dip

Serves 27. ***Hands-on time:*** *40 minutes.*
Total time: *3 hours, 45 minutes (includes soaking and cooking of beans).*

A hit with adults and kids alike, we've lightened up this party dish so you can take part in the fiesta without worrying about your waistline.

INGREDIENTS:

• 1 cup dried pinto beans
• 3 medium tomatoes, seeded and chopped (about 2½ cups)
• 1 small white onion, chopped (about ¾ cup)
• 2 to 3 jalapeño peppers, seeded and chopped (about ⅓ cup)
• ¾ packed cup fresh cilantro leaves, chopped, divided
• Juice 2 limes, divided
• ½ tsp sea salt, plus additional to taste, divided
• Fresh ground black pepper, to taste
• 2 ripe avocados, pitted and peeled
• 6 oz reduced-fat cheddar cheese, grated (about 1½ cups)
• 1½ cups reduced-fat sour cream

INSTRUCTIONS:

ONE: Rinse beans in a colander and discard any debris or small stones. Place in a medium saucepan and add enough water to cover beans. Bring to a boil over high heat and cook for two minutes. Turn off heat and let beans rest for one hour. Drain beans in a colander and rinse. Wash saucepan, return beans to saucepan and add enough water to cover by two inches. Bring to a boil over high heat. Reduce heat to low to maintain a steady simmer. Cover and cook for one-and-a-half to two hours or until beans are very tender. Reserve about two-thirds of a cup cooking liquid, drain beans and set aside to cool.

TWO: In a medium bowl, combine tomatoes, onion, jalapeños and about two-thirds of cilantro. Squeeze juice of one lime over tomato mixture and season, to taste, with salt and black pepper. Set aside.

THREE: In a food processor or blender, combine avocados, remaining cilantro and remaining juice of one lime. Purée until slightly chunky. Season with salt and black pepper, to taste. Set aside.

FOUR: Place beans and one-third of a cup reserved cooking liquid in a food processor (or use a powerful blender or mash by hand with a potato masher). Process until you have a slightly chunky purée, adding additional cooking liquid, one tablespoon at a time as needed to reach desired consistency. Add half teaspoon salt and black pepper. Pulse several times to combine. Transfer beans to a 9 x 13-inch casserole dish or large glass bowl and spread into an even layer.

FIVE: Sprinkle cheese evenly over beans. Dollop scoops of avocado mixture over cheese and use a spatula to spread into a thin layer. Dollop scoops of sour cream over avocado and spread into a thin layer. With a slotted spoon (to drain any liquid), spread tomato mixture evenly over sour cream. Serve immediately or cover and chill for up to four hours.

Nutrients per ¼-cup serving: Calories: 86, Total Fat: 4.5 g, Sat. Fat: 1.5 g, Carbs: 8 g, Fiber: 2 g, Sugars: 1.5 g, Protein: 4 g, Sodium: 87 mg, Cholesterol: 8 mg

Crustless Broccoli & Cheese Mini Quiches

Serves 5. *Hands-on time:* 15 minutes. *Total time:* 40 minutes.

These low-fat quiches come with an impressive amount of protein for a meat-free snack. Use them as snacks throughout the day to keep cravings at bay, or pair a couple of quiches with some fresh fruit and a slice of multigrain bread or a bowl of oatmeal for a balanced start to your day (eggs are a breakfast favorite, after all!).

INGREDIENTS:

- Olive oil cooking spray
- 1 tsp olive oil
- 1½ cups chopped broccoli
- ⅔ cup shredded low-fat cheddar cheese, divided
- 1 cup low-fat Greek-style yogurt
- 2 Tbsp low-fat milk
- 1 whole egg
- 1 tsp dried oregano
- ¼ tsp sea salt
- Fresh ground black pepper, to taste

INSTRUCTIONS:

ONE: Preheat oven to 350°F. Spray 10 cups of a muffin tray lightly with cooking spray.

TWO: Heat oil in a medium skillet. Add broccoli and sauté for five minutes. Distribute broccoli evenly among prepared muffin cups; then distribute half of the cheese evenly on top.

THREE: In a medium bowl, whisk together yogurt, milk, egg and seasonings, then distribute evenly over top of broccoli and cheese. Top with remaining cheese and bake 20 to 25 minutes or until quiches are set and lightly browned around the edges. Cool five minutes and serve or cool and refrigerate until ready to enjoy.

Nutrients per 2 quiches: *Calories: 100, Total Fat: 3.5 g, Sat. Fat: 2 g, Carbs: 6 g, Fiber: 2 g, Sugars: 1 g, Protein: 11 g, Sodium: 240 mg, Cholesterol: 40 mg*

NUTRITIONAL BONUS: Protein isn't just for athletes or those logging extra-long workouts. The macronutrient can be found in every cell in your body and is needed to repair those cells or create new ones. While meat products tend to offer larger amounts, a serving of our mini quiches is a clean vegetarian alternative that packs a protein punch.

Yummy Hummus

Serves 10. *Hands-on time:* 5 to 8 minutes. *Total time:* 5 minutes.

Everyone needs a standard hummus recipe. Try ours – it's healthy and delicious.

INGREDIENTS:

- 1 cup chickpeas, drained and rinsed (low sodium)
- 2 cloves fresh garlic, chopped
- 1 Tbsp sesame seeds
- 2 Tbsp 100% pure orange juice
- ¼ tsp sea salt
- ⅛ tsp fresh ground black pepper
- ⅛ tsp cumin
- 2 Tbsp extra-virgin olive oil
- 1 Tbsp chopped fresh parsley

INSTRUCTIONS:

ONE: Combine all the ingredients in a blender or mini food processor and purée until smooth.

Nutrients per 2-Tbsp serving: *Calories: 59, Total Fat: 3 g, Sat. Fat: 0 g, Carbs: 5 g, Fiber: 1 g, Sugars: 0.5 g, Protein: 2 g, Sodium: 56 mg, Cholesterol: 0 mg*

NEW!

Roasted Red Pepper & White Bean Hummus
WITH CRUDITÉS

Serves 16. *Makes* 2 cups. *Hands-on time:* 10 minutes. *Total time:* 10 minutes.

The flavor of this spicy, zesty dip beats any store-bought or restaurant variety by a long shot – the creamy cannellini beans give it a smooth and nutty taste. Chock-full of healthy fiber, this dip is significantly lower in both calories and fat, too.

INGREDIENTS:

- 1 (15-oz can) cannellini or white kidney beans, drained and rinsed
- 1 small clove garlic, minced
- 1 roasted red pepper (packed in water), drained
- Juice 1 lemon
- ½ tsp ground cumin
- ½ tsp sea salt, plus more to taste
- ¼ tsp fresh ground black pepper, plus more to taste
- 1 to 2 Tbsp extra-virgin olive oil
- Assorted crudités (carrots, celery, snap peas, bell peppers and/or fennel)

Continued ▶

Roasted Red Pepper & White Bean Hummus

Nutritional Bonus:

Aside from the array of vivid colors that make them so appealing, bell peppers are also an excellent source of vitamins C and A, two very powerful anti-oxidants that work to neutralize free radicals in the body.

INSTRUCTIONS:

ONE: In a food processor, pulse beans, garlic, red pepper, lemon juice, cumin, salt and black pepper for three to five minutes until mixture is thick and fluffy paste. While processor is running, drizzle in one tablespoon oil and, if too thick, add one more tablespoon. Taste and season with salt and black pepper, if desired. Pour mixture into a bowl and serve with crudités. (NOTE: The longer you process your dip, the smoother it will become.)

TIP: When using canned goods, look for brands that use BPA-free cans, such as Eden foods. And remember to drain and rinse the beans well.

Nutrients per 2-Tbsp serving: Calories: 46, Total Fat: 1 g, Sat. Fat: 0.1 g, Carbs: 8 g, Fiber: 2 g, Sugars: 2.5 g, Protein: 2 g, Sodium: 153 mg, Cholesterol: 0 mg

Your Guide to Flours

Almond Flour/Meal

Typically, almond flour is made from finely ground blanched almonds, while almond meal has a more coarse texture with the skins retained during grinding. Naturally gluten free and high in protein and monounsaturated fats, almond flour is the lowest carbohydrate option in our flour roundup.

TRY IT: A great addition to short-breads, pastry crusts, pastas and an alternate breading for chicken or fish. In quick breads, it adds nutty flavor as well as a tender texture.

STORE IT: Keep refrigerated in an airtight container for up to six months or freeze for up to one year.

Brown Rice Flour

Ground from rice with the germ and bran layers left intact, brown rice flour is a naturally gluten-free source of fiber, manganese, selenium and B vitamins.

TRY IT: Mildly flavored, finely ground brown rice flour adds a nice crunch to cookies and crackers. Using it in quick breads lessens or eliminates gluten without compromising taste or texture. Brown rice flour is also a natural substitute for white rice flour.

STORE IT: Keep refrigerated in an airtight container for up to five months or freeze for up to one year.

Buckwheat Flour

First domesticated in Southeast Asia, buckwheat is most closely related to the rhubarb plant. With a high proportion of eight amino acids, buckwheat, combined with other whole-grain flours such as wheat or spelt, creates a complete protein. Buckwheat is a good source of fiber, iron, calcium, magnesium, phosphorous and B vitamins.

TRY IT: The flavor of buckwheat is distinctly nutty and malt-like and pairs well with ginger, pumpkin and chocolate quick breads. Buckwheat not only gives a nutritional boost to cookies, pancakes, muffins and handmade noodles; if pure, it can be used in a gluten-free diet.

STORE IT: Keep refrigerated in an airtight container for up to three months or freeze for up to one year.

Kamut Flour

An ancient relative of wheat, most similar to durum, kamut is an organic product that originated in Egypt. Kamut flour is a high-gluten option that is easy to digest, so some people with wheat intolerances may be able to eat it. It also has up to 30 percent more protein than other wheat varieties and is high in potassium, B vitamins, vitamin E, zinc, magnesium and iron. Kamut's flavor is similar to that of white flour, but expect yeast breads to be a bit denser when using the flour interchangeably with white or whole-wheat types.

STORE IT: Store in an airtight container in a cool, dry place for up to one year or freeze for up to 18 months.

Quinoa Flour

A seed originating in the Andes region of South America, quinoa is made into a flour that is rich in a multitude of minerals, B vitamins and vitamin E, as well as omega-3 fatty acids. Most importantly, quinoa contains a balanced set of amino acids, making it a complete protein source, with a protein content higher than that of any other flour. If quinoa flour cannot be found, grind whole quinoa as needed using a high-speed blender or flour mill.

TRY IT: With a slightly grassy yet not overpowering flavor, quinoa flour pairs well with banana, zucchini and carrot breads and makes wonderful gluten-free tortillas.

STORE IT: Keep refrigerated in an airtight container for up to four months or freeze for up to six months.

Oat Flour

High in potassium, calcium, protein and B vitamins, oats are easy to digest and exceptionally versatile. Due to their impressive amount of soluble fiber, oats may help lower "bad" LDL cholesterol and provide long-lasting energy. If oat flour cannot be found, grind whole oats in a food processor (one-and-a-quarter cups oats will yield one cup oat flour).

TRY IT: Oat flour adds moisture to bar cookies and brownies and helps whole-grain baked goods stay fresh longer.

STORE IT: In an airtight container in a cool, dry place for up to three months or freeze for up to 18 months.

Spelt Flour

An ancient grain dating back to medieval times in Europe, spelt has made a comeback as a healthy alternative to whole wheat. Although it is a species of wheat, it is easier to digest for some with wheat intolerances. A good source of protein, B vitamins and fiber, spelt also contains mucopoly-saccharides, a type of carbohydrate that aids in blood clotting and stimulates the immune system. The gluten in spelt flour is fragile, so take special care not to over-mix.

TRY IT: When using spelt flour in a yeast bread recipe, increase yeast by 25 percent (if two teaspoons yeast are called for, increase to two-and-a-half teaspoons) or expect a denser loaf.

STORE IT: Store in an airtight container in a cool, dry place for up to three months or refrigerate or freeze for up to one year.

Millet Flour

Millet was first cultivated in China thousands of years ago. It is a seed, most commonly used as a cereal in Asia and Africa. Rich in iron, potassium, magnesium, calcium, phosphorous, manganese, zinc, B vitamins and fiber, millet has a protein content close to that of wheat. Millet is easy to digest, naturally gluten free and imparts a sweet taste. If you can't find millet flour, grind whole millet as needed using a high-speed blender or flour mill.

STORE IT: Keep refrigerated in an airtight container for up to two months or freeze for up to six months.

Quick Flour Substitution Guide

ALMOND FLOUR/MEAL	1 cup wheat flour = ¼ cup almond flour + ¾ cup wheat flour
BROWN RICE FLOUR	1 cup wheat flour = ¼ cup brown rice flour + ¾ cup wheat flour
BUCKWHEAT FLOUR	1 cup wheat flour = ½ cup buckwheat flour + ½ cup wheat flour Yeast breads: 1 cup wheat flour = ⅓ cup buckwheat flour + ⅔ cup wheat flour
KAMUT FLOUR	1 cup wheat flour = 1 cup Kamut flour
MILLET FLOUR	Cornbread, cookies, flatbreads and pancakes: 1 cup wheat flour = ½ cup millet flour + ½ cup wheat flour Biscuits and yeast breads: 1 cup wheat flour = ¼ cup millet flour + ¾ cup wheat flour
OAT FLOUR	Quick breads, cookies and pancakes: 1 cup wheat flour = ½ cup oat flour + ½ cup wheat flour Biscuits and yeast breads: 1 cup wheat flour = ¼ cup oat flour + ¾ cup wheat flour
QUINOA FLOUR	Non-yeast recipes: 1 cup wheat flour = 1 cup quinoa flour Yeast breads: 1 cup wheat flour = ½ cup quinoa flour + ½ cup wheat flour
SPELT FLOUR	1 cup wheat flour = 1 cup spelt flour

If your clean recipe calls for one cup of whole-wheat flour but you'd like to give quinoa or buckwheat flour a try, how much should you use? Just give our guide a quick peek for all of your flour substitution needs.

NOTE: **For those with wheat sensitivities, rye and barley flours work well in place of whole-wheat flour in most quick bread recipes. Also, while spelt flour is a species of wheat, it is easier for some with wheat intolerances to digest and can be used interchangeably with wheat flour.**

If you suffer from a gluten intolerance or celiac disease, try a gluten-free baking mix such as Bob's Red Mill All-Purpose Gluten-Free Baking Flour or make your own at home:

Gluten-Free Baking Mix for Quick Breads

Makes 1 cup.

- ½ cup brown rice or millet flour
- 4 Tbsp potato starch
- 4 Tbsp almond flour/meal
- ¼ tsp guar or xanthan gum (optional)

Nutrients per ¼ cup:

FLOUR	ALMOND	BROWN RICE	BUCKWHEAT	KAMUT	MILLET	OAT	QUINOA	SPELT
CALORIES	160	140	90	100	100	190	120	100
TOTAL FAT	14	1	1	0.5	1	2.5	2	0
SAT. FAT	1	0	0	0	0	0	0	0
CARBS	6	31	15	19	20	16	21	21
FIBER	3	2	4	3	2	2	4	2
SUGARS	1	0	0	0	0	0	0	2
PROTEIN	6	3	4	3	3	3	4	4
SODIUM	0	5	0	0	0	0	10	0
CHOLESTEROL	0	0	0	0	0	0	0	0

On-the-Go Clean Snacks

Fast food doesn't have to be unhealthy. Stay free and clear of the take-out window by keeping these quick snacks on hand when you're short on time – they require virtually no prep or cooking time.

- **HALF A MULTIGRAIN BAGEL** with unsalted almond butter

- **SCOOP OF DRY, WHOLE-GRAIN CEREAL** with added raisins and a handful of nuts

- **CUP OR TWO OF PLAIN POPCORN** (did you know it's a whole grain?) topped with a pinch of sea salt

- **SIX MULTIGRAIN CRACKERS** with two tablespoons natural, unsalted peanut or almond butter and a quarter cup of dried fruit

- **TEN UNSALTED ALMONDS AND ONE APPLE**, cut into slices

- **HALF A CAN OF SALMON OR TUNA** (canned in water) stuffed into a multigrain pita

- **TWO OUNCES OF LOW-FAT CHEESE CUBES** with half a cup of grapes or berries

- **FOUR WHOLE-WHEAT, ORGANIC GRAHAM CRACKERS** sandwiched with natural, unsalted peanut butter

- **HALF A CUP OF LOW-FAT COTTAGE CHEESE** with banana slices or berries

- **BAKED SWEET POTATO** topped with nonfat Greek yogurt and chives (a healthier take on the classic, loaded side)

- **FOUR OUNCES OF PLAIN, LOW-FAT YOGURT** mixed with whole-grain granola, flaxseeds and mixed berries

- **SELECTION OF CRUDITÉS** with two tablespoons of hummus for dipping

Shrimp & Avacado
"Sushi" Wrap, p. 182

Recipes for One or Two People

Curried Egg
White Sandwich, p. 182

Whether you are planning a romantic meal for that special someone or you're used to cooking for one, it's a constant challenge to find a recipe that fits your short guest list. Most recipes are created to serve four or more people. We've put together our best selection of meals for one or two just for you. And if you are serving a family of four (or more!), don't feel left out – many of our recipes are easily doubled! Our Curried Egg White Sandwich with Apricots is perfect for a fast dinner or weekend brunch, or try our Salmon & Artichoke Quesadillas for a new twist on a Mexican favorite. Dining solo never sounded more appetizing!

Cherry Tomato Meatballs

Serves 4. ***Hands-on time:*** *10 minutes.* ***Total time:*** *40 minutes.*

A new take on a classic favorite, these stuffed meaty delights work well with whole-wheat spaghetti or in a meatball sandwich. We've chosen lean sirloin to keep the flavor without the typical fat content found in most ground meats.

INGREDIENTS:

• Olive oil cooking spray
• 1¼ cups chopped onion
• 2 egg whites
• ¾ cup soft bread crumbs
• ½ cup skim milk
• Salt and pepper
• 1 Tbsp parsley
• ½ tsp oregano
• 1 lb lean ground sirloin
• 12 cherry tomatoes

INSTRUCTIONS:

ONE: Preheat oven to 375°F. Spray a baking dish with Pam.

TWO: In a bowl, combine all ingredients, except meat and tomatoes. Add mixture to ground sirloin and mix well.

THREE: Shape a quarter cup of the mixture evenly around each tomato so that the tomato is hidden inside the meatball.

FOUR: Place meatballs in baking dish and bake for 25 to 30 minutes.

Nutrients per 3-meatball serving: Calories: 283, Total Fat: 8 g, Sat. Fat: 4 g, Carbs: 14 g, Fiber: 1 g, Sugars: 4 g, Protein: 36 g, Sodium: 202 mg, Cholesterol: 73 mg

Cherry
Tomato
Meatballs

Nutritional Bonus:
Like other sea vegetables, kombu is rich in iron, a mineral that has been found to help decrease the risk of ovulatory infertility. And, broccoli contains the compound sulforaphane, a powerful antioxidant that has been shown to provide some protection against certain cancers, such as breast and prostate.

TIP:
Kombu can pack a lot of sodium, so cut down your portion of this sea veggie if you're watching your salt intake.

Kombu Melt

Kombu Melt

Serves 2. ***Hands-on time:*** *15 minutes.* ***Total time:*** *20 minutes.*

Perfect in place of your standard Saturday night pasta, this dish is packed with healthy nutrients.

INGREDIENTS:

- 1 head broccoli, cut into florets
- 1 cup low-sodium marinara sauce
- 1 pkg of kombu (seaweed), rinsed
- 1 cup whole or sliced shiitake mushrooms
- 1 oz raw cheddar-style goat cheese, grated

INSTRUCTIONS:

ONE: Preheat oven to 250°F. On the stovetop, steam broccoli in a steamer and heat pasta sauce in a saucepan.

TWO: When broccoli is nearly soft, place kombu in steamer (with broccoli) just long enough to heat it (about one minute).

THREE: Place kombu in an ovenproof plate or in a baking dish. Top with broccoli, mushrooms and heated marinara sauce. Sprinkle with cheese and place plate or dish in the oven with the door ajar for three minutes, or until cheese has melted.

Nutrients per serving: Calories: 245, Total Fat: 6 g, Sat. Fat: 3 g, Carbs: 39 g, Fiber: 17 g, Sugars: 11 g, Protein: 11 g, Sodium: 1,052 mg, Cholesterol: 11 mg

Suddenly St. Tropez Salad

Serves 2. ***Hands-on time:*** *10 minutes.* ***Total time:*** *10 minutes.*

Beets have a high sugar content but are low in calories, which gives this salad a sweet flavor while keeping you slim at the same time.

INGREDIENTS:

- 4 oz mesclun or baby romaine lettuce
- 1 cup halved grape tomatoes
- 1 medium beet, peeled and finely julienned into spaghetti-like strips
- 1 oz raw cheddar-style goat cheese, grated
- 2 Tbsp balsamic vinegar
- 3 to 4 packets Stevia
- 1 Tbsp diced fresh garlic
- Sea salt and fresh pepper to taste
- 2 Tbsp diced sweet onion (optional)
- ¼ cup chopped fresh basil (optional)
- 2 Tbsp chopped fresh oregano or chives (optional)

INSTRUCTIONS:

Toss all ingredients together in a large salad bowl and serve.

Nutrients per serving: Calories: 107, Total Fat: 3 g, Sat. Fat: 2 g, Carbs: 15 g, Fiber: 4 g, Sugars: 9 g, Protein: 5 g, Sodium: 98 mg, Cholesterol: 6 mg

Potato & Egg Italiano Sandwich

Makes 2 sandwiches. ***Hands-on time:*** *20 minutes.* ***Total time:*** *20 minutes.*

Potatoes and eggs are a match made in heaven – just think of your Grandmother's potato salad recipe. We've skipped the fatty mayo and turned this combo into a sandwich filling. Great for a fancy Sunday breakfast.

INGREDIENTS:

- 1 whole egg
- 2 egg whites
- ¼ cup peeled and diced potato
- 1½ tsp olive oil, divided
- 1 Tbsp water
- ¼ cup diced sweet red pepper
- ¼ cup diced onion
- 1 clove garlic, finely minced
- 1½ tsp finely chopped fresh basil
- 1½ tsp low-fat parmesan cheese
- Dash of ground black pepper
- 2 small whole-wheat Italian rolls, each cut in half
- 8 leaves raw spinach (about ½ cup)
- 4 slices tomato

INSTRUCTIONS:

ONE: Beat together whole egg and egg whites in a small bowl; set aside.

TWO: Sauté potato in medium pan with water and half teaspoon oil over medium heat. After five minutes, add red pepper, onion and garlic, cook until soft, then pour in eggs.

THREE: Meanwhile in a separate bowl, mix basil, cheese, black pepper and remaining teaspoon of oil.

FOUR: Stir eggs gently, then flip and cook until done.

FIVE: Spread half of basil-cheese mixture on top half of each roll. Then put half of egg mixture, four spinach leaves and two slices of tomato on other half of each roll, cover with roll top.

Nutrients per sandwich: Calories: 230, Total Fat: 8 g, Sat. Fat: 1.5 g, Carbs: 29 g, Fiber: 5 g, Protein: 12 g, Sodium: 310 mg, Cholesterol: 95 mg

NUTRITIONAL BONUS: Loaded with veggies, our egg sandwich is packed with 199 mcg of vitamin K, which is 250 percent of your daily requirement. Known as the clotting vitamin (for its blood clotting abilities), vitamin K also helps keep bones healthy and strong.

Shrimp, Artichoke & New Potato Stew for Two

Serves 2. **Hands-on time:** *15 minutes.* **Total time:** *15 minutes.*

Stew doesn't have to simmer for hours. This one cooks up in a jiffy, thanks to quick-cooking ingredients like shrimp and small potato wedges.

INGREDIENTS:

- 1 Tbsp olive oil
- ¼ onion, cut into ½-inch pieces
- 2 cloves garlic, thinly sliced
- 1 cup no-salt-added diced tomatoes (with juices)
- ⅔ cup low-sodium vegetable broth
- 4 oz small white or red creamer potatoes, cut into ½-inch wedges
- 1 Tbsp chopped fresh oregano
- ¼ tsp fine sea salt
- ¼ tsp ground black pepper
- 1 Tbsp chopped Italian parsley, divided
- 8 oz raw shrimp
- 1 cup frozen artichoke hearts, thawed (about ½ 8-oz pkg)

INSTRUCTIONS:

ONE: In a medium (3- to 4-quart) saucepan over medium heat, warm oil. Add onion and cook, stirring occasionally, until almost translucent, one-and-a-half to two minutes. Add garlic and cook for one minute.

TWO: Add tomatoes, broth, potatoes, oregano, salt, pepper and half of parsley. Bring to a boil over high heat; reduce heat to low to maintain a simmer, cover and cook, stirring occasionally, until potatoes are almost tender, four to six minutes.

THREE: Add shrimp and artichoke hearts, and return to a simmer. Cover and cook, stirring occasionally, until shrimp is barely opaque, two to three minutes. Serve garnished with remaining parsley.

Nutrients per 2-cup serving: Calories: 320, Total Fat: 9 g, Sat. Fat: 1.5 g, Carbs: 27 g, Fiber: 3 g, Sugars: 5 g, Protein: 29 g, Sodium: 760 mg, Cholesterol: 170 mg

TIP:
Creamer potatoes are simply potatoes that are harvested earlier on, before they mature. This allows for small and tender potatoes that are generally higher in moisture and less starchy than their fully grown cousins. Creamer potatoes also go by the names "baby potatoes," "new potatoes," "chats" and "earlies."

Quick & Healthy Pasta Carbonara
WITH MIXED VEGETABLES

*Serves 2. **Hands-on time:** 20 minutes. **Total time:** 20 minutes.*

Pasta carbonara is usually made with bacon, eggs and loads of cheese. Here, to make the dish both taste-bud friendly and good for you, we've switched the bacon to chicken, cut down on the eggs and cheese, and added easy-to-use mixed vegetables – and plenty of 'em.

INGREDIENTS:

- 1 (6-oz) boneless, skinless chicken breast, cut into ½-inch pieces
- 4 oz whole-wheat spaghetti, linguini or fettuccini
- 1½ cups mixed frozen vegetables
- 1 large egg
- ⅓ cup finely grated Parmigiano-Reggiano cheese
- 2 cloves garlic, finely minced
- ½ tsp fresh ground black pepper
- ⅛ tsp fine sea salt

INSTRUCTIONS:

ONE: In a medium nonstick skillet over medium-high heat, cook chicken, stirring occasionally, until browned and cooked through, about four minutes. Transfer to a large bowl; set aside.

TWO: In a large pot of boiling water, cook pasta according to package directions. Stir in vegetables two minutes before pasta is al dente (very slightly chalky in the center).

THREE: While pasta is cooking, add egg, cheese, garlic, pepper and salt to bowl with chicken, stirring to combine.

FOUR: Reserve half a cup of pasta-cooking water, then drain pasta. Immediately add pasta and half of reserved pasta water to chicken mixture, tossing to combine. Add more pasta water, as desired. Serve immediately.

Nutrients per 1½-cup serving: Calories: 410, Total Fat: 8 g, Sat. Fat: 3 g, Carbs: 38 g, Fiber: 9 g, Sugars: 5 g, Protein: 35 g, Sodium: 373 mg, Cholesterol: 47 mg

Nutritional Bonus:
Compared to white-flour pasta, the whole-wheat variety is loaded with minerals, particularly magnesium, which is essential to the production and use of insulin.

Cavatappi
WITH SPINACH RICOTTA PESTO & SEARED FILET MIGNON

*Serves 2. **Hands-on time:** 20 minutes. **Total time:** 30 minutes.*

Spinach has the unique ability to stay green in pesto much longer than an herb such as basil. Puréeing the tender leaves transforms a whole serving of salad greens into just the right amount of sauce. Add just a bit of lean beef and you've got a satisfying meal with complementary flavors. Remember, they serve creamy spinach at steak houses for a delicious reason!

INGREDIENTS:

- 4 oz whole-wheat cavatappi pasta (or whole-wheat rotini or fusilli pasta)
- 1 clove garlic
- ½ cup fresh parsley leaves
- 2 cups fresh spinach
- ¼ cup part-skim ricotta cheese
- 1 Tbsp low-sodium vegetable broth
- 4 oz filet mignon (or lean steak)

INGREDIENTS:

ONE: Cook pasta according to package directions; drain well.

TWO: In a food processor, combine garlic, parsley and spinach and grind to a paste. Add ricotta and broth and process to make a smooth purée. In a large bowl, toss pesto with pasta.

THREE: Heat a cast-iron skillet over high heat. When hot, add filet. Sear for about two minutes per side, depending on thickness and level of doneness preferred. When well browned and cooked, remove steak to a cutting board. Let stand for at least three minutes to allow meat to re-absorb its juices, then slice thinly across the grain. Serve pasta topped with steak strips.

Nutrients per 2-cup serving: Calories: 334, Total Fat: 6 g, Sat. Fat: 2 g, Carbs: 48 g, Fiber: 7 g, Sugars: 2 g, Protein: 23 g, Sodium: 128 mg, Cholesterol: 40 mg

Baked Salmon
WITH ORANGE GLAZE

*Serves 2. **Hands-on time:** 5 minutes. **Total time:** 30 minutes.*

The flavors of salmon and citrus complement each other beautifully. Serve this dish with brown rice or over fresh greens.

INGREDIENTS:

- 2 (5-oz) large salmon fillets
- 2 cups chopped spinach
- 1 cup sliced mushrooms
- 2 medium Roma tomatoes, chopped
- Homemade orange glaze (see recipe, below)

INSTRUCTIONS:

Preheat oven to 375°F. Place salmon fillets (skin side down) in a 13- x 9-inch baking dish sprayed with cooking spray. Mix remaining ingredients until well blended and spoon over salmon. Bake for 20 to 25 minutes or until salmon flakes easily. Top with orange glaze.

Nutrients per serving: Calories: 397, Total Fat: 14 g, Sat. Fat: 2 g, Carbs: 25 g, Fiber: 6 g, Sugars: 15 g, Protein: 43 g, Sodium: 212 mg, Cholesterol: 99 mg

Orange Glaze

Try this sweet glaze on fish, chicken or tofu.

INGREDIENTS:

- 4 Tbsp of Smucker's Low Sugar Sweet Orange Marmalade
- ½ tsp minced fresh ginger
- ½ tsp minced fresh garlic
- 1 tsp tahini

INSTRUCTIONS:

Combine all ingredients in a microwaveable bowl. Stir well with a whisk or fork. Heat for three minutes, stopping to stir every minute. Let cool.

Nutrients per serving: Calories: 71, Total Fat: 2 g, Sat. Fat: 0 g, Carbs: 12 g, Fiber: 0 g, Sugars: 10 g, Protein: 0 g, Sodium: 0 mg, Cholesterol: 0 mg

Baked
Salmon with
Orange
Glaze

Apple
Grilled
Cheese

Apple Grilled Cheese
WITH GRAINY MUSTARD

Makes 2 sandwiches. **Hands-on time:** *5 minutes.* **Total time:** *10 minutes.*

The "white-bread-and-butter fried cheese sandwich" of years past is transformed with spelt bread, low-fat cheddar cheese, whole-grain mustard and thinly sliced tart apples. And, while we may have updated this classic sandwich for modern and health-conscious tastes, we didn't dare tamper with its trademark simple assembly or minimal ingredients. Five ingredients and 10 minutes is all you'll need to get our grilled cheese on the table!

INGREDIENTS:

- 4 slices spelt bread or sprouted whole-grain bread
- 1 tsp olive oil
- 1 tsp whole-grain Dijon mustard
- 2 oz low-fat cheddar cheese, finely grated, divided
- ½ medium Granny Smith apple or other tart apple, halved, cored and thinly sliced lengthwise

TIP: Try to slice the apple as thinly as possible using a mandolin or sharp knife.

INSTRUCTIONS:

ONE: Lay bread out on clean work surface and lightly brush top side of each piece with oil. Turn two pieces of bread over and spread with mustard. Divide half of cheese between both mustard-covered slices, arranging cheese in a thin layer. Cover cheese with a layer of apples, dividing evenly between both slices, followed by remaining cheese. Top each with other half of bread, oiled-side-up, making two sandwiches.

TWO: Heat a nonstick skillet over medium-low heat. Place sandwiches in pan and cook until light golden brown on bottom. Flip, using a spatula, and continue to cook until cheese has melted and bread is golden brown on other side, about six minutes total. Cut sandwiches in half and serve.

OPTION: If you have a panini grill, try using it in lieu of the nonstick skillet for even easier no-flipping-required cooking.

Nutrients per sandwich: *Calories: 220, Total Fat: 7 g, Sat. Fat: 2 g, Carbs: 27 g, Fiber: 4 g, Sugars: 6 g, Protein: 14 g, Sodium: 450 mg, Cholesterol: 5 mg*

Open-Face Tuna Veggie Melt

Serves 2. **Hands-on time:** *8 minutes.* **Total time:** *18 minutes.*

We've made our tuna salad with apples, mixed vegetables and thick yogurt, topping it with low-fat cheese. This amps up the flavor and cuts back on the fat, leaving you with a healthy midday meal.

INGREDIENTS:

- 1 (6-oz) can or pouch unsalted tuna in water, drained
- 3 Tbsp diced celery
- 3 Tbsp diced red onion
- 2 Tbsp peeled and diced carrots
- 2 Tbsp seeded and diced tomato
- 2 Tbsp unpeeled and diced Golden Delicious apple
- ⅓ cup nonfat Greek-style yogurt
- 1½ tsp white wine vinegar
- ½ tsp dried oregano
- ¼ tsp parsley flakes
- ⅛ tsp ground black pepper
- ¼ loaf fresh-baked whole-wheat bread (4 oz)
- 2 thin slices tomato
- 2 (1-oz) slices Jarlsberg Light or reduced-fat Swiss cheese

INSTRUCTIONS:

ONE: In a medium bowl, stir together first 11 ingredients until well combined.

TWO: Slice bread horizontally, making a top and bottom. Place both halves crust-side-down, divide tuna salad equally among halves and spread onto each. Top each with one slice tomato and one slice cheese.

THREE: In an oven or toaster oven, broil topped bread halves on low for five to ten minutes or until cheese is melted and slightly browned.

Nutrients per serving (½ cup tuna salad, 1 slice tomato, 1 oz cheese, 2 oz bread): *Calories: 340, Total Fat: 4.5 g, Sat. Fat: 2 g, Carbs: 31 g, Fiber: 5 g, Sugars: 7 g, Protein: 41 g, Sodium: 410 mg, Cholesterol: 35 mg*

Salmon & Artichoke Quesadillas

*Serves 2. **Hands-on time:** 25 minutes. **Total time:** 30 minutes.*

Quesadillas are so versatile; they'll work with almost any filling. We've chosen salmon and artichokes for ours – perfect for a light summer lunch.

INGREDIENTS:

- 1 (6-oz) wild Alaskan salmon fillet
- 6 artichoke hearts, chopped
- 1 Tbsp chopped fresh dill
- ½ tsp extra-virgin olive oil, divided
- 4 whole-wheat tortillas
- 2 wedges Laughing Cow Light Garlic & Herb cheese, each sliced into 5 pieces, divided
- ¼ cup diced plum tomatoes, divided
- ¼ cup diced scallions, divided (reserve green stems for garnish)
- ½ cup chopped baby spinach, divided
- 2 Tbsp nonfat Greek-style yogurt
- ½ cup low-sodium salsa (optional)

INSTRUCTIONS:

ONE: In a nonstick skillet over medium-high heat, cook salmon skin-side-down for five minutes. Flip salmon and add artichokes and dill to pan. Remove salmon skin with fork, discard, and cook salmon and artichokes for another five minutes or until salmon is flaky. Flake salmon with fork while still in skillet. Transfer salmon-artichoke mixture to a bowl.

TWO: Carefully wipe skillet clean and return to medium-high heat. Add a quarter teaspoon oil and spread around skillet. Place first tortilla in skillet and cook one minute per side, until air pockets form; remove tortilla. Place second tortilla in skillet, cook for one minute, flip, then turn heat down to medium-low. Place five pieces cheese on tortilla. Add about three quarters of a cup salmon-artichoke mixture, two tasblespoons tomatoes, two tablespoons scallions and a quarter cup spinach, making sure that ingredients are evenly distributed around tortilla. Place first tortilla over top and cook for one minute, pressing down with spatula. Carefully flip quesadilla and cook for one to two more minutes. Remove first complete quesadilla from skillet and place on serving plate. Turn heat back up to medium-high, add remaining quarter teaspoon oil and repeat entire process with remaining tortillas and accompaniments.

THREE: Let quesadillas cool for a few minutes before cutting each into six wedges with a sharp knife. Dollop each quesadilla with one tablespoon yogurt and serve with salsa, if desired.

Nutrients per quesadilla (including 1 Tbsp yogurt): Calories: 483, Total Fat: 15 g, Sat. Fat: 2 g, Carbs: 51 g, Fiber: 16 g, Sugars: 4 g, Protein: 34 g, Sodium: 536 mg, Cholesterol: 64 mg

Champagne Chicken, Artichoke & Mushroom Salad

*Serves 2. **Hands-on time:** 15 minutes. **Total time:** 1 hour (includes marinating).*

Traditional champagne chicken is made with heavy cream. We've turned our version into a light salad using the champagne flavor in the dressing.

INGREDIENTS:

SALAD

- ¼ lb assorted red and purple potatoes (about 4 small potatoes)
- ½ lb boneless, skinless chicken breasts
- 6 artichokes, halved
- 8 baby bella mushrooms, quartered
- 3 cups baby spring mix
- 1 plum tomato, sliced

VINAIGRETTE

- ⅓ cup champagne vinegar
- 2½ tsp extra-virgin olive oil
- 1 tsp Dijon mustard
- ¼ cup chopped flat-leaf parsley
- 2 Tbsp chopped fresh dill
- ¼ tsp ground black pepper
- ¼ tsp sea salt (optional)

INSTRUCTIONS:

ONE: In a medium saucepan over high heat, add potatoes and completely cover with water. Bring to a boil and cook for 15 minutes or until fork tender. Drain and let cool before cutting potatoes into bite-size pieces.

TWO: In a medium saucepan over medium-high heat, add chicken and enough water to cover it. Poach chicken for 10 to 15 minutes or until no longer pink. Drain and let cool before cutting chicken into bite-size pieces. In a large bowl, add potatoes, chicken, artichokes and mushrooms; mix gently.

THREE: Prepare vinaigrette: In a medium bowl, whisk together vinegar, oil and Dijon. Then add parsley and dill and season with pepper and salt, if desired. Pour vinaigrette over potato-chicken mixture. Stir gently to coat. Cover and let marinate for 30 to 60 minutes in refrigerator.

FOUR: To serve, place one-and-a-half cups baby spring mix on each of two plates. Add two cups chicken mixture to each plate. Top each with half of tomato.

Nutrients per serving (1½ cups greens, 2 cups chicken salad, ½ tomato): Calories: 283, Total Fat: 8 g, Sat. Fat: 1 g, Carbs: 21 g, Fiber: 5 g, Sugars: 4 g, Protein: 31 g, Sodium: 167 mg, Cholesterol: 66 mg

Simple Yet Elegant
Sole & Asparagus
BAKED IN PARCHMENT

*Serves 2. **Hands-on time:** 15 minutes. **Total time:** 25 minutes.*

Ideal for a date night – you can prepare this recipe entirely in advance, then simply pop it into the oven about 15 minutes before you're ready to serve.

INGREDIENTS:

- 4 tsp olive oil, divided
- 4 thin asparagus spears, trimmed and halved lengthwise
- 2 (6-oz) Pacific sole fillets
- 1 small shallot, thinly sliced, divided
- ¾ tsp chopped fresh tarragon, divided
- ¾ tsp fine sea salt, divided
- ¼ tsp ground black pepper, divided
- 1 tsp white wine vinegar
- 2 lemon slices, ¼-inch thick, halved

INSTRUCTIONS:

ONE: Preheat oven to 375°F. Cut two 14-inch pieces of parchment or foil. Arrange parchment on a rimmed baking sheet and brush each with some oil, leaving a two-inch border; set remaining oil aside.

TWO: In a small saucepan of boiling water, cook asparagus until crisp-tender, about one minute. Drain, rinse with cold water and drain again; then set aside.

THREE: Place fish fillets on a work surface. Sprinkle with shallot, tarragon, salt and pepper, reserving a pinch of each. Divide asparagus spears between fillets, arranging them crosswise to the fish. Arrange fish in center of oiled parchment. Drizzle with vinegar and remaining oil. Sprinkle with remaining shallot, tarragon, salt and pepper. Arrange lemon slices on top.

FOUR: To seal packet, bring top and bottom edges of parchment together and fold down towards fillet in half-inch sections. Then fold each side of parchment in toward the fillet in half-inch sections. Ensure packets are securely closed but not too tight to fillet for proper steaming.

FIVE: Bake for 13 to 15 minutes, until a paring knife inserted through packet slips easily into fish. Present packets at the table, hot and puffy from the oven, for your date to slit open and enjoy.

Nutrients per parchment packet (6 oz sole and juices, plus 2 spears asparagus): Calories: 230, Total Fat: 11 g, Sat. Fat: 1.5 g, Carbs: 2 g, Fiber: 1 g, Sugars: 1 g, Protein: 29 g, Sodium: 360 mg, Cholesterol: 80 mg

Cooling Vegetable Salad

Cajun Catfish Po' Boy

Cajun Catfish Po' Boy & Cooling Vegetable Salad

Serves 2. ***Hands-on time:*** *20 minutes.* ***Total time:*** *25 minutes.*

Catfish Po' Boy sandwiches are a staple in Cajun and South Louisiana cuisine. Savor this southern spicy sandwich between cooling bites of this fresh veggie side salad.

INGREDIENTS:

COOLING VEGETABLE SALAD

- 1 cup peeled and halved cucumbers
- 10 grape tomatoes, halved
- ¼ cup shredded carrots
- ¼ cup minced flat-leaf parsley
- ¼ cup diced red onion
- ¼ tsp ground black pepper
- ¼ tsp garlic powder
- ½ tsp extra-virgin olive oil
- 1 Tbsp rice wine vinegar

CAJUN CATFISH

- 2 (3-oz) catfish fillets
- 1 tsp extra-virgin olive oil
- 1½ tsp Cajun spices
- 4 oz bakery-fresh whole-wheat baguette, sliced into 4 pieces and toasted
- 4 slices red onion
- 4 slices tomato (each slice ¼-inch thick)
- 2 Boston lettuce leaves

GOAT CHEESE SPREAD

- 1 oz goat cheese
- 3 Tbsp nonfat Greek-style yogurt
- 1 tsp fresh lemon juice
- 2 Tbsp minced flat-leaf parsley
- 3 Tbsp shredded carrots
- 2 Tbsp diced cucumbers
- ½ tsp ground black pepper

INSTRUCTIONS:

ONE: Ensure that two racks are in middle positions in oven. Preheat oven to 400°F.

TWO: Prepare Cooling Vegetable Salad: In a medium bowl, combine cucumbers, tomatoes, carrot, parsley and onion. Then add pepper, garlic powder, oil and vinegar and stir until vegetables are evenly coated. Place in refrigerator to let flavors meld until ready to serve meal.

THREE: Prepare Cajun Catfish: Place catfish on a foil-lined cookie sheet. Brush fillets with oil and sprinkle with spices. Bake 12 to 15 minutes, until flaky and no longer translucent.

FOUR: Prepare Goat Cheese Spread: In a small bowl, stir together cheese, yogurt, lemon juice, parsley, carrot, cucumber and pepper until combined. Set aside.

FIVE: To assemble each sandwich, spread Goat Cheese Spread on one side of a baguette slice and set aside. Place a catfish fillet on another slice of baguette. Top fillet with two onion slices, two tomato slices and one lettuce leaf; then top with reserved baguette slice, spread-side-down. Repeat with remaining catfish fillet and accompaniments. Serve with Cooling Vegetable Salad. Keep stored in refrigerator for two to four days to ensure freshness.

Nutrients per serving (2 oz baguette, 3 oz catfish, 1 cup salad, 2 slices onion, 2 slices tomato, 1 lettuce leaf, ¼ cup goat cheese spread): Calories: 345, Total Fat: 14 g, Sat. Fat: 5 g, Carbs: 35 g, Fiber: 7.5 g, Sugars: 8 g, Protein: 31 g, Sodium: 592 mg, Cholesterol: 64 mg

Light Tuna Salad Wrap

Serves: 1. ***Hands-on time:*** *5 minutes.* ***Total time:*** *5 minutes.*

There are easy ways to lighten up any wrap or sandwich. Simply swap out ingredients that are high in fat and sub in fresh, flavorful, healthy ones in their place.

INGREDIENTS:

- 1 low-carb whole-wheat spinach wrap
- ⅔ cup solid light tuna packed in water, low sodium
- 1 Tbsp chopped celery
- 1½ tsp shredded carrots
- 1 Tbsp chopped tomato
- 4½ tsp brown rice
- 1 Tbsp dill relish
- 2 Tbsp fat-free mayonnaise

INSTRUCTIONS:

Combine all ingredients in a medium-sized mixing bowl. Scoop onto spinach wrap. Fold and enjoy!

Nutrients per serving: Calories: 330, Total Fat: 5.5 g, Sat. Fat: 0.3 g, Carbs: 27.4 g, Fiber: 10.2 g, Protein: 42.9 g, Sugars: 8.3 g, Sodium: 448 mg, Cholesterol: 80 mg

Shrimp & Avocado "Sushi" Wrap

*Serves 2. **Hands-on time:** 15 minutes. **Total time:** 30 minutes.*

Enjoy the flavors of a homemade sushi roll (minus the mayonnaise often added in western sushi) without the bamboo mat or labor-intensive process by wrapping your ingredients in a healthy whole-wheat tortilla, making assembly and packing a snap.

INGREDIENTS:

- 1 tsp raw honey
- 1 Tbsp rice vinegar
- 2 tsp fresh ginger (peeled and finely sliced into rounds, then sliced into thin strips)
- 2 Tbsp thinly shaved red onion
- ¼ cup nonfat plain Greek-style yogurt
- 1 tsp wasabi paste (or to taste)
- 2 whole-wheat tortillas (6 inches each)
- ¼ small avocado, pitted and thinly sliced
- ½ cup thinly sliced carrot sticks
- 1 cup seeded and thinly sliced cucumber,
- 1 cup chopped baby spinach
- 4 large shrimp (85 g), cooked, peeled, deveined and chopped

INSTRUCTIONS:

ONE: In a small bowl, whisk together honey and vinegar (if honey does not dissolve, microwave for about 45 seconds). Add ginger and onion and toss to coat. Let stand for at least 20 minutes.

TWO: In another small bowl, stir together yogurt and wasabi.

THREE: On each tortilla, pile half of each of the following: avocado, carrots, cucumber and spinach. Then top with shrimp and ginger mixture, dividing evenly. Drizzle each with yogurt sauce and roll up tortilla.

Nutrients per sandwich: Calories: 284, Total Fat: 7.5 g, Sat. Fat: 1 g, Carbs: 38 g, Fiber: 6 g, Sugars: 8.5 g, Protein: 15 g, Sodium: 326 mg, Cholesterol 65 mg

TIP: Just remember that wasabi pastes can vary greatly in terms of heat. So, unless you are a wasabi veteran, think about starting out with half the wasabi paste indicated and add more, to taste, if you want to add a kick.

For a photo of this recipe, see p. 166.

Curried Egg White Sandwich
WITH APRICOTS

*Serves 2. **Hands-on time:** 20 minutes. **Total time:** 30 minutes.*

Traditional egg salad recipes call for excessive amounts of mayo and egg yolks. Skipping the mayo entirely and sticking to just whites doesn't mean less flavor: curry, apricots and lemon keep things interesting, while water chestnuts add crunch and texture.

INGREDIENTS:

- 4 large eggs
- ½ tsp ground turmeric
- ½ cup cauliflower (broken into very small florets)
- 2 Tbsp shredded carrot
- 2 Tbsp chopped, sliced water chestnuts
- 3 unsweetened dried apricots, chopped
- 2 Tbsp nonfat plain Greek-style yogurt
- ½ tsp lemon zest
- 1½ tsp fresh lemon juice
- ¾ tsp raw honey
- 1 tsp chopped fresh ginger
- ½ tsp curry powder
- 2 Tbsp chopped fresh cilantro leaves
- 4 slices multigrain bread, toasted
- 4 lettuce leaves

INSTRUCTIONS:

ONE: Place eggs in a 2-quart saucepan and cover with cold water. Bring to a rolling boil. As soon as eggs start to boil, cover and remove from heat. Let stand for 15 minutes, then drain and rinse with cold water. Chill eggs in refrigerator or in a bowl of ice water until cool enough to handle, about 10 minutes.

TWO: In a 1-quart pot, bring two cups water to a boil. Add turmeric and cauliflower, boil for three minutes, then drain and chill until ready to use.

THREE: Peel eggs and remove whites (save yolks for another use or discard). Coarsely mash whites in a large bowl. Add cauliflower, carrot, water chestnuts and apricots. In a small bowl, stir together yogurt, lemon zest and juice, honey, ginger, curry powder and cilantro. Pour yogurt mixture over egg mixture and stir to combine.

FOUR: Divide egg salad into two portions and spread onto two slices of bread, then add lettuce and top with remaining slices of bread.

PACK FOR LUNCH: This sandwich can be packed completed or the egg salad can be packed separately and spread onto bread just before serving. If you have a toaster at the office, you can toast the bread just before assembly for a warm lunch.

Nutrients per sandwich: Calories: 270, Total Fat: 2 g, Sat. Fat: 0.5 g, Carbs: 43 g, Fiber: 11 g, Sugars: 11 g, Protein: 18 g, Sodium: 409 mg, Cholesterol: 0 mg

For a photo of this recipe, see p. 167.

One-Skillet Lamb Chops
WITH PEARS & BALSAMIC PAN SAUCE

Serves 2. ***Hands-on time:*** *10 minutes.* ***Total time:*** *10 minutes.*

Here, we're using lamb loin chops, which look like miniature T-bone steaks. They're full of flavor and the fat is relatively easy to trim off.

INGREDIENTS:

- 4 medium or 6 small ¾-inch thick lamb loin chops (1 to 1¼ lb), fat trimmed
- ¼ tsp fine sea salt
- ¼ tsp ground black pepper
- ¼ cup 100% unsweetened apple juice
- ¼ cup low-sodium beef broth
- 1½ tsp balsamic vinegar
- ½ firm-ripe pear, peeled, cored and cut into ¼-inch slices
- ¾ tsp chopped fresh rosemary, thyme or combination

INSTRUCTIONS:

ONE: Sprinkle lamb with salt and pepper. Heat a large nonstick skillet over medium-high heat. Add lamb; cook to desired doneness, about two-and-a-half minutes per side for medium rare or four minutes per side for medium. Transfer lamb to plates and cover to keep warm.

TWO: Discard any fat from skillet and return to medium heat. Add apple juice, broth, vinegar and pear to skillet, and cook, scraping up any browned bits in the bottom of the pan until liquid is reduced by about half, two to three minutes. Remove from heat and stir in herbs. Top lamb with pears and pan sauce, and serve. Garnish with additional rosemary or thyme, if desired.

Nutrients per serving (4½ oz lamb, ¼ pear and 2 Tbsp sauce): *Calories: 230, Total Fat: 6 g, Sat. Fat: 2.5 g, Carbs: 11 g, Fiber: 2 g, Sugars: 8 g, Protein: 31 g, Sodium: 360 mg, Cholesterol: 115 mg*

Nutritional Bonus: This dish is an excellent source of both protein and niacin, a water-soluble B-vitamin that helps your digestive system run properly.

Nutritional Bonus:
Portobello mushrooms are packed with selenium, potassium, copper and three B-complex vitamins: riboflavin for healthy skin and vision, niacin for aiding the digestive and nervous systems, and pantothenic acid, which is vital for hormone production.

Roasted Chicken & Portobello Focaccia

Roasted Chicken & Portobello Focaccia

Serves 2. ***Hands-on time:*** *15 minutes.* ***Total time:*** *25 minutes.*

Vegetarians can often be found dining on grilled portobellos for good reason: the mushrooms add savory texture and actually pack quite a protein punch. You can also use portobello mushrooms alongside lean meat in recipes to enhance the meaty taste and texture, all while stretching your dollar.

INGREDIENTS:

- 8 oz boneless, skinless chicken breast
- 1 (4 oz) medium portobello mushroom
- 1 Tbsp fresh rosemary
- 1 tsp fresh thyme
- 1 tsp extra-virgin olive oil
- 1 tsp balsamic vinegar
- 2 (3-oz) whole-wheat focaccia (about 4 x 5 inches each)
- 4 oz part-skim mozzarella cheese, thinly sliced
- 1 large tomato, thinly sliced
- 2 small scallions, chopped
- ½ cup thinly sliced fresh basil

INSTRUCTIONS:

ONE: Preheat oven to 400°F. Line a sheet pan with nonstick foil, if desired. Slice chicken into half-inch strips, across the grain, and place in a large bowl. Slice mushroom in slightly thinner strips and add to chicken. Sprinkle with rosemary and thyme. In a small bowl, stir together oil and vinegar, then drizzle over chicken-mushroom mixture. Spread mixture out on prepared pan, not allowing strips to touch, and roast for 15 minutes, stirring halfway through. Remove from oven to cool slightly.

TWO: Slice focaccia horizontally, creating top and bottom halves, and toast in a toaster or under a hot broiler for one minute to crisp, if desired. To assemble, place toasted focaccia on plates. Place half of cheese on each bottom half, followed by half of chicken-mushroom mixture. Divide tomato, scallions and basil between the two sandwiches and cover with top halves.

PACK FOR LUNCH: **Bag or store bread, chicken-mushroom mixture and toppings separately and assemble just before eating to avoid sogginess.**

Nutrients per sandwich: Calories: 470, Total Fat: 12 g, Sat. Fat: 5 g, Carbs: 42 g, Fiber: 7 g, Sugars: 7 g, Protein: 47 g, Sodium: 686 mg, Cholesterol: 81 mg

Chia Fizz

Serves 1. ***Hands-on time:*** *5 minutes.* ***Total time:*** *15 minutes (including chill time).*

Sprinkled on cereal, salads and soups or added to baked goods, the nutty-tasting black and white seeds, which can also be sprouted and added to sandwiches and salads, are as nutritious as they are versatile. When soaked in water, chia seeds form a gel that adds substance and sass to smoothies, juices and drinks.

INGREDIENTS:

- 12 fresh mint leaves
- ½ lime, left unpeeled and cut in thirds, divided
- 1 tsp light agave syrup
- 1 Tbsp chia seeds
- 8 oz seltzer or natural sparkling water

INSTRUCTIONS:

ONE: In a large glass, muddle mint leaves and two lime wedges with a muddler or back of a spoon.

TWO: Add agave, seeds and seltzer. Stir.

THREE: Chill in fridge for 10 minutes to allow chia seeds to gel.

FOUR: Garnish with remaining lime wedge, stir and serve.

Nutrients per 9- to 10-oz serving: Calories: 100, Total Fat: 4.5 g, Sat. Fat: 0 g, Carbs: 15 g, Fiber: 6 g, Sugars: 5 g, Protein: 2 g, Sodium: 0 mg, Cholesterol: 0 mg

Avocados & Mangos

Take a stroll through the exotic aisle in the produce section! Picking and prepping these delicious fruits is a breeze.

If you're one of those people who save the joy of eating a mango until your trip to the tropics because you think the prep work is just too tedious or confusing, you're about to save a couple thousand dollars every year. You can eat mangos to your heart's content, and avocados too (an amazing source of healthy fats) as we show you how to choose the best ones and properly peel them so the delicious fruit doesn't go to waste.

Shopping for mangos

Janet Miller, a food stylist based in Los Angeles, says that you can determine if a mango is ripe by sniffing its stem end. It should be fragrant and sweet-smelling. She recommends choosing mangos with taut skins that show some yellow and red and give slightly when pressed.

Shopping for avocados

Miller, who is also a women's health care nurse practitioner in Beverly Hills, CA (a major avocado hub), says that it's best to buy avocados three days before you plan to eat them so they have time to ripen. Interesting fact from Miller: "To enhance the ripening process of avocados after purchase, remove the small piece of stem that is usually left for shipping purposes to actually retard ripening."

To avoid buying unripe fruit, watch for these qualities: "They will be lacking all of the qualities of ripe fruit: fragrance, and therefore taste. The texture will be too firm in the unripe fruit, as avocados are as much about the texture as the taste. I have tried placing avocados in a brown paper bag with a very ripe banana or apple. The gas released by the ripe fruit will enhance the ripening process of the green fruit."

Miller warns that the avocado will oxidize (turn brown) in air once opened. Try rubbing cut pieces with lemon or lime juice to slow the browning process. Mangos, however, will not turn brown after cutting.

Avocado

ONE: Cut to the pit with an 8-inch chef's knife; slice all the way around the middle of the avocado from stem to blossom end (or top to bottom); and then slice all the way through the flesh of the avocado, tracing the pit.

TWO: Twist the top half off.

THREE: With a short, sharp, careful chopping motion, embed the knife in the pit; remove the pit and discard.

FOUR: Scoop the avocado flesh from the skin with a large serving spoon. Or, if you want quarters or slices, score the skin and simply peel it off from top to bottom in one clean motion.

Mango

ONE: Using a sharp 3-inch paring knife, cut a thin slice off the bottom of the mango to create a flat surface. Stand the mango on a cutting board, stem-side up.

TWO: Beginning at the stem, use the knife to trim away the skin, following the contour of the fruit to the bottom.

THREE: The mango has two soft cheeks that run from the top to the bottom of the fruit. To trim the fleshy cheeks away, place the knife at the top of the mango, slightly off-center. Slice off one of the cheeks in a clean, single cut, running the knife along the pit as you cut (some of the flesh will cling to the pit).

FOUR: Remove the pit, slice the mango into smaller pieces and enjoy.

Holiday Meals

Pomegranate-Glazed Stuffed
Roast Turkey, p. 201

Hosting this year's holiday feast and feeling stumped on what to serve? Our holiday menus are 100 percent *Clean Eating*-approved, so you'll feel good about every delicious bite. We'll show you one way to prepare green beans, two ways to dish out potatoes, stuffing and cranberry sauce, three distinct ways to prepare and serve turkey, and some spectacular desserts! Try our Pomegranate-Glazed Stuffed Roast Turkey for a sweet take on a holiday classic or wow your guests with our Mushroom & Leek Stuffing. Follow our three mouthwatering menus as outlined or exchange dishes to suit the pleasures of your palate. Happy holidays and happy clean eating!

Menu One:

Rosemary, Sage & Orange Turkey

Serves 14. *Hands-on time:* 20 minutes. *Total time:* 4 hours, 10 minutes.

Preparing a Thanksgiving turkey can be overwhelming for some, but we've broken it down into easy, manageable steps for a stress-free holiday. See page 206 for our Step-By-Step Turkey Prep Guide.

INGREDIENTS:

- 1 (14- to 16-lb) organic turkey
- 6 sprigs fresh rosemary
- 1 bunch fresh sage
- 1 orange
- 2 cloves garlic, minced
- 1 tsp extra-virgin olive oil
- ½ tsp each sea salt and ground black pepper
- 12 cups Traditional Bread Stuffing (recipe p. 193)

INSTRUCTIONS:

ONE: Remove neck and giblets from turkey. Discard or save for gravy, if you wish. Rinse turkey inside and out with cold running water. Pat dry with paper towels. Place turkey, breast side up, on a rack in a large roasting pan. Cut rosemary sprigs into smaller pieces. Coarsely chop sage, including stems. Using a vegetable peeler, slice four thick strips of peel from orange. Carefully cut away any white pith – you just want the fragrant peel. Place rosemary, sage and orange peel into a bowl. Add garlic, oil, salt and pepper. Mix well. Using your fingers, loosen skin from each breast. Tuck herb mixture under skin.

TWO: Lightly pack neck cavity with just enough stuffing to fill. Remember that the stuffing will expand during roasting. Bring neck skin up over back and secure with skewers or sew shut. Fill body cavity with remaining stuffing. Tuck legs under skin flap. After stuffing, ensure that the turkey is still breast side up.

THREE: Lightly brush or spray turkey with a little more oil. (Don't worry: This won't add fat because the skin will be discarded later.) Tent pan with foil. Roast in a preheated 325°F oven for two hours.

FOUR: Discard foil. Continue roasting (you don't have to baste) until a thermometer inserted in thigh registers 180°F – this will take anywhere from two to four hours, depending on the size of the bird. Make sure to check on the turkey after three-and-a-half hours of total roasting time to determine how much more cooking time is needed. If the turkey starts to brown too much before it's fully cooked, cover dark spots with foil.

FIVE: When done, cover with foil and let stand at least 20 minutes before carving. Discard skin and herb mixture and scoop stuffing into a serving bowl before carving.

TIME-SAVING TIP: **Never stuff a turkey ahead and let it sit – bacteria will grow in any stuffing left in an uncooked turkey. However, it's OK to prepare the herb and orange mixture and tuck it under the skin. Cover and refrigerate overnight. Stuff turkey with Traditional Bread Stuffing just before roasting.**

Nutrients per serving (6 oz skinless white meat, ½-cup stuffing): *Calories: 309, Total Fat: 4.5 g, Sat. Fat: 1 g, Carbs: 20.5 g, Fiber: 4.5 g, Sugars: 5 g, Protein: 44 g, Sodium: 334 mg, Cholesterol: 102 mg*

Rosemary, Sage & Orange Turkey

Nutritional Bonus:
Our Thanksgiving turkey won't add another notch to your belt loop and it's good for you: One small serving provides more than 80 percent of the protein you need in a day. Plus, it's a good source of B-vitamins (especially niacin and vitamin B6), selenium, zinc and iron.

Gingery Roasted Squash p. 198

Traditional Bread Stuffing

THE BEST OF CLEAN EATING

Nutritional Bonus:

The leafy green watercress has been found to offer some cancer-prevention potential, so you may want to add this often-overlooked superfood – which is bursting with more than 15 essential vitamins and minerals – to your regular shopping list.

Golden Mashed Potatoes

Nutritional Bonus:

Potatoes are an exceptionally healthy high-fiber, low-calorie food that offers significant protection against cardiovascular disease and cancer.

Golden Mashed Potatoes

Serves 18. **Makes** *9 cups.* **Hands-on time:** *15 minutes.* **Total time:** *40 minutes.*

Yukon Gold potatoes are so creamy that you can skip the heavy cream and butter used in traditional mashed-potato recipes without forgoing taste or texture. Light sour cream and Dijon mustard give these Golden Mashed Potatoes some extra tanginess.

INGREDIENTS:

- 8 large Yukon Gold potatoes (4½ to 5 lbs)
- 3 large cloves garlic, peeled and smashed
- 1 cup light sour cream
- ½ cup skim milk
- 1 Tbsp Dijon mustard
- ½ tsp sea salt
- 1½ Tbsp each chopped fresh thyme leaves and chopped chives

INSTRUCTIONS:

ONE: Scrub potatoes but don't peel them. Cut into halves and place in a very large, wide saucepan. Add garlic. Cover with water and bring to a boil. Reduce heat, partially cover and simmer until fork tender, 20 to 25 minutes.

TWO: Drain potatoes and garlic. Return to saucepan set to low heat. Using a potato masher, coarsely mash. Add sour cream, milk, mustard and salt. Mash to desired consistency. Stir in thyme and chives.

TIME-SAVING TIP: Prepare mashed potatoes ahead of time, but don't add thyme or chives. Just before serving, reheat in a medium microwave, stirring often. Add more skim milk if the mixture is too dry. Stir in thyme and chives, then turn into a warm serving bowl.

Nutrients per ½-cup serving: *Calories: 115, Total Fat: 1 g, Sat. Fat: 0.5 g, Carbs: 22 g, Fiber: 1 g, Sugars: 1 g, Protein: 4 g, Sodium: 92.5 mg, Cholesterol: 4.5 mg*

Traditional Bread Stuffing

Serves 24. **Makes** *12 cups (enough for a 14- to 16-lb turkey).* **Hands-on time:** *25 minutes.* **Total time:** *45 minutes.*

Whether you prefer yours cooked in or out of the turkey, stuffing is a natural fit. In our Traditional Bread Stuffing we used sprouted whole grains in lieu of white bread, which gives a mild nutty flavor but also boosts the side dish's fiber content. And, instead of the usual whole eggs, we used extra-virgin olive oil to cut out cholesterol and saturated fat.

INGREDIENTS:

- 680 g loaf sprouted whole-grain bread, such as Ezekiel, defrosted
- 2 Tbsp extra-virgin olive oil
- 4 stalks celery, finely chopped
- 2 small onions, finely chopped
- 1 Tbsp poultry seasoning
- 1 tsp sea salt
- 1 apple, such as McIntosh or Granny Smith, cored and chopped (skin on)
- 1 cup dried cherries
- ½ cup low-sodium chicken broth

INSTRUCTIONS:

ONE: Cut crusts from bread. Tear bread into small pieces that measure about 10 cups. Spread out on two baking sheets and lightly toast in a preheated 350°F oven for 10 minutes. Turn into a very large bowl.

TWO: Heat oil in a large, wide frying pan set over medium heat. Add celery, onions, poultry seasoning and salt. Stir often until onions are soft, 12 to 15 minutes. Add apple and cherries. Stir occasionally, until apple starts to soften, five to seven minutes. Turn over toasted bread and drizzle with half of the broth. Stir to mix evenly. The stuffing should be moist, not soggy. Cool mixture completely before stuffing turkey.

TIME-SAVING TIP: Prepare stuffing and let cool. It will keep well, covered and refrigerated, for up to three days. Bring to room temperature before stuffing turkey.

Nutrients per ½-cup serving: *Calories: 104, Total Fat: 1.5 g, Sat. Fat: 0 g, Carbs: 19 g, Fiber: 4.5 g, Sugars: 4 g, Protein: 4 g, Sodium: 158 mg, Cholesterol: 0 mg*

Lighten-Up Pumpkin Pie

*Serves 12. **Hands-on time:** 15 minutes. **Total time:** 1 hour, 30 minutes.*

Forget pie filling! Using pumpkin purée – the real thing – is better in every way, especially in terms of taste and health.

INGREDIENTS:

- 1½ cups crushed ginger snaps or graham crackers, such as Sha Sha Co. Spelt Ginger Snaps or Health Valley Original Oat Bran Graham Crackers
- 1½ Tbsp canola oil
- 2 egg whites
- 1 whole egg
- 1 scant cup loosely packed organic brown sugar
- 1 tsp finely grated orange or lemon peel
- 1 tsp each ground ginger, cinnamon, ground cardamom and sea salt
- ⅛ tsp each ground allspice and mace
- 1 (12 oz) can evaporated milk, preferably skim
- 1 (14 oz) can organic pumpkin purée (not pie filling), such as Tree of Life

INSTRUCTIONS:

ONE: Place crumbs in a deep-dish 9- or 10-inch pie plate. Drizzle with oil. Using a fork, stir to moisten. Using your hands, press crumbs against the bottom and up the sides of the pan – the crust should look crumbly. Refrigerate while making the filling, allowing the crust to set a little.

TWO: Lightly beat egg whites and whole egg. Whisk in brown sugar, grated peel, spices and sea salt. Whisk in milk and pumpkin purée. Pour over crust. Place pie on a baking sheet. Bake in center of a preheated 300°F oven until center is almost set when pan is jiggled, 60 to 75 minutes. Let cool, then refrigerate until ready to serve.

TIME-SAVING TIPS: Pie tastes best the same day it's made. However, it will keep well if covered and refrigerated overnight. The flavors blend as it sits, so a good alternative is to make the pie filling and crust the day before. Wrap and refrigerate each separately. Fill crust and bake on serving day.

Nutrients per 4-oz serving (about ¾-inch slice): *Calories: 231, Total Fat: 5 g, Sat. Fat: 0.25 g, Carbs: 41 g, Fiber: 4 g, Sugars: 20 g, Protein: 6.5 g, Sodium: 180 mg, Cholesterol: 15.5 mg*

NUTRITIONAL BONUS: The orange hue of pumpkin is a strong indicator that it's a good source of beta-carotene – a carotenoid and antioxidant. Your body can convert the phytonutrient into vitamin A, which is essential for good eyesight, cell development and immunity. Since vitamin A is more actively and readily available through animal products, beta-carotene consumption through plant food is especially important for vegetarians.

Roasted Maple Cranberry Sauce

*Makes 1 cup. **Hands-on time:** 10 minutes. **Total time:** 1 hour, 10 minutes.*

It's so easy to make your own cranberry sauce. Try ours with the infused flavors of tarragon and maple and you'll never go back to canned sauce again.

INGREDIENTS:

- 3 cups fresh or frozen cranberries (340 g pkg)
- ¼ cup and 2 Tbsp real maple syrup
- 2 Tbsp water
- 1 lime
- 1 shallot, minced
- ½ tsp dried tarragon
- ¼ tsp sea salt

INSTRUCTIONS:

ONE: Place cranberries on a pie plate and drizzle with quarter cup maple syrup and water. Using a zester, peel strips of lime; stir into mixture.

TWO: Bake, uncovered, in a preheated 350°F oven, stirring occasionally, until cranberries break down and sauce is bubbly, about one hour. Remove from oven. Squeeze in juice from lime and stir in remaining two tablespoons syrup, along with shallot, tarragon and salt.

TIME-SAVING TIP: The sauce will keep well, covered and refrigerated, for up to two weeks – the flavors will blend and improve the longer it sits. Bring to room temperature before serving.

Nutrients per 2-Tbsp serving: *Calories: 28, Total Fat: 0 g, Sat. Fat: 0 g, Carbs: 7 g, Fiber: 1 g, Sugars: 5 g, Protein: 0 g, Sodium: 25 mg, Cholesterol: 0 mg*

Roasted
Maple
Cranberry
Sauce

Menu Two:

Citrus-Splashed Roasted Turkey Breast

Serves 10. **Hands-on time:** 40 minutes. **Total time:** 1 hour, 50 minutes.

Turkey breasts are a good source of lean protein. The meat tastes mild, which makes it a great flavor absorber. Mixing hot chile flakes with tangy tarragon and a three-citrus marinade adds layers of flavor.

INGREDIENTS:

- 1 each lemon, lime and orange
- 2 Tbsp olive oil
- 1 Tbsp chile flakes
- 1 Tbsp dried tarragon
- 5 to 6 lbs whole, boneless turkey breasts (2 breasts)
- 1 Tbsp honey

INSTRUCTIONS:

ONE: Finely grate the peels from a lemon, lime and orange into a bowl. Stir in oil, chili flakes and tarragon. Discard skin from turkey. Place turkey in a large bowl or baking dish. Rub citrus peel mixture over meat. Cover and refrigerate overnight to let flavors blend.

TWO: Squeeze the juices from the lemon, lime and orange – the juices should measure about a half cup. Pour the juices into a small saucepan; add honey. Bring to a boil, stirring often. Reduce heat and simmer, stirring often, until the mixture is thick and syrupy and has reduced to about a quarter cup. Set aside to cool.

THREE: Preheat oven to 325°F. Place turkey breasts in a shallow-sided roasting pan. Loosely cover with foil. Roast in oven for one hour.

FOUR: Increase heat to 400°F. Discard foil and brush turkey with a bit of the citrus-honey mixture (about two tablespoons). Brush with the glaze every five minutes or so for the next 10 to 20 minutes. The turkey breasts are done when an instant-read thermometer inserted into the thickest part of the breast registers 170°F. The total cooking time is one hour and 10 to 20 minutes.

TIME-SAVING TIP: Prepare the turkey marinade and citrus glaze up to three days before using. Cover and refrigerate. For a casual meal, roast before serving and dish up cold.

Nutrients per serving: *Calories: 281, Total Fat: 4 g, Sat. Fat: 0.5 g, Carbs: 4.5 g, Fiber: 1 g, Sugars: 2.5 g, Protein: 56 g, Sodium: 94 mg, Cholesterol: 90 mg*

196

THE BEST OF CLEAN EATING

Harvest Caponata

Serves 10. *Makes* 6 cups. *Hands-on time:* 10 minutes. *Total time:* 50 minutes.

Caponata is a southern-Italian-style eggplant relish. Lightly roasted with a few other fall vegetables, it makes a refreshing change from the sweet cranberry sauce that is typically served. Any leftovers are great for cold turkey sandwiches the next day.

INGREDIENTS:

- 3 plum tomatoes, cut lengthwise into halves
- 2 red bell peppers, seeded and cut in half
- 1 large eggplant, thickly sliced
- 1 large red onion, sliced into thick rings
- 1 to 2 Tbsp olive oil
- ¼ tsp each sea salt and ground black pepper
- 3 Tbsp red wine vinegar
- ¼ cup chopped Italian parsley or cilantro
- 8 black olives, pitted and chopped
- 2 Tbsp capers

INSTRUCTIONS:

ONE: Arrange oven racks in top and bottom third of oven. Preheat oven to 400°F. Toss tomatoes, peppers, eggplant and onion with one tablespoon oil; sprinkle with sea salt and black pepper. Add more oil only if mixture looks too dry.

TWO: Pick out and divide peppers, eggplant and onions between two lightly oiled (about one teaspoon) baking sheets and spread mixture out. Roast on top and bottom racks of preheated oven for 20 minutes. Remove from oven and add tomatoes. Return to oven (switching original position of sheets on racks) and roast, stirring occasionally, until vegetables are tender and browned around edges, 15 to 20 additional minutes.

THREE: Chop vegetables into small pieces and place in a bowl. Drizzle with vinegar; add parsley, olives and capers. Toss to mix. Serve at room temperature.

TIME-SAVING TIP: Prepare the relish, but don't add parsley. Cover and refrigerate for up to three days – the flavors blend more the longer it sits. Stir in parsley before serving so that it looks fresh.

Nutrients per ½-cup serving: *Calories: 43, Total Fat: 2 g, Sat. Fat: 0 g, Carbs: 6.5 g, Fiber: 3 g, Sugars: 3 g, Protein: 1 g, Sodium: 122 mg, Cholesterol: 0 mg*

Puy Lentils
WITH BRUSSELS SPROUTS

Serves 10. *Makes* 8 cups. *Hands-on time:* 5 minutes. *Total time:* 35 minutes.

Replace empty-carb stuffing with low-fat, high-protein lentils. While these aren't actually used to stuff the turkey, they do make a hearty side dish that's just as satisfying. Unlike regular brown lentils, the green, French Puy type keeps its shape when cooked and has a lovely peppery flavor that's positively robust with the addition of smoked paprika.

INGREDIENTS:

- 2 cups Du Puy lentils
- 6 cups water or low-sodium chicken broth (or 3 cups of each)
- 8 dried apricots, cut into quarters
- 1 tsp smoked sweet paprika
- 1 carrot, finely chopped
- 10 Brussels sprouts, shredded
- 2 large shallots, minced
- ¼ tsp sea salt

INSTRUCTIONS:

ONE: Rinse lentils, pick out any debris (if necessary) and place in a large saucepan. Stir in water or chicken broth, apricots and paprika. Bring to a boil. Reduce heat and simmer, uncovered, until most of the liquid is absorbed and lentils are tender, 25 to 30 minutes. Add carrot for the last 15 minutes of cooking. Drain well.

TWO: Meanwhile, place shredded Brussels sprouts and shallots in a large serving bowl. Sprinkle with salt. When lentils are drained, add to shallot mixture in bowl. Toss to mix evenly. Serve warm.

TIME-SAVING TIP: Cook lentils one or two days ahead, then turn them into a large bowl. Cover and refrigerate for up to two days. Prepare Brussels sprouts and shallots the day before serving; wrap separately and refrigerate. Reheat lentils in the microwave, stirring occasionally, until warmed through. Stir in shallots, Brussels sprouts and salt just before serving so that they stay fresh, or keep it casual and prepare the entire recipe without reheating. Serve as a cold salad.

Nutrients per ¾-cup serving: *Calories: 167, Total Fat: 0.5 g, Sat. Fat: 0 g, Carbs: 30 g, Fiber: 13 g, Sugars: 2 g, Protein: 11 g, Sodium: 61 mg, Cholesterol: 0 mg*

NUTRITIONAL BONUS: Also known as French green lentils or simply Puy lentils, the first ingredient in this side dish is blue-green and really holds its shape during cooking. Can't find them at your local grocer? You can sub in any other small lentil, but remember that the cooking time may have to be adjusted.

Roasted Cauliflower, Leek & Garlic Soup

***Serves** 10.* ***Makes** 8 cups.* ***Hands-on time:** 15 minutes.* ***Total time:** 1 hour.*

Serving soup before a main course is a great way to whet the appetites of your guests. This festive first course is comforting and healthy.

INGREDIENTS:

- 3 leeks, white part only, washed and thickly sliced
- ½ head garlic, cut so cloves are exposed
- 1 large head cauliflower, cut into florets
- 1 to 2 Tbsp olive oil
- ¼ tsp each sea salt, ground black pepper and ground nutmeg
- 3 cups low-sodium chicken broth
- 3 bay leaves
- 1 cup skim or 1% milk
- 3 cups shredded fresh basil
- 3 Tbsp hot water

INSTRUCTIONS:

ONE: Preheat oven to 425°F. Place a large baking sheet in the oven while it's preheating. Toss leeks, garlic and cauliflower with one tablespoon oil, sea salt, black pepper and nutmeg. Add remaining oil only if mixture looks dry. Carefully spread out on hot baking sheet. Roast in center of oven, stirring occasionally, until cauliflower is browned and almost tender, 25 to 30 minutes.

TWO: Remove garlic from baking sheet and set aside. Scrape leeks and cauliflower into a large saucepan. Add chicken broth and bay leaves. When cool enough, squeeze garlic from skins into saucepan and discard skins. Bring to a boil, then reduce heat. Cover and simmer until leeks are very tender, 10 to 15 minutes. Working in batches, purée in a food processor and pour into a saucepan. Stir in milk. Reheat before serving.

THREE: Place basil in a blender. Add hot water. Purée until smooth. Ladle soup into warm bowls. Add a spoonful of basil into each; using a toothpick, swirl decoratively into soup.

TIME-SAVING TIP: Prepare soup ahead of time and refrigerate for up to five days or freeze for up to one month. Prepare basil purée the day before.

Nutrients per ¾-cup serving: Calories: 76, Total Fat: 2 g, Sat. Fat: 0 g, Carbs: 11.5 g, Fiber: 3 g, Sugars: 4 g, Protein: 5 g, Sodium: 114 mg, Cholesterol: 0.5 mg

Gingery Roasted Squash
WITH WATERCRESS

***Serves** 8 to 10.* ***Hands-on time:** 10 minutes.* ***Total time:** 45 minutes.*

Roasted squash is a welcome addition to any Thanksgiving feast. Its naturally buttery flavor makes it feel like a decadent dish and the addition of ginger gives it an extra tasty boost.

INGREDIENTS:

- 2 large butternut squash
- 2 large onions, thickly sliced into wedges
- 1 Tbsp olive oil
- ¼ tsp each sea salt and ground black pepper
- ¼ cup julienned fresh ginger
- 2 bunches watercress, washed and trimmed

INSTRUCTIONS:

ONE: Position oven racks in top and bottom thirds of oven. Place a baking sheet on each rack while oven is preheating to 425°F. Peel squash and slice in half lengthwise. Scoop out and discard seeds. Cut squash into chunky pieces. Toss squash and onions with oil, sea salt and black pepper. Carefully divide mixture onto hot baking sheets.

TWO: Roast in oven for 15 minutes without stirring. Stir two tablespoons ginger into squash and onion mixture on each sheet. Switch positions of sheets, then continue roasting until squash is browned around edges and tender, another 15 to 18 minutes. Turn into a large bowl and add watercress. Stir to mix. Serve warm.

TIME-SAVING TIP: You can cut squash and onions the night before the big day. Place them in a large bag and add oil only. Julienne ginger and wrap tightly in plastic wrap. Wash and trim watercress. Wrap in a kitchen towel and refrigerate everything overnight. Don't forget to season the squash mixture with salt and pepper before roasting.

Nutrients per 1¼-cup serving (¹⁄₁₀ of recipe): Calories: 128, Total Fat: 2 g, Sat. Fat: 0 g, Carbs: 30 g, Fiber: 5 g, Sugars: 6 g, Protein: 3 g, Sodium: 59 mg, Cholesterol: 0 mg

For a photo of this recipe, see page 192.

Cranberry Orange Cheesecake Pears

Serves 10. **Hands-on time:** *20 minutes.*
Total time: *1 hour, 15 minutes (including chilling time).*

Sometimes a bite of cake is just as fulfilling as an entire slice. These hot and sweet pears with a creamy filling are sure to satisfy your end-of-meal craving.

INGREDIENTS:

PEARS

- 10 Bosc pears
- 2 cinnamon sticks
- 2 cups each 100% cranberry juice and 100% orange juice
- 1 vanilla bean, split lengthwise

CHEESECAKE STUFFING

- 1 cup light cream cheese, at room temperature
- 1 tsp vanilla extract
- ½ tsp dried ground ginger
- ⅛ tsp almond extract (optional)
- ⅓ cup dried unsweetened cranberries
- ½ cup unsalted, sliced almonds, toasted

INSTRUCTIONS:

ONE: Peel pears. Trim bottoms so that they sit flat. Using a small spoon or a melon baller, scoop out and discard cores. Place pears in a very large, wide, heavy-bottomed saucepan. Add cinnamon sticks and juices. Scrape out seeds from vanilla bean and stir in; add scraped bean husks, too.

TWO: Bring to a boil, then reduce heat. Cover and simmer, occasionally turning pears over carefully to ensure even cooking, until almost tender but still a little firm, about 20 to 25 minutes.

THREE: In a bowl, stir cream cheese with vanilla extract, ginger and almond extract (if using) until mixed. If the mixture is too thick to stir easily, add a few spoonfuls of hot pear cooking liquid. Stir in cranberries and almonds.

FOUR: Carefully spoon pears onto a large platter. Cover and refrigerate to cool completely. Boil remaining pear liquid in pan, stirring often, until it reduces to half a cup. The sauce will foam and bubble toward the end of cooking, so be sure to stir often. Remove from heat and discard cinnamon sticks and vanilla husks.

FIVE: To serve, fill pears with cream cheese mixture. Place on plates and spoon sauce over the top.

TIME-SAVING TIP: In the days leading up to Thanksgiving, prepare the cheesecake mixture but don't add almonds. Cover and refrigerate for up to three days. Poach pears and make the sauce. Refrigerate overnight. Stuff pears and keep refrigerated for up to six hours. Bring both pears and sauce to room temperature before serving.

Nutrients per stuffed pear: Calories: 208, Total Fat: 6 g, Sat. Fat: 3 g, Carbs: 38 g, Fiber: 5 g, Sugars: 27 g, Protein: 4 g, Sodium: 74 mg, Cholesterol: 13 mg

Nutritional Bonus:
Did you know that, ounce for ounce, pomegranate juice has 17 percent more polyphenols than red wine? These powerful antioxidants scavenge for cell-damaging free radicals, which may help slow or reduce the risk of assorted diseases. You can also enjoy our moist, juicy turkey without packing on the pounds: A filling serving of white meat (and stuffing!) covers nearly 25 percent of your daily protein needs yet contains only about 320 calories.

Cranberry Sauce

Pomegranate-Glazed Stuffed Roast Turkey

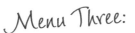

Menu Three:

Pomegranate-Glazed Stuffed Roast Turkey

Serves *14.* ***Hands-on time:*** *30 minutes.* ***Total time:*** *4 to 4½ hours (includes roasting).*

Preparing a Thanksgiving turkey can be overwhelming for some, but we've broken it down into easy, manageable steps for a stress-free holiday. Here are a few more helpful hints for mastering the main event: To avoid overcooking, check your turkey early and often and test doneness with a meat thermometer, if possible. And, to avoid unnecessary mess (or dropping the main course!), many turkeys are sold with a string for lifting the finished bird out of the pan.

INGREDIENTS:

TURKEY

- 2 Tbsp chopped fresh rosemary
- Zest of 1 lemon
- 1 tsp fresh ground black pepper
- ¾ tsp sea salt
- 1 (14- to 16-lb) turkey, defrosted and brought to room temperature
- Olive oil cooking spray
- ¼ cup low-sodium chicken broth
- 1 recipe Mushroom & Leek Stuffing (see p. 202) at room temperature

POMEGRANATE GLAZE

- 1½ cups 100% pomegranate juice
- ½ cup low-sodium chicken broth
- ¼ cup no-sugar-added strawberry jam
- 2 Tbsp raw organic honey

INSTRUCTIONS:

TURKEY

ONE: Preheat oven to 325°F. In a small bowl, stir together rosemary, lemon zest, pepper and salt. Set aside.

TWO: Prep turkey, following the Step-By-Step: Turkey Prep Guide on p. 206.

THREE: Transfer turkey to oven and roast for a total time of three-and-a-half to four-and-a-half hours. While turkey roasts, make Pomegranate Glaze (instructions follow). After two hours of cooking, loosely cover turkey with foil to prevent over-browning. When turkey is 20 to 30 minutes from being done (meat temperature registers about 160°F), uncover and baste with half of Pomegranate Glaze. The turkey is done when juices run clear and a meat thermometer registers 180°F when inserted into the deepest part of the thigh and 165°F when inserted into the center of stuffing in the body cavity.

FOUR: Remove turkey from oven and let rest for 20 minutes. Add a quarter cup broth to remaining Pomegranate Glaze and reheat on low until hot but not bubbling. Spoon stuffing out of neck and body cavity and transfer to a serving bowl. Remove turkey skin and carve. Drizzle each serving with two teaspoons Pomegranate Glaze and serve.

POMEGRANATE GLAZE

In a small saucepan, combine pomegranate juice, half cup broth, jam and honey. Bring to a simmer over medium-high heat. Reduce heat to medium-low and simmer until mixture reduces by half, 10 to 15 minutes. Remove from heat and let rest at room temperature for 20 minutes to allow glaze to thicken.

NOTE: The fat-free pomegranate glaze doubles as a flavorful sauce.

TIME-SAVING TIP: Glaze may be made one day ahead. Cover and refrigerate. Before basting turkey, reheat glaze in a small saucepan on low heat until it reaches a slightly thick but pourable consistency.

Nutrients per serving (4 oz skinless white meat, ½ cup stuffing, 2 tsp glaze):
Calories: 320, Total Fat: 4 g, Sat. Fat: 2 g, Carbs: 36 g, Fiber: 5 g, Sugars: 10 g, Protein: 25 g, Sodium: 530 mg, Cholesterol: 60 mg

Cranberry Sauce
WITH APPLES & GINGER

Serves *8 to 10.* ***Makes*** *2 cups.* ***Hands-on time:*** *17 minutes.* ***Total time:*** *3 hours, 17 minutes (includes chilling time).*

The short harvest season for cranberries coincides perfectly with the Thanksgiving feast – and we wouldn't have it any other way! Whether you use the fresh or frozen type, these berries break down as they cook, while the apples stay slightly firm, creating a pleasing variety of textures and tastes in our revamped cranberry sauce. Plus, the slight spiciness of fresh ginger gives this not-too-sweet fat-free condiment a pleasant kick.

INGREDIENTS:

- 12 oz cranberries, fresh or frozen and defrosted
- 1 apple, cored and chopped into ⅓-inch pieces
- ½ cup raw organic honey
- ½ cup water
- 1½ Tbsp finely minced fresh ginger
- Zest and juice of ½ lemon
- ⅛ tsp sea salt

INSTRUCTIONS:

Add all ingredients to a large saucepan and bring to a boil over medium-high heat. Reduce heat to medium-low and cook for eight to ten minutes, or until cranberries break down, apples soften and mixture thickens (sauce will continue to thicken slightly as it chills). Stir often to prevent sticking on bottom of pan. Transfer to a serving dish or storage container, cover and chill for at least three hours.

TIME-SAVING TIP: Cranberry sauce keeps up to five days, covered, in the refrigerator. Bring to room temperature to serve.

Nutrients per 3-Tbsp serving: *Calories: 84, Total Fat: 0 g, Sat. Fat: 0 g, Carbs: 21 g, Fiber: 2 g, Sugars: 18 g, Protein: 0 g, Sodium: 24 mg, Cholesterol: 0 mg*

Mushroom & Leek Stuffing

Serves 24. *Makes* 12 cups (enough for a 14- to 16-lb turkey).
Hands-on time: 40 minutes. *Total time:* 40 minutes.

For Thanksgiving traditionalists, skipping stuffing is out of the question, so we upped the nutrition content with whole-wheat sourdough bread and meaty portobello mushrooms. Look for whole-wheat sourdough at your local bakery. But there's no need to stress if you can't track it down: You can substitute regular whole-wheat bread (a pantry staple), if necessary.

INGREDIENTS:

- 1 (680-g) loaf whole-wheat sourdough bread or regular whole-wheat bread
- 1 Tbsp olive oil, divided
- 1 lb portobello mushrooms, cut into ½-inch pieces (about 4 cups)
- 1 cup finely chopped carrots,
- 1 cup finely chopped celery
- 1 large leek, trimmed, halved lengthwise and chopped
- ½ cup low-sodium chicken broth
- 1 tsp fresh ground black pepper
- 1½ tsp dried thyme
- 1 tsp dried rosemary
- 1 tsp chile powder
- 1 tsp onion powder
- ½ tsp sea salt

INSTRUCTIONS:

ONE: Preheat oven to 350°F. Slice bread (if not already sliced) and discard crusts. Cut bread into three-quarter-inch cubes. Spread bread cubes out in a single layer on two rimmed baking sheets. Bake for ten minutes or until lightly toasted, tossing halfway through. Transfer to a very large bowl.

TWO: Heat a half tablespoon oil in a large skillet over medium heat. Add mushrooms and cook, stirring often, until tender and lightly browned, eight to ten minutes. Add mushrooms to bowl with bread. Wipe out skillet with paper towel and heat remaining oil on medium-high. Add carrots, celery and leek. Cook until vegetables are tender and lightly browned, eight to ten minutes. Add to bread bowl.

THREE: Add remaining ingredients to bread bowl and stir gently to combine. Bread should be moist, not dry or soggy. Cool completely before stuffing turkey, about one-and-a-half hours.

OPTION: **If you'd rather not stuff the turkey, you can bake the stuffing separately: Bring stuffing to room temperature and, when the turkey finishes cooking, raise oven temperature to 400°F. Coat a large (about 9 x 13-inch) baking dish with olive oil cooking spray and add stuffing. Cover tightly with foil and bake for 20 minutes. Then remove foil and bake for 10 to 15 minutes more, or until lightly browned.**

TIME-SAVING TIP: **Stuffing may be prepared up to two days in advance. After cooling, cover and refrigerate. Bring to room temperature before stuffing turkey.**

WASTE NOT, WANT NOT: **Don't just throw your bread crusts away; turn them into fresh bread crumbs by blitzing them in a food processor. Then store the homemade crumbs in an airtight container in the fridge for five days or freeze for two months. Use them to coat vegetables or fish or in meatballs and meatloaf.**

Nutrients per ½-cup serving: Calories: 150, Total Fat: 3 g, Sat. Fat: 0 g, Carbs: 28 g, Fiber: 5 g, Sugars: 5 g, Protein: 6 g, Sodium: 360 mg, Cholesterol: 0 mg

Spiced Pumpkin Mousse

Serves 10. *Hands-on time:* 20 minutes. *Total time:* 2 hours, 20 minutes (includes chilling).

The secret to rich desserts without the fat? Silken tofu. Unlike the firm tofu used in stir-frys, this softer type can be blended to a smooth, thick consistency – perfect for creamy desserts. Lightly sweetened with pure maple syrup and your favorite pumpkin pie spices, our mousse is so rich and delicious your family will never be able to guess the secret ingredient.

INGREDIENTS:

- 2 (15-oz) cans 100% pure pumpkin purée (not pumpkin pie filling)
- 1 (1-lb) pkg silken tofu, drained well
- ½ cup pure maple syrup
- 1½ tsp ground cinnamon
- ¾ tsp ground ginger
- ¼ tsp ground nutmeg
- ¼ tsp ground cloves
- ¼ tsp sea salt
- ½ cup nonfat plain Greek-style yogurt
- 1 oz dark chocolate, cut into thin shards (about ¼ cup)

INSTRUCTIONS:

ONE: In the bowl of a food processor, combine pumpkin and tofu. Process until combined, about 30 seconds. Add maple syrup, cinnamon, ginger, nutmeg, cloves and salt. Process until combined, about 30 seconds more.

TWO: Transfer mousse to a resealable container, cover and refrigerate for at least four hours.

THREE: Drain any water that has accumulated from mousse. Give it a quick stir and scoop half a cup of mousse into each of 10 small glasses or ramekins. (You may have some mousse left over.) Top each serving with two teaspoons yogurt and one teaspoon chocolate. Keep refrigerated until ready to serve.

Nutrients per serving (½ cup mousse, 2 tsp yogurt, 1 tsp chocolate): Calories: 130, Total Fat: 3.5 g, Sat. Fat: 1.5 g, Carbs: 22 g, Fiber: 4 g, Sugars: 14 g, Protein: 4 g, Sodium: 60 mg, Cholesterol: 0 mg

Nutritional Bonus:
The ample amount of mushrooms in this stuffing packs a big, meaty flavor punch for very few calories. The tasty fungi also happen to be high in riboflavin, a B vitamin that maintains healthy blood cells. In addition, one portobello contains more potassium than a banana!

Mushroom & Leek Stuffing

Coconut Cardamom Sweet Potatoes

Serves *10.* **Hands-on time:** *20 minutes.* **Total time:** *1 hour, 10 minutes.*

Your holiday table will seem incomplete without a creamy sweet potato casserole. We put a new spin on the eye-catching orange-hued spuds with light coconut milk and the sweet, spicy flavors of vanilla, cardamom and cayenne. Finish it off with chopped pecans and you have a delightfully crunchy topping.

INGREDIENTS:

- 5 medium sweet potatoes (3½ to 4 lbs), peeled and cut into ¾-inch pieces
- ¾ cup light coconut milk
- 2 tsp ground cardamom
- 1 tsp pure vanilla extract
- ½ tsp sea salt
- ⅛ tsp fresh ground black pepper
- ⅛ tsp cayenne pepper
- ⅓ cup unsalted pecan halves, chopped

INSTRUCTIONS:

ONE: Preheat oven to 325°F. Bring a large pot of water to a boil over high heat. Add sweet potatoes, return to boiling and cook until soft, about 10 minutes. Drain and transfer potatoes to the bowl of a stand mixer (or use a large bowl and a hand-held electric mixer).

TWO: Add coconut milk, cardamom, vanilla, salt, black pepper and cayenne to potatoes. Mix on medium speed until smooth, scraping down sides of bowl once or twice. Transfer to a 9 x 9-inch baking dish. Sprinkle pecans evenly over sweet potato mixture.

THREE: Bake 45 to 50 minutes, or until edges are slightly browned. Cool on a rack for 10 minutes and serve.

TIME-SAVING TIP: Sweet potatoes may be prepared through Step Two up to two days ahead of your big dinner. Cover and refrigerate. To heat, transfer directly from refrigerator to oven and add 10 minutes to baking time. And, because the turkey also cooks at 325°F, you can multitask by putting your potatoes in the oven along with your turkey!

Nutrients per ½-cup serving: *Calories: 100, Total Fat: 3.5 g, Sat. Fat: 1 g, Carbs: 15 g, Fiber: 2 g, Sugars: 5 g, Protein: 2 g, Sodium: 120 mg, Cholesterol: 0 mg*

NUTRITIONAL BONUS: The sweet potatoes in this dish boost the vitamin A content to over 200 percent of your daily need. Better yet, the vitamin A appears in its beta-carotene form, which promotes bone growth and teeth development. You'll also get almost 10 percent of your fiber needs taken care of with just one serving, along with healthy doses of zinc and manganese.

Green Beans
WITH ROASTED CHESTNUTS

Serves *10.* **Hands-on time:** *20 minutes.* **Total time:** *30 minutes.*

A light lemon-garlic sauce made with chicken broth adds savory flavor to the mild chestnuts and tender-crisp green beans, making for an elegant side dish. If thin French-style beans are unavailable, feel free to use the regular variety. Look for roasted and peeled European chestnuts, not water chestnuts, in cans or vacuum-packed jars (no draining required) around the holidays.

INGREDIENTS:

- 1½ lbs French green beans
- 1 Tbsp olive oil
- 2 large shallots, thinly sliced (about ½ cup)
- 1½ cups canned or jarred vacuum-packed roasted chestnuts, sliced
- 4 cloves garlic, minced
- ⅓ cup low-sodium chicken broth
- Juice ½ lemon
- ¼ tsp sea salt
- ¼ tsp fresh ground black pepper

INSTRUCTIONS:

ONE: Bring a large pot of water to a boil over high heat. Fill a bowl with ice water. Add beans to pot and boil for three to four minutes or until tender-crisp. Drain and immediately transfer beans to ice water for two minutes. Drain again and set beans aside.

TWO: Heat oil in a large skillet over medium-low heat. Add shallots and cook for three minutes, stirring often. Add chestnuts and garlic and cook for one minute. Add broth, bring to a simmer and cook until reduced by half, stirring occasionally.

THREE: Add beans to shallot mixture and toss well until heated through, about two minutes. Add lemon juice, salt and pepper and remove from heat. Serve hot.

TIME-SAVING TIP: Green beans may be blanched (Step One) up to two days in advance. After draining ice water, transfer beans to a zip-top bag along with a paper towel to absorb any moisture and refrigerate. Bring beans to room temperature before tossing with shallot mixture.

Nutrients per ¾-cup serving (loosely packed): *Calories: 170, Total Fat: 2 g, Sat. Fat: 0 g, Carbs: 33 g, Fiber: 6 g, Sugars: 2 g, Protein: 7 g, Sodium: 55 mg, Cholesterol: 0 mg*

Nutritional Bonus:
Green beans, relative of kidney and black beans, are highly nutrient-dense yet low in calories. You'll get 25 percent of the vitamin K, 20 percent of the vitamin C, 16 percent of the fiber and 16 percent of the vitamin A you need each day in a one-cup serving. These beans also supply half your daily need of iron, which helps carry oxygen from your lungs.

Green Beans

Step-By-Step: Turkey Prep Guide

If the idea of preparing a turkey from scratch is a bit overwhelming, follow our simple steps to get the bird from freezer aisle to family table with ease.

ONE: Remove and discard neck and giblets.

TWO: Rinse turkey and pat dry.

THREE: Place turkey breast-side up in a large roasting pan fitted with a rack. Gently lift skin covering each breast and tuck half of rosemary mixture under skin with your fingers.

FOUR: Rub remaining rosemary mixture over turkey's skin and coat lightly with cooking spray.

FIVE: Fill neck cavity with Mushroom & Leek Stuffing (see recipe, p. 202). Do not over-pack, as stuffing expands during cooking.

NOTE: Since you will remove the turkey skin before carving, rubbing the mixture over the skin will have a smaller effect on the overall flavor. But it will add beautiful aromatic notes to your home and a visual appeal when presenting your turkey at your holiday table.

SIX: Pull neck skin down over cavity opening. Firmly turn wings back to hold neck skin in place and stabilize turkey in roasting pan. If necessary, cover neck skin with foil to prevent stuffing from spilling out.

SEVEN: Fill body cavity with stuffing.

EIGHT: Cover opening with foil. Proceed with Step Three of Pomegranate-Glazed Stuffed Roast Turkey recipe (see p. 201).

Bird is the Word

When you're talking turkey, it's all in the name. But what exactly do those names mean?

Heritage Turkeys

While all domesticated turkeys originally descended from the wild turkey, heritage birds are not to be confused with the popular Broad-breasted White turkey at the grocery store. Offering rich flavor and beautiful plumage, birds such as Bourbon Red, Jersey Buff and Standard Bronze set the bar for heritage birds. All heritage turkeys must breed naturally and grow slowly over five to seven years for hens and three to five years for toms. These birds are not easily available, but, thanks to the efforts of Slow Food USA, the American Livestock Breeds Conservancy and concerned farmers, these originals are making a comeback.

Free-Range Turkeys

According to the United States Department of Agriculture, "free range" means that birds have "access" to the outdoors. Above and beyond that, it's up to the farmer to determine how often and how far the turkeys actually roam. While free-range turkeys should be the antithesis of industrially raised birds, ironically most aren't raised much differently. When buying free-range, it's best to do your research and find out what farm they come from.

Organic Turkeys

Luckiest of the flock, these birds are fed grains free of antibiotics, pesticides and chemical-fertilizers. Most organic turkeys are also free range.

Fresh Turkeys

These have never been chilled below 26°F – and that's good because some experts argue that frozen turkeys are drier.

Kosher Turkeys

Similar to organic turkeys, these birds are fed antibiotic-free grains and are allowed to roam freely. They're processed under rabbinical supervision and soaked with a salt brine that adds moistness and helps retain that moisture during cooking.

> When buying free-range, it's best to do your research and find out what farm they come from.

Sweet Potatoes

Consider trading in white potatoes for the sweet kind more often. You'll boost your healthy carb intake and much more.

Generally, two menus call for sweet potatoes. One is Thanksgiving dinner, where they are a near-mandatory complement in the form of a stand-alone marshmallow-topped dish or a pie. While we understand the sweet tooth well, here at *Clean Eating* we prefer the second menu option, where sweet potatoes become part and parcel of a healthy lifestyle. Because sweet potatoes are a great source of complex carbs and are packed with nutrients, they work well at many meals alongside lean protein, like chicken, and healthy fats, found in fish.

Sweet potato shopping

Sweet potato shopping is pretty easy. As with all produce, keep an eye out for bruises and soft spots. According to Diane Forley, a chef consultant based in New York, sweet potatoes are best when the flesh is firm, with minimal scarring and no cut ends.

Sweet potato prep

Sweet potatoes are often the most delicious part of a clean menu. Not only do they fulfill a meal's healthy-carb requirement, but they can also help to satisfy your cravings for sweets. Additionally, they are high in vitamins A and C and potassium. However, the sweeter the potato, the higher its sugar content, says Forley. So if you're watching your sugar intake, keep your sweet potato consumption at a moderate level.

If you're new to these heavenly taters, be forewarned – they are much harder than potatoes and very tricky to cut. (Rookie mistake: putting them in the fridge, which makes

SHOPPING TIP: If you're not using the sweet potatoes right away, it's best to store them in a cool, dark place, like a cupboard. They should never be kept in the fridge; the cold can alter their taste in a manner that won't be pleasing to your palate. For the best flavor and freshness, use sweet potatoes within 10 days of purchase.

them even harder.) "You can always use a vegetable peeler to remove the skin," says Forley. "If the potato is large, cut it in half. Lay the flat side down on your cutting board and continue to slice the vegetable into the desired size." (Try cutting them into fry-sized strips.)

Cooking

Sweet potatoes, just like starchier regular potatoes, can be prepared in several ways – boiled, baked, sautéed, steamed and fried (obviously, we're cautious about recommending the latter). To retain flavor and moisture, Forley prefers to bake sweet potatoes whole in their jackets. Once they have cooled, peeling the skin is a snap.

For some recipes, baking is preferable to boiling, since boiling causes potatoes to absorb excess water, which can affect the end result, says Forley. Boiling, which is unavoidable at times, may also result in the reduction of certain key nutrients.

Next time you're looking to get experimental with your sweet potatoes, try adding them to a salad. Combine sliced avocados, cooked sweet potato cubes, cherry tomatoes and arugula with a squeeze of lemon juice, a sprinkle of olive oil and parsley leaves.

> **TIME-SAVING TIP: No time to bake or boil? No problem. Poke a few holes in a raw sweet potato with a fork and pop it in the microwave for five minutes. Once it's cool, slice the sweet potato in half and dig in!**

Yam or sweet potato?

While sweet potatoes and yams are thought of interchangeably, the two are different. Botanically, the yam is a member of the lily family, and the sweet potato is kin to the morning glory vine. Available year-round but at their best between late August and March, true yams, according to Forley, are typically starchier and less sweet than a sweet potato. It's important to note that what is often labeled "yam" at the supermarket is usually an orange-skinned sweet potato, so it's wise to check with your grocer.

Delicious
Low-Fat Desserts

Orange Chocolate
Ricotta Cheesecake, p. 225

The words "clean eating" and "deprivation" do not belong in the same sentence. Let's get rid of the notion that all desserts are "bad" for you – it's simply not true. Clean eating is not about giving up the foods you love or ignoring your cravings; it's about giving in to them – using your smarts. Our desserts use naturally sweet, unprocessed and unrefined ingredients that work for your body, not against it, allowing you to indulge in pleasures that only taste sinful. Our Almond Butter Chocolate Chip Cookies were one of our greatest hits ever, as were our Chocolate Sour Cream Cupcakes. For something a little lighter, try our Peach & Blackberry Cobbler or our Chocolate-Drizzled Roasted Cherries. These sweets can't be beat!

Easy Egg Custard
WITH FRESH PEACHES

Serves 6. **Hands-on time:** *10 minutes.* **Total time:** *40 minutes.*

Egg custard is a classic dessert, but traditional recipes call for excessive amounts of butter, sugar, flour, whole milk and egg yolks. Skipping the high-calorie/high-fat ingredients and sticking to just two egg yolks doesn't mean less flavor. Honey, vanilla and nutmeg keep things interesting, while peaches add a topping that's soft and sweet.

INGREDIENTS:

- 2 eggs
- 2 egg whites
- 3 Tbsp raw honey
- 1 tsp pure vanilla extract
- Pinch sea salt
- 1½ cups low-fat milk
- ½ tsp fresh grated nutmeg
- Boiling water, as needed
- 2 peaches, pits removed and sliced

INSTRUCTIONS:

ONE: Preheat oven to 350°F. In a large bowl, beat together eggs, egg whites, honey, vanilla and salt.

TWO: In a medium saucepan, heat milk over high heat until just about to boil, about 10 minutes. Remove milk from heat immediately.

THREE: Slowly pour milk into egg mixture, a few tablespoons at a time, while whisking.

FOUR: Place six ramekins in a deep baking dish. Pour custard evenly into each ramekin so each ramekin is about two-thirds full and top with nutmeg, dividing evenly. Pour boiling water into the deep dish so that the level of the water comes up to the level of the custard in the ramekins. Carefully transfer baking dish with ramekins to oven and bake until custards are set and a knife inserted into a center comes out clean, about 30 minutes.

NOTE: **If you have a slide-out rack in your oven, place baking dish with ramekins on rack, then carefully fill it with boiling water and slide rack into oven to bake.**

FIVE: Remove baking dish from oven and let cool until ramekins can safely be removed from hot water bath. Serve custard warm with peach slices or chill in refrigerator overnight to enjoy the next day.

Nutrients per serving (1 ramekin with 2 or 3 peach slices): *Calories: 106, Total Fat: 2 g, Sat. Fat: 1.2 g, Carbs: 17 g, Fiber: 0.8 g, Sugars: 16 g, Protein: 6 g, Sodium: 122 mg, Cholesterol: 73 mg*

Nutritional Bonus:
Although they taste delightfully sweet, peaches are actually low in calories and boast a healthy dose of vitamin A, fiber and phytochemicals, which have important disease-fighting properties.

Easy Egg Custard

Vanilla Bean-Spiked Autumn Apple Pie

Serves 12. ***Hands-on time:*** *35 minutes.*
Total time: *2 hours, 35 minutes (including chilling time.)*

Tart apple pie heralds the onset of fall's chill like few other sweets. Fresh vanilla bean enriches and deepens this version's flavor – a surprising twist. Put the dough together the night before. Roll and fill, then let the pie bake while you sit down to dinner. The house will fill with the fragrance of the autumn harvest and your family will enjoy a warm, low-fat, reduced-sugar, homemade dessert.

INGREDIENTS:

CRUST

- 1 cup whole-wheat flour
- ½ cup ground oatmeal
- ½ tsp sea salt
- 2 tsp apple cider vinegar
- 2 Tbsp ice water
- ½ cup Do-It-Yourself Olive-Butter Spread

NOTE: To make the olive-butter spread, simply process ¼ cup olive oil with ¼ cup unsalted butter until smooth.

FILLING

- 8 cups peeled and thinly sliced Braeburn apples (6 to 8 medium)
- 3 Tbsp whole-wheat flour
- 3 Tbsp apple butter
- 1 Tbsp freshly squeezed lemon juice
- ⅛ tsp sea salt
- 2 Tbsp honey
- 1 vanilla bean, cut open lengthwise and seeds scraped out

INSTRUCTIONS:

CRUST

Stir the flour, oatmeal and sea salt together in a medium bowl. In a small bowl, whisk together the vinegar and water. Use a pastry blender to cut the olive-butter spread into the flour until the mixture resembles coarse meal. Drizzle in the vinegar mixture and toss with a fork until the dough is evenly moist. Stir until a dough forms. Divide into two pieces, one slightly larger in diameter than the other. Press each into a six-inch disk and wrap in plastic. Chill for at least one hour and up to two days.

ROLLING DOUGH

Between two sheets of plastic, roll the larger disk of dough into a 12-inch circle. Remove the top piece of plastic, lift the bottom piece from diagonal corners and invert it over a 9-inch pie dish. Press the dough into the pan and peel off the plastic. Roll the second piece of dough in the same way, slide it onto a sheetpan and refrigerate for later use as the pie's top crust.

TIP:
When apples ripen in the fall, they come in abundance! Luckily, there are plenty of ways to make the most of them, such as the pie and crisp on these pages. To store for a long time, wrap each apple individually in a small piece of newsprint, place in a cardboard box and store in a cool location. A cellar or cold room is perfect.

FILLING & ASSEMBLY

ONE: Preheat oven to 450°F.

TWO: Put the apple slices in a big bowl, sprinkle with the flour and toss. In a small bowl, stir together the apple butter, lemon juice, sea salt, honey and vanilla bean. Stir into the apples. Spoon the apples into the crust and press them down gently.

THREE: Grab the second piece of dough from the fridge and slide it over the filled pie. Press the dough into place firmly. Trim, seal and crimp the edges. Use a paring knife to cut four slits in the top of the pie.

FOUR: Bake for 15 minutes. Reduce temperature to 350°F and bake for an additional 45 minutes, until brown and bubbly. Let cool one hour before slicing.

Nutrients per serving (¹/₁₂ **of pie):** *Calories: 183, Total Fat: 9 g, Sat. Fat: 3 g, Carbs: 25 g, Fiber: 3 g, Sugars: 13 g, Protein: 2 g, Sodium: 122 mg, Cholesterol: 10 mg*

Apple Cranberry Crumble

***Serves** 12. **Hands-on time:** 15 minutes. **Total time:** 50 minutes.*

For those craving some all-American apple pie, our clean crumble is a much easier seasonal alternative. Pop it into the oven just before sitting down to dinner and, as you're about to clear the table, you'll have a comforting dessert ready to warm your family on even the chilliest winter night.

INGREDIENTS:

- Olive oil cooking spray
- ⅓ cup Sucanat
- 2 Tbsp whole-wheat flour
- ½ tsp cinnamon
- 2 Granny Smith apples, peeled, cored and sliced thin
- 2 cups fresh cranberries
- ½ cup old-fashioned oats
- ¼ cup maple flakes
- ¼ tsp baking powder
- ¼ tsp sea salt
- 1½ Tbsp canola oil
- 1 Tbsp 100% apple juice

INSTRUCTIONS:

ONE: Preheat oven to 375°F. Lightly coat an 8-inch baking pan with cooking spray.

TWO: In a large mixing bowl, combine Sucanat, flour and cinnamon; add apple slices and cranberries, mix together and spread evenly in prepared baking pan.

THREE: In a medium bowl, mix together oats, maple flakes, baking powder and salt.

FOUR: In a separate bowl, combine oil and apple juice; then add it to oat mixture, distributing evenly until mixture appears crumbly.

FIVE: Sprinkle oat mixture over apples and cranberries, and bake for 35 minutes until bubbly. Dessert may be served warm or chilled.

Nutrients per 2 x 2-inch square serving: Calories: 100, Total Fat: 2 g, Sat. Fat: 0 g, Carbs: 20 g, Fiber: 2 g, Sugars: 15 g, Protein: 1 g, Sodium: 45 mg, Cholesterol: 0 mg

Nutritional Bonus:
Sweet and tart cranberries surprisingly offer an impressive amount of fiber. One cup of whole cranberries rings in at almost five grams of fiber, which is more than two slices of store-bought, whole-wheat bread that offers a little less than four grams of the macronutrient. So eat up!

CE "Ice Cream" Sandwiches

Makes 8 sandwiches. **Hands-on time:** 25 minutes.
Total time: 4 hours, 35 minutes (includes chilling time.)

Summer will never be the same with our version of this tasty treat. A hit with kids and adults alike, these sandwiches are perfect for a mid-afternoon cooldown on a hot day or after-dinner dessert.

INGREDIENTS:

• 1 recipe Vanilla Frozen Yogurt (see far right)
• 1 recipe Chocolate-Spiked Oatmeal Cookies (see right)

INSTRUCTIONS:

To assemble sandwiches, spoon three tablespoons frozen yogurt between two cookies. (If yogurt is too hard to scoop, allow it to warm slightly for a few minutes on counter until desired consistency.) Repeat for remaining cookies. Eat immediately or transfer to freezer-safe container and store in freezer until ready to eat. For best results, eat within two to three hours of filling cookies.

Nutrients per 1 CE "Ice Cream" Sandwich: Calories: 268, Total Fat: 3.75 g, Sat. Fat: 1.4 g, Carbs: 51 g, Fiber: 5.5 g, Sugars: 27 g, Protein: 8.4 g, Sodium: 100 mg, Cholesterol: 3 mg

Chocolate-Spiked Oatmeal Cookies

Makes 16 cookies. **Hands-on time:** 15 minutes. **Total time:** 25 minutes.

Adding chocolate gives this classic cookie a delightful new twist. Try it as part of our CE "Ice Cream" Sandwich (see left) or dunk it into a refreshing glass of milk.

INGREDIENTS:

- Olive oil cooking spray
- 1¼ cups quick-cook old-fashioned oats
- ½ cup whole-wheat pastry flour
- 2 tsp flaxseed meal
- 1 tsp cinnamon
- ½ tsp baking powder
- ¼ tsp sea salt
- ½ cup agave nectar
- 1 large egg white
- 2 tsp unsalted almond butter
- 1 tsp pure vanilla extract
- ¼ cup dark bittersweet chocolate chips (about 40 grams)

INSTRUCTIONS:

ONE: Preheat oven to 350°F and lightly spray two baking sheets with cooking spray.

TWO: In a large mixing bowl, combine oats, flour, flaxseed meal, cinnamon, baking powder and salt.

THREE: In a small mixing bowl, whisk together agave, egg white, almond butter and vanilla.

FOUR: Add egg mixture to dry ingredients all at once and combine. Stir in chocolate chips.

FIVE: Divide batter equally into 16 mounds (about one rounded tablespoon in size) and arrange evenly spaced on prepared baking sheets. Using the back of a slightly dampened spoon, flatten each mound into two-and-a-half-inch circles. Bake nine to ten minutes, until golden. Cool on sheets for an additional 10 minutes before transferring to racks to cool completely. Stored in an airtight container, cookies will keep fresh for two to three days.

Nutrients per 2-cookie serving: Calories: 206, Total Fat: 3 g, Sat. Fat: 1 g, Carbs: 40 g, Fiber: 5 g, Sugars: 16 g, Protein: 6 g, Sodium: 68 mg, Cholesterol: 0 mg

Vanilla Frozen Yogurt

Makes 1½ cups. **Hands-on time:** 10 minutes.
Total time: 4 hours, 35 minutes (includes chilling time.)

Frozen yogurt is a superb substitute for ice cream, especially when you're paying attention to your health and weight. Eat our natural version of this frozen treat with berries, on crumbles and pies and as the center of our CE "Ice Cream" Sandwiches (see far left).

INGREDIENTS:

- 1½ cups strained low-fat plain yogurt
- ¼ cup agave nectar
- 2 tsp pure vanilla extract

INSTRUCTIONS:

ONE: In a mixing bowl, combine strained yogurt, agave and vanilla. Stir until well blended, then spoon mixture into a shallow 9 x 9-inch non-reactive freezer-safe container.

TWO: Transfer container to freezer and chill until mixture is starting to freeze slightly around the edges, about 45 minutes. Scrape ice crystals from edges with a spatula and mix thoroughly back into yogurt mixture. Continue to blend until creamy again, about two minutes. Return container to freezer and repeat this process two more times, for a total of three times. Each time the mixture will get thicker and a little harder to blend. After the third mixing, return container to freezer until ready to eat, about two to three hours. For best results, store tightly sealed in freezer and use within two to three days.

Nutrients per 3-tablespoon serving: Calories: 62, Total Fat: 0.75 g, Sat. Fat: 0.4 g, Carbs: 11 g, Fiber: 0.5 g, Sugars: 11 g, Protein: 2.4 g, Sodium: 32 mg, Cholesterol: 3 mg

Chocolate Hazelnut Crispy Squares

*Serves 24. **Hands-on time:** 30 minutes.*
***Total time:** 30 minutes (plus 30 minutes to 1 hour to set).*

Instead of reaching for marshmallows (white sugar and corn syrup traps!) for your revamped rice squares, sneak in some puréed dates (no one will taste them!) to give these treats all the sweetness you'd expect with a bit of fiber as an extra bonus. Plus, the hazelnuts help give this recipe a decadent dessert feel, all resulting in bars that taste like fudge (and who doesn't love fudge?).

INGREDIENTS:

- ½ cup unsalted raw hazelnuts, coarsely chopped
- 1½ cups unsweetened brown rice cereal
- ¾ cup rolled oats
- 2½ oz dark chocolate (70% cocoa or greater), chopped into chunks (75 g or ⅓ cup plus 2 Tbsp)
- 1 cup unsweetened dried pitted dates (Medjool or honey), puréed until smooth
- ½ cup unsalted hazelnut butter or your favorite unsalted natural nut butter
- 2 Tbsp raw honey

INSTRUCTIONS:

ONE: In a medium mixing bowl, add hazelnuts, cereal and oats and stir until combined. Set aside.

TWO: Melt chocolate in a medium bowl over a double boiler. Remove bowl from double boiler and, using a wooden spoon, add puréed dates, hazelnut butter and honey to melted chocolate. Carefully stir until combined. As mixture stiffens, set bowl over double boiler again as needed.

THREE: Add chocolate mixture to bowl with cereal mixture and, using a wooden spoon, fold in until thoroughly combined. Scrape mixture into baking pan (9 x 11 x 2 inches), pressing down firmly with your hands and smoothing the top. Cover and refrigerate for 30 minutes to one hour to allow mixture to set. Cut into one-and-a-half-inch squares and serve immediately. Squares can be kept, covered, in refrigerator for three to five days.

TIP: Try serving our squares with a bit of strained low-fat plain yogurt sweetened with raw honey.

OPTION: Instead of using a baking pan, you can also roll your chocolate-cereal mixture into truffle-like balls before refrigerating (one-and-a-half tablespoons mixture each; makes about 24 balls).

Nutrients per 1½-inch square: Calories: 110, Total Fat: 6 g, Sat. Fat: 1 g, Carbs: 13 g, Fiber: 2 g, Sugars: 7 g, Protein: 2 g, Sodium: 0.25 mg, Cholesterol: 0 mg

Peach & Blackberry Cobbler

*Serves 12. **Hands-on time:** 15 minutes. **Total time:** 1 hour, 10 minutes.*

This sweet treat is the perfect late-summer dessert. Try it with our Vanilla Frozen Yogurt (p. 217).

INGREDIENTS:

BOTTOM FRUIT LAYER

- Olive oil cooking spray
- 6 medium fresh or frozen peaches (do not peel)
- 2 cups fresh or frozen blackberries (do not thaw if frozen)
- 2 Tbsp light spelt flour
- 2 Tbsp light agave nectar
- ½ tsp ground ginger

TOP BISCUIT LAYER

- 2 Tbsp extra-virgin coconut oil, melted
- ¼ cup light agave nectar
- ½ cup unsweetened plain rice milk
- 1 Tbsp finely ground flaxseed
- 1 tsp pure vanilla extract
- ½ tsp pure almond extract
- 1 cup spelt flour (light or whole grain)
- ¼ cup old-fashioned rolled oats (not instant or quick cook)
- 1 Tbsp baking powder
- ½ tsp ground cinnamon
- ¼ tsp fine sea salt

INSTRUCTIONS:

ONE: Preheat oven to 350°F. Lightly mist a 2-quart (8-cup) casserole or heat-proof glass pan with cooking spray.

TWO: Prepare bottom fruit layer: Wash, pit and slice peaches about a quarter-inch thick, then place in a medium bowl. Add flour, agave and ginger; toss to coat fruit. Turn mixture into prepared pan and set aside.

THREE: Prepare top biscuit layer: In a small bowl, whisk together coconut oil, agave, rice milk, flaxseed, and vanilla and almond extracts. Set aside while you measure dry ingredients or for at least two minutes.

FOUR: In the bowl of a food processor, whirl flour and oats until you have a coarse meal. Add baking powder, cinnamon and salt and whirl briefly to combine. Pour in agave-milk mixture and blend to create a thick batter.

FIVE: Using a tablespoon, drop spoonfuls of batter randomly over fruit in prepared pan. (Don't worry if fruit isn't entirely covered with batter; typically, the fruit filling will bubble up over the topping while it bakes.)

SIX: Place pan on a baking sheet (to catch any spills if fruit bubbles over edge) and bake for 50 to 55 minutes, rotating pan about halfway through, until top is deep golden brown. Cool slightly before serving. May be served warm or at room temperature. Store, covered, in refrigerator for up to five days; return to room temperature before serving.

Nutrients per ⅔-cup serving: Calories: 130, Total Fat: 3 g, Sat. Fat: 2 g, Carbs: 26 g, Fiber: 3 g, Sugars: 14 g, Protein: 3 g, Sodium: 45 mg, Cholesterol: 26 mg

Peach &
Blackberry
Cobbler

Nutritional Bonus: Raisins rank among the best food sources of antioxidants, according to testing done by the United States Department of Agriculture. Antioxidants may protect cells and their components from oxidative damage, which in turn may help slow the processes associated with aging in both the body and brain. But don't overdo it with the shriveled treats. Dried fruit can pack a lot of sugar.

Oatmeal Raisin Cookies

Oatmeal Raisin Cookies

Makes 3 dozen. *Hands-on time:* 10 minutes. *Total time:* 25 minutes.

Oatmeal cookies typically call for butter and two different types of sugar – brown and white. We've lightened our version by using canola oil, which is low in saturated fat, high in cholesterol-lowering mono-unsaturated fat and a good source of healthy omega-3 fats.

INGREDIENTS:

- Nonstick cooking spray
- ½ cup canola oil
- ⅓ cup plus 2 Tbsp Sucanat (or dehydrated cane juice)
- 1 egg white
- ¾ tsp vanilla extract
- 3 Tbsp water
- 2 cups Old Fashioned Quaker Oats (large flakes)
- ⅔ cup whole-wheat baking flour
- ¼ tsp sea salt
- ½ tsp baking soda
- ⅔ cup raisins
- 1 tsp cinnamon

INSTRUCTIONS:

Preheat oven to 350°F. Grease baking sheet with nonstick spray. In a bowl, hand-mix oil and Sucanat. Add egg white, vanilla and water; mix well. Add oats, flour, salt, baking soda, raisins and cinnamon, and mix until just blended to retain the texture of oats. Drop batter by teaspoonfuls onto baking sheet. Bake for 10 to 15 minutes or until bottoms are lightly browned.

Nutrients per cookie: Calories: 70, Total Fat: 3.5 g, Sat. Fat: 0 g, Carbs: 9 g, Fiber: 1 g, Sugars: 4 g, Protein: 1 g, Sodium: 34 mg, Cholesterol: 0 mg

Chocolate Sour Cream Cupcakes

Makes 12 cupcakes. *Hands-on time:* 15 minutes . *Total time:* 1 hour.

Rich and tangy organic sour cream keeps these cupcakes moist.

INGREDIENTS:

- 1 cup unsweetened natural cocoa powder
- 1¼ cups Sucanat, divided
- ¼ cup whole-wheat pastry flour
- ¼ tsp kosher salt
- ¼ tsp baking soda
- 1 cup organic low-fat sour cream
- ⅓ cup plus 2 tsp skim milk, divided
- 1 Tbsp olive oil
- ½ tsp pure vanilla extract
- 1 whole egg plus 2 egg whites
- 1 oz bittersweet chocolate, chopped, plus more for garnish if desired

INSTRUCTIONS:

ONE: Preheat oven to 350°F. Line a 12-cup muffin pan with paper cupcake liners. In a large mixing bowl, combine cocoa powder, one cup Sucanat, flour, salt and baking soda.

TWO: In a medium mixing bowl, whisk together sour cream, one-third cup milk, oil, vanilla and whole egg. Make a well in the center of the dry ingredients and pour in wet ingredients. Combine everything with a rubber spatula.

THREE: Add egg whites to a large clean, dry mixing bowl or the bowl of a stand mixer. Whip whites with hand beater or whisk attachment of stand mixer until they begin to get foamy. Add remaining quarter cup Sucanat very gradually to whites. Continue whipping whites into medium-stiff peaks. Fold whites in thirds into cake batter, gently but assertively with rubber spatula.

FOUR: Fill each of the 12 cupcake liners three-quarters-full with batter. Tap bottom of filled muffin pan on countertop and transfer immediately to oven. Bake for 45 minutes or until a toothpick inserted in the center of a cupcake comes out clean. Remove from oven and let cupcakes cool completely.

FIVE: When cupcakes are completely cool, combine chocolate and remaining two teaspoons milk in a microwave-safe bowl. Microwave on 50 percent power for 30 seconds. Stir until melted chocolate is completely smooth. Spread a thin layer on top of each cupcake. Sprinkle additional chocolate shavings on top, if desired.

TOPPING TAKE-TWO: Substitute half a cup of low-fat sour cream mixed with one tablespoon honey for the chocolate glaze. Put a quarter-teaspoon dollop on each cupcake and top with sliced strawberries.

Nutrients per cupcake: Calories: 160, Total Fat: 6 g, Sat. Fat: 3 g, Carbs: 28 g, Fiber: 3 g, Sugars: 22 g, Protein: 4 g, Sodium: 85 mg, Cholesterol: 10 mg

Hidden Gem Cupcakes

*Makes 12. **Hands-on time:** 25 minutes. **Total time:** 1 hour.*

Everyone loves a surprise, especially when that surprise is a sweet berry filling. Perfect for birthday (or surprise) parties!

INGREDIENTS:

- Olive oil cooking spray (optional)
- 3 Tbsp canola oil
- ⅔ cup light agave nectar
- ½ cup plus 1 Tbsp unsweetened applesauce
- 1 Tbsp finely ground flaxseed
- 1 Tbsp pure vanilla extract
- 1 Tbsp apple cider vinegar
- 2 cups light spelt flour, scooped and then leveled
- 1 tsp baking powder
- 1 tsp baking soda
- ½ tsp fine sea salt
- 1 cup berries (blueberries, raspberries, blackberries, chopped strawberries or combination), fresh or frozen (do not thaw), divided, plus 12 raspberries for garnish
- 3 oz dark chocolate (70% cocoa), chopped
- 2 Tbsp unsweetened almond or rice milk

INSTRUCTIONS:

ONE: Preheat oven to 350°F. Line 12 cups of a muffin tray with paper liners or mist with cooking spray.

TWO: In a small bowl, whisk together oil, agave nectar, applesauce, quarter cup water, flaxseed, vanilla and vinegar. Set aside for at least two minutes while measuring dry ingredients.

THREE: In a large bowl, sift together flour, baking powder, baking soda and salt. Stir briefly to combine. Pour wet mixture over dry mixture and stir to blend well.

FOUR: Fill each muffin cup with about one tablespoon batter, spreading to cover bottom and part way up the side of each cup. Place a heaping teaspoon of berries (about four to five berries) over the center of the batter, taking care not to let berries touch the sides of the cup. Top with another spoonful of batter, and gently spread batter to cover berries completely. Make sure to use all the batter, dividing evenly among 12 muffin cups.

FIVE: Bake for 30 to 35 minutes, rotating tray about halfway through, until cupcakes are golden and a tester inserted in the center comes out clean (it may be moist but shouldn't have any batter on it). Remove and allow to cool at room temperature for five minutes before removing cupcakes from tray to a cooling rack to cool completely.

SIX: Combine chocolate and milk in a large heatproof bowl set over a small pot of simmering water over low heat. Stir until chocolate melts and mixture is smooth and can be drizzled; add more milk if necessary to achieve desired texture.

SEVEN: Once cupcakes are cool, drizzle chocolate glaze in free-form lines across the top of each cupcake, then top with a raspberry. May be served immediately or stored in an airtight container at room temperature if serving later the same day. Cupcakes can also be stored, wrapped individually in plastic wrap, for up to three days in the refrigerator but should be enjoyed at room temperature.

Nutrients per cupcake: Calories: 210, Total Fat: 6 g, Sat. Fat: 1.5 g, Carbs: 37 g, Fiber: 3 g, Sugars: 20 g, Protein: 3 g, Sodium: 190 mg, Cholesterol: 0 mg

Black Bean Fudge Cakes

*Serves 8. **Hands-on time:** 10 minutes. **Total time:** 40 minutes.*

These fudge cakes are chocolately, delicious and surprisingly healthy thanks to the addition of black beans, which gives them a boost of fiber and a punch of protein.

INGREDIENTS:

- Olive oil cooking spray
- 1 oz dark organic chocolate (70% cocoa or greater)
- 1½ cups soft-cooked black beans, rinsed and drained
- 2 eggs
- 1 egg white
- 2 Tbsp olive oil
- ¼ heaped cup unsweetened cocoa powder
- 1 tsp baking powder
- 1 tsp pure vanilla extract
- ¼ cup unsweetened applesauce
- ½ cup raw organic honey
- ¼ to ½ cup chopped unsalted walnuts

INSTRUCTIONS:

ONE: Preheat oven to 350°F. Mist eight individual ramekins or one 8-inch square baking dish with cooking spray.

TWO: Melt dark chocolate in a small saucepan over low heat with one tablespoon water mixed in.

THREE: Combine melted chocolate, beans, eggs, egg white, oil, cocoa powder, baking powder, vanilla, applesauce and honey in a food processor; process until smooth. Stir in walnuts and pour mixture into prepared ramekins or baking dish.

FOUR: Bake in preheated oven until the tops are dry and the edges start to pull away from the sides, about 20 minutes for ramekins and 30 minutes for baking dish. Garnish each piece with a dollop of nonfat Greek-style yogurt, if desired.

Nutrients per serving: Calories: 230, Total Fat: 12 g, Sat. Fat: 2 g, Carbs: 28 g, Fiber: 4 g, Sugars: 19 g, Protein: 5 g, Sodium: 120 mg, Cholesterol: 45 mg

Almond Butter Chocolate Chip Cookies

GLUTEN FREE

Makes 24 cookies. ***Hands-on time:*** *10 minutes.* ***Total time:*** *22 minutes.*

This recipe is a reader favorite! With only six ingredients, these cookies are easy to make and even easier to enjoy.

INGREDIENTS:

- 1 cup unsalted almond butter, stirred well
- ¾ cup Sucanat
- 1 large egg
- ½ tsp baking soda
- ¼ tsp sea salt
- 3 oz dark chocolate (70% cocoa or greater), broken into small pieces

INSTRUCTIONS:

ONE: Preheat oven to 350°F. In a medium bowl, stir together first five ingredients until blended. Stir in chocolate.

TWO: Drop dough by rounded tablespoonfuls onto parchment-lined baking sheets. Bake for 10 to 12 minutes or until lightly browned. Let cool on baking sheets for five minutes. Remove to a wire rack and let cool for 15 more minutes.

Nutrients per cookie: Calories: 110, Total Fat: 8 g, Sat. Fat: 1.5 g, Carbs: 10 g, Fiber: 1 g, Sugars: 3g, Protein: 2 g, Sodium: 55 mg, Cholesterol: 10 mg

Nutritional Bonus:

While dark chocolate contains potent antioxidants, think twice before enjoying it with milk. Researchers have found that the bittersweet treat's free-radical fighters may bind with the protein in milk, interfering with antioxidant absorption and possibly negating any associated health benefits.

Orange Chocolate Ricotta Cheesecake

Serves 16. *Makes* 1 (9-inch) cake. *Hands-on time:* 45 minutes.
Total time: 1 hour, 45 minutes (plus 2 hours or overnight to set).

This subtly sweet ricotta cheesecake makes use of agar (also called agar agar), a vegetarian gelatin derived from seaweed. The small clear flakes can be found in most health food stores, specialty food shops or the health and organic foods aisle of most supermarkets.

INGREDIENTS:

CRUST

- ¼ cup Dutch-processed cocoa powder (or unsweetened cocoa powder)
- ½ cup almond meal/flour
- ¾ cup rolled oats
- ¼ cup raw honey
- Pinch sea salt

FILLING

- 1 medium navel orange, zested and juiced
- ¼ cup skim milk
- ¼ cup raw honey
- 3 Tbsp agar agar flakes
- 3 oz dark chocolate (70% cocoa or greater), chopped (about 100 g or ½ cup)
- 1½ cups extra-smooth low-fat ricotta cheese
- ¾ cup low-fat cream cheese, softened

GARNISH

- 3 Tbsp Dutch-processed cocoa powder (or unsweetened cocoa powder)
- 8 slices navel orange, each slightly twisted* (optional)

*NOTE: To create a twisted orange slice, make a cut from center of orange slice to one edge. Twist cut edges away from each other and set orange twist onto plate.

EQUIPMENT:

- 1 (9-inch) springform pan

INSTRUCTIONS:

ONE: Prepare crust: Combine cocoa, almond meal and oats in a food processor and pulse until combined and almost smooth. Add honey and salt and continue to pulse until combined. Press mixture evenly into the bottom of springform pan. Cover with plastic wrap and refrigerate for one hour. (Crust may be prepared ahead and kept, covered and refrigerated, for 24 hours.)

TWO: Prepare filling: Add orange zest and juice, milk and honey to a small saucepan. Stir in agar agar and let rest for 15 minutes at room temperature. Bring to a boil over medium-high heat, stirring continuously. Reduce heat to low and continue to simmer and stir for about three to five minutes or until agar agar is dissolved. Set aside at room temperature.

THREE: Meanwhile, melt dark chocolate in a medium-size bowl over a double boiler. Set aside.

FOUR: In the bowl of a stand mixer with the whisk attachment (or in a large mixing bowl, if using an electric hand mixer), whip together ricotta and cream cheeses until combined and fluffy. While mixer is running on medium speed, slowly pour in orange mixture until combined. Then slowly pour in warm, melted dark chocolate until combined.

FIVE: Pour filling over crust in springform pan and smooth with a spatula until even. Cover with plastic wrap and refrigerate for a minimum of two hours or overnight until set. Cheesecake will keep, covered and refrigerated, for up to two days.

SIX: To serve, carefully loosen the cheesecake from the sides of the pan with a knife. Remove sides of springform pan. Over a bowl, pour remaining three tablespoons cocoa into a fine mesh strainer. Lightly dust entire top of cake so that no filling is visible. Fill a pitcher or bowl with warm water. With a sharp knife, slice cake into 16 wedges, dipping knife into water and carefully wiping it clean and dry with a towel after each slice. Garnish each piece of cheesecake with a slightly twisted orange slice, if desired.

Nutrients per serving (1½-inch slice; about 3 oz): *Calories: 166, Total Fat: 7 g, Sat. Fat: 3.5 g, Carbs: 21 g, Fiber: 2 g, Sugars: 13 g, Protein: 6.5 g, Sodium: 114 mg, Cholesterol: 14 mg*

Carrot Cake with Cream Cheese Honey Drizzle

Slow-Cooker Carrot Cake
WITH CREAM CHEESE HONEY DRIZZLE

Serves 10. **Hands-on time:** *20 minutes.* **Total time:** *3 hours.*

Carrot cake is delicious served warm, and this one is made right in your slow cooker! But if you'd like to save some for later enjoyment, our cake can be wrapped tightly and refrigerated for three to four days or frozen for up to one month.

INGREDIENTS:

- Olive oil cooking spray
- 1¼ cups all-purpose spelt flour
- ⅓ cup shredded unsweetened coconut
- 1½ tsp ground cinnamon
- 1½ tsp baking powder
- 1 tsp baking soda
- ¼ tsp sea salt
- ½ cup unsweetened sultana raisins (golden raisins)
- 1 large egg white
- 1 tsp flaxseed, ground, mixed with 2 tsp water
- ½ cup raw organic honey
- ⅓ cup unsweetened applesauce
- ¼ cup buttermilk or low-fat plain yogurt
- 2 Tbsp olive oil
- 1 tsp pure vanilla extract
- 4 oz carrot, peeled and finely shredded (about ½ cup packed)
- ⅓ cup Cream Cheese Honey Drizzle (see recipe, right)

INSTRUCTIONS:

ONE: Cut parchment to fit bottom and sides of stoneware insert or ceramic dish of a small 4- to 6-quart slow cooker. Spray insert or dish with cooking spray and line with prepared parchment. If using a larger 5- to 7-quart slow cooker, select a foil or glass baking pan that easily fits inside stoneware insert. Mist baking pan with cooking spray and similarly line with parchment.

TWO: Place flour, coconut, cinnamon, baking powder, baking soda and salt in a bowl and whisk lightly to combine. Stir in raisins.

THREE: In a separate large bowl, combine egg white and flax-water mixture and whisk until bubbles form. Add honey, applesauce, buttermilk, oil and vanilla and whisk until well blended. Stir in dry ingredients, until just mixed. Fold in carrot and pour mixture into prepared stoneware dish or baking pan. Cover entire top of slow cooker with three layers of paper towel and secure with lid. This will catch the extra condensation in the slow cooker and prevent the cake from getting too moist. Bake for two to two-and-a-half hours on low or until a knife inserted in centre of cake comes out dry. Remove stoneware dish or baking pan from heat and place on cooling rack until cool.

FOUR: Slice cake into ten equal portions, about three ounces each, and serve warm or at room temperature with one tablespoon Cream Cheese Honey Drizzle.

Cream Cheese Honey Drizzle

Makes ⅓ cup icing. **Hands-on time:** *5 minutes.* **Total time:** *5 minutes.*

Our drizzle icing can be prepared ahead of time and kept chilled in an airtight container for up to three days.

INGREDIENTS:

- ¼ cup low-fat plain cream cheese
- 1 Tbsp raw organic honey
- 1 lemon, finely zested and juiced, divided

INSTRUCTIONS:

In a small bowl, heat cream cheese on high in microwave until slightly warm, about 10 to 15 seconds. Remove from microwave and use a rubber spatula to stir honey into cream cheese until smooth. Add pinch lemon zest and two teaspoons lemon juice and continue to stir. Slowly add two tablespoons water, a bit at a time, until mixture is consistency of thick cream. Taste topping and add more zest and juice if a more lemony taste is desired.

Nutrients per serving (3 oz cake and 1 Tbsp drizzle): *Calories: 190, Total Fat: 5 g, Sat. Fat: 2 g, Carbs: 35 g, Fiber: 2 g, Sugars: 17 g, Protein: 4 g, Sodium: 210 mg, Cholesterol: 5 mg*

Orange-Infused Chocolate Almond Cake

Serves 12. Hands-on time: 15 minutes. Total time: 1 hour, 5 minutes.

Our clean chocolate cake is dense, fudgy and so visually appealing you'll want to serve it on a platter. While the taste and texture are truly indulgent, one slice rings in at a mere 160 calories and five grams of fat.

INGREDIENTS:

CAKE

- Olive oil cooking spray
- 2 Tbsp organic coconut oil, melted
- 2 Tbsp smooth, unsalted almond butter
- ½ cup agave nectar
- ¼ cup prune purée (or all-natural prune baby food)
- ⅔ cup orange juice, freshly squeezed
- 2 Tbsp finely ground flaxseed
- 2 tsp real vanilla extract
- ½ tsp balsamic vinegar
- 4 tsp freshly grated orange zest
- 1 cup plus 2 Tbsp light spelt flour, scooped and then leveled
- ⅓ cup unsweetened, dark cocoa powder, scooped and then leveled
- ¾ tsp baking soda
- 1 tsp baking powder
- ¼ tsp sea salt
- Orange zest for garnish, grated (optional)
- Blanched almonds for garnish (optional)

GLAZE

- ¾ cup orange juice, freshly squeezed
- 2 Tbsp agave nectar

INSTRUCTIONS:

CAKE

ONE: Preheat oven to 350°F. Line the bottom of an 8½-inch springform pan with parchment paper; then mist paper and sides of pan with cooking spray.

TWO: In a small bowl, whisk together oil, almond butter and agave nectar until smooth. Add prune purée, juice, flaxseeds, vanilla, vinegar and zest, and mix well. Set aside, while you measure dry ingredients, for at least two minutes.

THREE: In a large bowl, sift together flour, cocoa, baking soda, baking powder and salt. Stir briefly to combine.

FOUR: Pour wet mixture over dry one and stir well to blend. Pour into prepared pan and smooth the top.

FIVE: Bake for 30 minutes; then rotate pan 180 degrees to ensure even baking and continue to bake for another 15 to 20 minutes, until cake springs back when pressed lightly in center. Remove from oven and allow to cool at room temperature while you prepare glaze.

GLAZE

Combine juice and agave nectar in a small, heavy pot. Bring to boil over medium-high heat, then lower heat to simmer. Allow mixture to bubble gently, stirring occasionally, until it reduces to about a third of a cup, about 20 minutes. The mixture will turn deep golden and should coat a spoon.

ASSEMBLY

Remove sides of pan from cooled cake. Slide a knife or metal spatula between parchment and bottom of the pan, then slip a serving plate into the gap and slide the cake onto it. Pour warm glaze over top of cake and gently spread toward the sides, allowing any excess to drip over the edges. Garnish with additional zest and almonds, if desired.

Nutrients per slice (½₁₂ of cake): Calories: 160, Total Fat: 5 g, Sat. Fat: 2.5 g, Carbs: 30 g, Fiber: 2 g, Sugars: 18 g, Protein: 3 g, Sodium: 120 mg, Cholesterol: 0 mg

Chocolate Almond Meringues

Makes 30. Serves 6. Hands-on time: 15 minutes. Total time: 4.25 hours.

Flavored with a touch of almond extract, our unique meringues are low in fat and calories but sinfully sweet enough to satisfy your sweet tooth.

INGREDIENTS:

- 3 egg whites
- ⅛ tsp cream of tartar
- 2 Tbsp cocoa powder
- ½ cup natural brown sugar
- ¼ tsp almond extract

INSTRUCTIONS:

ONE: Preheat oven to 150°F (or lowest oven setting) and place oven rack in top third of oven. Line a cookie sheet with parchment paper.

TWO: Using a mixer, beat egg whites with cream of tartar until they form stiff peaks. Sift cocoa powder and sugar into the egg white mixture and beat until combined. Stir in almond extract.

THREE: Place heaping tablespoonfuls of the batter, evenly spaced, onto the lined cookie sheet. Bake for two hours, turning the baking sheet halfway through baking time to ensure even drying.

FOUR: Turn off oven and leave meringues to dry for two hours or overnight. Serve at room temperature. (Meringues may be frozen for up to one month.)

Nutrients per serving: Calories: 77, Total Fat: 0 g, Sat. Fat: 0 g, Carbs: 18 g, Fiber: 1 g, Protein: 2 g, Sugars: 17 g, Sodium: 28 mg, Cholesterol: 0 mg

Chocolate
Almond
Meringues

Nutritional Bonus:
Coconut oil is becoming increasingly popular because of its unique flavor, antioxidant properties and a host of other possible health benefits.

Coconut Chai Chocolate Cake

Coconut Chai Chocolate Cake

Serves 12. Makes 1 9-inch cake. Hands-on time: 15 minutes. Total time: 45 minutes.

Coconut and chocolate are one of the world's most perfect pairings, and this cake is jaw-droppingly delectable. But aside from the taste, the health benefits of coconut also deserve a gold star. Coconut oil is made up of medium chain fatty acids that are converted to energy instead of being stored as fat. These fatty acids are said to increase metabolism and aid fat loss, not that you need any more convincing to try this tempting cake!

INGREDIENTS:

- Olive oil cooking spray
- 1 Tbsp plus 1¼ cups whole-wheat flour, divided
- ½ cup unsweetened cocoa powder
- 1 tsp baking powder
- 1 tsp baking soda
- ½ tsp ground cinnamon
- ⅛ tsp ground ginger
- ⅛ tsp ground cardamom
- ⅛ tsp fresh grated nutmeg
- ½ tsp sea salt
- 1 egg
- 1 egg white
- ½ cup low-fat milk
- ⅓ cup unsweetened applesauce
- ¼ cup raw honey
- 1 tsp finely grated orange zest,
- 2 Tbsp organic virgin coconut oil, melted
- ½ tsp pure coconut extract
- 10 unsweetened dates, finely chopped
- ¼ cup unsweetened flaked coconut
- Toasted unsweetened flaked coconut for garnish, optional

INSTRUCTIONS:

ONE: Preheat oven to 350°F. Coat a 9-inch round baking pan with cooking spray and one tablespoon flour, discarding any excess that doesn't stick to pan.

TWO: Combine remaining one-and-a-quarter cups flour, cocoa powder, baking powder, baking soda, spices and salt in a large bowl. Add egg, egg white, milk, applesauce, honey, orange zest, oil and coconut extract. Using a whisk or electric hand-held mixer, beat until combined.

THREE: In a small saucepan, bring one cup water and dates to a boil over high heat. Then gently whisk date-water mixture into cake batter along with flaked coconut. (Batter will be thin.)

FOUR: Pour batter into prepared pan and bake for 30 to 35 minutes or until a toothpick inserted into the center comes out clean. Cool for 10 minutes and remove from pan to wire rack.

FIVE: To serve, slice cake into 12 pieces and top each with toasted coconut, if desired.

Nutrients per ¹⁄₁₂ cake (without coconut garnish): Calories: 160, Total Fat: 7 g, Sat. Fat: 5 g, Carbs: 25 g, Fiber: 4 g, Sugars: 11 g, Protein: 4 g, Sodium: 219 mg, Cholesterol: 18 mg

Ginger Thyme Lemonade Granita

Serves 10. Hands-on time: 20 minutes.
Total time: 5 hours, 50 minutes (including chilling time.)

Originally from Sicily, a granita is a semi-frozen dessert made from sugar, water and a variety of flavorings.

INGREDIENTS:

- ⅓ cup agave nectar
- 16 sprigs fresh thyme, divided
- 2 Tbsp chopped fresh ginger
- 2 medium lemons
- 1 tsp chopped fresh thyme

INSTRUCTIONS:

ONE: Pour agave and two-and-a-half cups water into a medium-sized saucepan and whisk to combine. Add 12 thyme sprigs and ginger to pan. Bring to a boil over medium-high heat, reduce heat and simmer for 10 minutes. Remove pan from heat and let cool for flavors to infuse, about 15 to 20 minutes.

TWO: Meanwhile, zest lemons and coarsely chop zest. Set aside. Juice lemons into a mixing bowl, strain out all seeds and pulp, and discard, leaving only juice (about a half cup juice). Add zest to juice and set aside.

THREE: Once agave mixture is cool, strain it into juice, discarding solids. Add one teaspoon chopped thyme and whisk until combined. Pour mixture into a shallow, flat freezer-safe container large enough that liquid is only about one-inch deep (9 x 9-inch is ideal). Loosely cover and place in freezer for one hour. Remove from freezer, scrape sides and stir mixture with a fork to break up ice crystals. Return to freezer for about three to four hours, scraping mixture with a fork every hour or so until frozen. Mixture should be granular and slightly slushy.

FOUR: When ready to serve, scrape with a fork, scoop into martini-style glasses, garnish with remaining thyme sprigs and serve immediately. Re-freeze any unused portions immediately, storing covered in a sealable freezer-safe container. Granita is best if consumed within two to three days.

Nutrients per ¹⁄₃-cup serving: Calories: 35, Total Fat: 0 g, Sat. Fat: 0 g, Carbs: 10 g, Fiber: 0 g, Sugars: 9 g, Protein: 0 g, Sodium: 0 mg, Cholesterol: 0 mg

Strawberry & Peach Lemon Shortcake
WITH CARDAMOM AGAVE YOGURT & FRESH MINT

*Serves 8. **Hands-on time:** 20 minutes. **Total time:** 1 hour, 45 minutes (including cooling time.)*

Shortcake is typically made with high-fat ingredients. Our substitutions, including whole wheat flour, flaxseed, agave nectar and egg whites, add healthy fiber, protein and fats without giving up flavor.

INGREDIENTS:

- 1 lb fresh strawberries, trimmed and thinly sliced
- 4 to 6 medium peaches, pitted and thinly sliced
- 8 sprigs fresh mint

YOGURT CRÈME:

- 2 cups plain low-fat yogurt, strained or nonfat Greek-style yogurt
- 4 Tbsp agave nectar
- 2 tsp pure vanilla extract
- ½ tsp ground cardamom

LEMON CAKE:

- 1½ cups whole-wheat flour
- ¼ cup ground flaxseed
- 2 tsp baking powder
- ¼ tsp sea salt
- 1 cup plain low-fat yogurt
- ½ cup agave nectar
- 1 large lemon, zested and juiced (⅓ cup juice)
- 1 tsp pure vanilla extract
- 6 large egg whites (¾ cup)
- ¼ cup olive oil
- Olive oil cooking spray

INSTRUCTIONS:

ONE: Preheat oven to 350°F. Prepare lemon cake: Sift together flour, flaxseeds, baking powder and salt in a medium bowl and set aside. In a larger bowl, combine yogurt, agave, lemon zest and juice and vanilla, whisking until combined.

TWO: Gradually mix wet ingredients into dry ingredients, until just combined; do not over-mix.

THREE: In a separate dry bowl, whisk egg whites until fluffy. Then, using a rubber spatula, gently fold egg whites and oil into batter.

FOUR: Lightly spray sides of baking pan (9½ x 8 x 2-inch) with cooking spray or line bottom of pan with parchment paper. Pour batter into pan and place pan into preheated oven. Bake for 45 minutes or until a toothpick inserted into the center comes out clean. Remove pan from oven and allow cake to cool to room temperature, about 30 minutes.

FIVE: Cut around edges of pan to loosen cake and turn cake out onto a cutting board. Cut into eight equal-sized pieces, trimming edges if necessary.

SIX: Prepare Yogurt Crème: In a small bowl, combine yogurt, agave, vanilla and cardamom. Whisk until incorporated, cover and refrigerate until needed.

SEVEN: Take one piece of cake and cut in half through the middle (as if you were cutting a bun for a sandwich). Layer each individual shortcake in the following manner: bottom half of cake, two tablespoons Yogurt Crème, strawberries, peaches, one tablespoon Yogurt Crème, top half of cake, two tablespoons Yogurt Crème, strawberries, peaches, one tablespoon Yogurt Crème. Top with a sprig of mint and repeat for desired number of portions.

Nutrients per serving: Calories: 380, Total Fat: 7 g, Sat. Fat: 2 g, Carbs: 62 g, Fiber: 7 g, Sugars: 37 g, Protein: 16 g, Sodium: 100 mg, Cholesterol: 0 mg

For a photo of this recipe see the cover.

Molten Lava Cakes

*Serves 4. **Hands-on time:** 10 minutes. **Total time:** 20 minutes.*

These ooey gooey cakes are traditionally made with butter, whole eggs and white sugar. We've leaned up this version – without sacrificing taste – by using olive oil, egg whites and Sucanat, a minimally refined cane sugar.

INGREDIENTS:

- Olive oil cooking spray
- ¼ cup plus 1 Tbsp unsweetened cocoa powder
- ⅓ cup Sucanat
- 3 Tbsp unsweetened applesauce
- 3 Tbsp olive oil
- 1 egg
- 1 egg white
- ½ cup white whole-wheat flour
- 1 tsp pure vanilla extract
- Orange or pear slices, for garnish (optional)

INSTRUCTIONS:

ONE: Preheat oven to 400°F. Lightly spray four 4-ounce custard cups or small ramekins with cooking spray. In a medium bowl, combine cocoa powder and Sucanat; whisk in applesauce and oil.

TWO: In a small bowl, lightly whisk egg and egg white and add to cocoa mixture, whisking until smooth. Stir in flour and vanilla until flour is combined completely – do not over mix.

THREE: Divide mixture evenly among prepared custard cups, place on a baking sheet and bake for nine minutes. Centers should be soft but sides firm. Invert cups onto serving plates; let stand a few minutes before removing cups. Garnish each cake with fruit slices, if desired; serve warm.

Nutrients per 4 oz cake: Calories: 250, Total Fat: 13 g, Sat. Fat: 2.5 g, Carbs: 32 g, Fiber: 5 g, Sugars: 17 g, Protein: 6 g, Sodium: 40 mg, Cholesterol: 32 mg

Nutritional Bonus:

Chock-full of flavonoids, cocoa may help keep your heart strong by influencing the body's production of nitric oxide, which regulates blood vessel tone.

Molten Lava Cakes

Nutritional Bonus:

The beautiful blues and reds of these delicious berries are not only visually appealing; they also mean good things for your health! Berries contain flavanoids and phytochemicals that may help reduce your risk of several types of cancers.

Mixed Berry Crisp

Mixed Berry Crisp
WITH DATE OAT STREUSEL

Serves 8. *Hands-on time:* 15 minutes. *Total time:* 1 hour.

Nobody will be able to resist the streusel topping on this warm and delicious dessert. Feed your body and your soul with our version of this classic last course – the dates add a natural sweetness that aids digestion and strengthens the heart.

INGREDIENTS:

- 16 oz fresh or thawed frozen mixed berries (raspberries, blueberries, blackberries and strawberries; about 3 cups)
- Zest and juice of 1 lemon
- 1 Tbsp arrowroot
- 2 Tbsp raw honey, divided
- 10 pitted unsweetened dates
- ½ cup whole oats
- ½ cup whole-wheat flour
- ½ tsp ground cinnamon
- ½ tsp ground nutmeg
- 3 Tbsp virgin coconut oil, melted
- Pinch sea salt

INSTRUCTIONS:

ONE: Preheat oven to 350°F. In a medium bowl, combine berries, lemon zest, lemon juice and arrowroot. Drizzle one tablespoon honey over top and toss to combine. Pour berry mixture into a baking dish.

TWO: In a food processor, chop dates into small pieces. Add oats, flour, cinnamon, nutmeg, oil, remaining one tablespoon honey and salt; blend to combine. Distribute crumble mixture evenly over berries in baking dish.

THREE: Place baking dish on a baking sheet to catch any spills. Bake for 45 minutes, until browned and bubbling. Serve warm and garnish with nonfat Greek yogurt, if desired.

NOTE: **This dessert can be stored at room temperature for one day, and if there's any left (wink, wink, because it's so good!) it will last in the refrigerator for up to three days.**

Nutrients per ½-cup serving: *Calories: 166, Total Fat: 6 g, Sat. Fat: 4.6 g, Carbs: 28 g, Fiber: 4.5 g, Sugars: 13 g, Protein: 2.5 g, Sodium: 43 mg, Cholesterol: 0 mg*

Chocolate-Drizzled Roasted Cherries

Serves 4. *Makes* 4 cups. *Hands-on time:* 20 minutes. *Total time:* 45 minutes.

After cooking, you can remove the aluminum foil and place the cherries into a fancy dish for a perfectly elegant dessert that is rich and sweet, like cherry pie, without all the added weight of a pastry.

INGREDIENTS:

- 4 cups sweet cherries (Bing, Lambert, Ranier or Royal Ann), pitted
- 1 Tbsp orange zest
- 1 Tbsp raw honey
- 1 cinnamon stick
- ⅛ tsp chile powder
- ⅛ tsp ground cinnamon
- Pinch cayenne pepper
- ¼ cup skim milk
- 2 oz dark chocolate (70% cocoa or greater), chopped (about ⅓ cup)

INSTRUCTIONS:

ONE: Preheat oven to 350°F. Prepare two foil pouches as per the "How to Make a Foil Pouch" guide on p. 41, making one pouch a quarter of the suggested size. In a mixing bowl, gently toss cherries with orange zest and honey. In the larger foil pouch, place seasoned cherries and cinnamon stick; seal. In a small mixing bowl, combine chile powder, cinnamon and cayenne pepper with milk and whisk to combine. In the smaller pouch, place chocolate and pour spiced milk over top, making sure to fold up sides of foil as per guide to avoid liquid spilling over.

TWO: Place pouch with cherries on a baking tray and onto middle rack of preheated oven. Roast cherries for 20 minutes.

THREE: After 20 minutes, place foil pouch containing chocolate mixture onto tray in the oven alongside pouch with cherries and roast both for five more minutes.

FOUR: Remove both pouches from oven. Carefully open pouch with cherries and let cool for two to three minutes at room temperature. Remove cinnamon stick and discard. Using a strainer, drain liquid from cherries into a small mixing bowl; set aside. Divide strained cherries among four serving dishes.

FIVE: Carefully open foil pouch with chocolate mixture and, using a spatula, scrape mixture into the small bowl with reserved cherry liquid. Whisk until smooth. Drizzle chocolate mixture over top of cherries and serve immediately.

Nutrients per 1-cup serving: *Calories: 191, Total Fat: 6 g, Sat. Fat: 4 g, Carbs: 35 g, Fiber: 5 g, Sugars: 28 g, Protein: 3 g, Sodium: 9 mg, Cholesterol: 0.5 mg*

NOTE: **Cherries may be served warm, at room temperature or chilled overnight once they have been roasted.**

Cacao's
Wow Factor

**Suppress your appetite while satisfying your sweet tooth...
with chocolate!**

> Cacao is actually one of
> the great weight-loss foods
> because it contains an
> abundance of minerals that
> appear to shut off the appetite.

Chocolate is probably not the first thing that comes to mind when you think about healthy, clean eating (though it may be on your mind when you're trying to diet!). The good news is that chocolate – and cacao, its natural counterpart – is considered by some to actually be a health food.

"Cacao, which is the seed of a South American tree fruit, contains no sugar and between 12 and 50 percent fat and oil, depending on variety and growth conditions," says David Wolfe, a noted natural foods expert. "Cacao is actually one of the great weight-loss foods because it contains an abundance of minerals, such as magnesium, iron and chromium, that appear to shut off the appetite."

Then why is it that most of us can't stop eating chocolate once we start? "The addictive properties in chocolate come from the sugar and fat that is added to most commercial chocolate – not from the cacao bean itself," explains chocolate expert Patricia Tsai, owner of Chocovivo.

Cacao, cocoa, chocolate – what's the difference? Cacao is the raw bean (or seed) from the cacao tree. When cacao beans are dried, fermented and ground, they become what is called "chocolate liquor." Cocoa is a powder that comes from separating out the cocoa butter from the chocolate liquor (that's why you can find fat-free cocoa powder sold in stores). Chocolate is made by blending together cocoa, cocoa butter and sugar.

Different manufacturers use different amounts of cocoa, cocoa butter and sugar to create their own special blends. For

The Ultimate in Healthy Decadence

Made with 100 percent organic blue agave nectar, dark chocolate and natural fruit, "SAINTLY SINS" is the award-winning handmade chocolate collection created by TRACEY DOWNEY OF IRVINE, **California-based Xan Confections. These treasures are** LOW GLYCEMIC, GLUTEN FREE **and** VEGAN **and contain only 29 calories, one gram of fat and eight grams of sugar per delicious piece. The "Jewel" collection chocolates are** VEGAN, **agave-based caramels with no refined sugar – clocking in at 55 calories, three grams of fat and six grams of sugar per piece.**

Web Bonus!
Pamper yourself with healthy chocolate cookies! Visit **cleaneatingmag.com/chocolatecookies** for the recipe!

From Bean to Bar

1 Cacao beans are seeds from Forastero trees that are picked, dried and roasted.

2 The center of the bean, known as the cocoa nib, is removed and ground to form chocolate liquor.

3 The chocolate liquor is made into a paste. The cocoa butter is removed and then dried into a powder we know as cocoa.

4 Dark chocolate is made by combining the cocoa with sugar and vanilla. The higher the percentage of cocoa, the darker the chocolate. For clean eaters, 70 percent and more is recommended.

a chocolate to be considered dark, it must contain at least 35 percent cocoa; milk chocolate has milk added to it, which adds additional fat and calories.

Unprocessed cacao beans, on the other hand, are considered to be a whole food and are prized by many as superior to good old-fashioned chocolate. "Cacao has been found to have about four times the beneficial procyanidin antioxidants found in regular roasted dark chocolate," explains ethnobotanist Nat Bletter, PhD, of the New York Botanical Garden. Yet the pure cacao bean may be an acquired taste for some, since it contains no sugar and has a nutty, somewhat bitter flavor unless mixed with something like dried fruit or other sweeteners.

Cacao is known to be high in fatty acids, which are beneficial for your brain, heart and mood. As for the claim that cacao can help suppress the appetite? The US National Institutes of Health reports that Japanese researchers found that regular consumption of cocoa may prevent obesity and weight gain. Rats were fed high-fat diets, supplemented with real or imitation cocoa. After three weeks, the rats eating real cocoa had lower body weight and less fat tissue than those eating artificial cocoa. Researchers concluded that cocoa helps prevent fatty acid synthesis and also speeds fat burning in the liver. Of course, this does not serve as an excuse to be gluttonous. As with all foods, be judicious here too, especially since these were non-human studies.

Enjoy an ounce of dark chocolate or cacao nibs a few times a week or add a tablespoon of cocoa or cacao powder to your morning smoothie. Try Navitas Naturals for a variety of cacao products and check out our chocoholic recipe for Almond Butter Chocolate Chip Cookies (p. 224)!

Get the Skinny on Sweeteners

Naturally sweet foods, such as dates, berries and bananas, can be even more satisfying than a stodgy cookie.

"Naturally sweet foods, such as dates, berries and bananas, can be even more satisfying than a stodgy cookie," says registered dietitian Deborah Cohen, MHSc. Many also happen to work well as clean and natural sweeteners. But, be advised, not all sweeteners are created equally.

Corn syrup converts to fat in the body in record time, while high fructose corn syrup (HFCS) – food manufacturers' cheaper answer to sugar – may be even worse. Research has found that HFCS goes directly to the liver, releasing enzymes that tell the body to store fat, which may increase harmful triglyceride and cholesterol levels. Instead, on the right you'll find the lowdown on five *CE*-approved sweeteners you can experiment with today.

Stevia

This natural powder is derived from the South American herb Stevia rebaudiana. With zero calories and a concentrated sweet kick, it's often best used diluted in water. One half-teaspoon can equal the sweetness of one cup of refined white sugar.

FIND IT: Health food stores.

Raw honey

Nature's original sweetener contains 21 calories per teaspoon. Researchers have found that raw honey, specifically, contains probiotic bacteria that help support a healthy digestive system.

FIND IT: Health and organic food aisle at supermarkets and health food stores.

Sucanat

A straightforward replacement for granulated sugar, it retains its molasses content, making it the closest thing to pure cane sugar. One teaspoon has 16 calories.

FIND IT: Health and organic food aisle at supermarkets, health food stores and wholesomesweeteners.com.

Maple sugar flakes

They've got the winning taste of pure syrup with a pleasing crunch at just seven-and-a-half calories per teaspoon – half the calories of refined sugar.

FIND IT: Large grocery and superstores and igourmet.com.

Organic evaporated cane juice

It's similar in appearance to sugar though a bit darker since it's not as processed or refined. You can use it as you would white sugar, though it has a deeper molasses-like flavor.

FIND IT: Health food stores.

Researchers have found that raw honey, specifically, contains probiotic bacteria that help support a healthy digestive system.

Summer BBQ

Chicken & Veggie Skewers, p. 242
Grilled Shrimp, p. 110

Summer is the season for sun, swimming and grilling. During this hot, lazy season, what's better than inviting friends and family over, firing up the BBQ and eating good food hot off the grill? Nothing we can think of! And that's why we included this special BBQ mini-section especially for you. Our summer recipes are easy on your waistline and simple to prepare. They're so easy to make, your toughest decision will be choosing between our Chicken & Veggie Skewers, the Ultimate Turkey Burgers and our Grilled Maple-Soy Salmon – and picking out a swimsuit to wear poolside, of course!

Chicken & Veggie Skewers

Serves 4. **Hands-on time:** 25 minutes. **Total time:** 60 minutes.

While it can be challenging to grill meat and veggies on the same skewer, the trick is all in the sizes. Cut boneless chicken into one-inch pieces to cook in perfect tandem with the vegetable chunks (see below). Soaking the wooden skewers in water before loading them will aid in even cooking and prevent the wood from burning. This recipe will fill about 12 10-inch skewers. Allow two or three per person and multiply the recipe as needed, depending upon the other dishes you're serving.

INGREDIENTS:

- 1 lb boneless, skinless chicken breast, cut into 1-inch pieces
- 1 small onion, chopped into ¾-inch pieces
- 8 medium mushrooms, cut in half
- 1 medium zucchini, cut into ½-inch chunks

MEDITERRANEAN-BALSAMIC MARINADE

- 1 Tbsp olive oil
- 2 Tbsp balsamic vinegar
- ½ tsp dried thyme
- ½ tsp dried rosemary

INSTRUCTIONS:

ONE: Place chicken in a shallow bowl and vegetables in a large bowl. In a small bowl, stir together marinade ingredients well.

TWO: Place 12 10-inch wooden skewers in a shallow container and cover with water. Set aside. Pour one tablespoon of marinade over chicken, tossing to mix well. Pour remaining marinade over vegetables and toss gently. Let chicken, vegetables and skewers sit for 20 minutes.

THREE: Thread chicken and veggies onto skewers, alternating each piece of chicken with two vegetables until all skewers are loaded. Note: Make sure to wash your hands with soap and warm water after handling chicken.

FOUR: Place skewers over medium-hot fire for four to five minutes. Turn over and grill for another four to five minutes. Rearrange skewers over heat as needed for final four to five minutes of cooking, removing them when chicken is firm and vegetables are tender.

TO CHECK FOR CHICKEN DONENESS: Lightly press the middle of the piece with a fork or spatula – it should feel firm and give only slightly, and juices should run clear.

Nutrients per 3-skewer serving: *Calories: 185, Total Fat: 5 g, Sat. Fat: 1 g, Carbs: 6 g, Fiber: 1 g, Sugars: 3 g, Protein: 28 g, Sodium: 83 mg, Cholesterol: 66 mg*

For a photo of this recipe, see p. 240.

Ultimate Turkey Burgers

Serves 6. ***Hands-on time:*** *10 minutes.* ***Total time:*** *50 minutes.*

Replacing ground beef with lean ground turkey is an easy way to reduce fat and calories without sacrificing taste. Try it in any recipe that calls for ground beef — no one will know the difference!

INGREDIENTS:

- 1½ lbs ground turkey
- 1 medium red pepper, diced into ¼-inch pieces
- 2 garlic cloves, minced
- 1 Tbsp finely minced parsley (or freeze-dried parsley)
- ½ tsp sea salt
- ½ tsp black pepper

INSTRUCTIONS:

ONE: In a medium bowl, combine all ingredients together well. Place about one-third of a cup of mixture between two sheets of waxed paper. Press firmly into a patty that is four inches wide and about a half-inch thick. Repeat with remaining mixture until you have six patties. Chill in freezer for 30 minutes before grilling time.

TWO: Using a spatula, place patties carefully on grill over medium-high heat. Grill three to four minutes, and then flip. Grill for another three to four minutes or until burgers are golden brown and firm in the middle.

TRY THIS: **Popping your turkey burger onto a whole-grain bun will add 114 calories, two grams of fat, 22 grams of carbs and some much-needed fiber (two grams) to your meal. Also try a selection of fresh vegetables for toppings, such as sliced tomato and onion sprouts.**

Nutrients per patty: *Calories: 177, Total Fat: 9 g, Sat. Fat: 3 g, Carbs: 2 g, Fiber: 0.5 g, Sugars: 1 g, Protein: 20 g, Sodium: 268 mg, Cholesterol: 90 mg*

Nutritional Bonus:

Salmon is a great source of omega-3s, essential fatty acids that have been found to help in everything from brain development and normal growth to lowering cholesterol and blood pressure, reducing the risk of heart disease, and aiding those suffering from arthritis and other inflammatory disorders – plus a bevy of other benefits!

Grilled Maple Soy Salmon

Grilled Maple Soy Salmon

Serves 4. **Hands-on time:** *5 minutes*. **Total time:** *25 minutes*.

Salmon is naturally high in oil, those good-for-you omega-3s – and that means not only juicier, flakier protein, but also easier, nonstick grilling. However, it's fine to go for your fish of choice – from halibut and sea bass to catfish and tilapia. Less oily types grill best when brushed more generously with olive oil (about a half-teaspoon per fillet). Place three-quarter-inch-thick fillets or steaks over a medium-hot fire for browning without burning. Thinner fillets may do best in a basket over a hotter fire – quick cooking results in fish that will be more moist.

INGREDIENTS:

- 4 salmon fillets or steaks (about 4 oz each)
- 1 Tbsp pure maple syrup
- 1 Tbsp soy sauce

INSTRUCTIONS:

ONE: Place salmon in a large, shallow glass container. In a small bowl, stir together syrup and soy sauce, and brush on both sides of salmon (or on skinless side only, if salmon has skin). Let sit for 15 minutes.

TWO: Place salmon directly on grate over medium-high heat for three to four minutes. Flip with tongs or a spatula and grill for two to three more minutes, or until salmon is no longer shiny or translucent in the middle. The flesh should be firm and just slightly flaky. Serve immediately.

Nutrients per fillet: Calories: 176, Total Fat: 7 g, Sat. Fat: 1 g, Carbs: 4 g, Fiber: 0 g, Sugars: 3 g, Protein: 23 g, Sodium: 276 mg, Cholesterol: 62 mg

Healthy Corn on the Cob

Serves 6. **Hands-on time:** *10 minutes*. **Total time:** *45 minutes*.

Corn on the cob is a summer staple. This corn tastes best as fresh as possible, so look to purchase it at a farmers' market or roadside stand.

INGREDIENTS:

- 6 ears of corn, cleaned as directed below

INSTRUCTIONS:

ONE: Remove husks from corn carefully, leaving two or three layers of inner husks in place. Cut tassels off top of ears, about one inch above end of cobs. Fill a sink or large tub with four quarts cool water. Place corn in water (it will float) and let soak for 20 minutes.

TWO: Remove corn from water and drain. Place wet, whole ears on grill over medium-high heat for four minutes. Turn ears over by thirds, and keep turning every three to four minutes until corn is golden brown and roasted, for about four turns and a total cooking time of 15 to 16 minutes.

THREE: Remove from grill and serve. Pull back the husks to reveal the tender steamed corn inside. (Caution: Corn will be very hot to the touch.)

Nutrients per ear: Calories: 123, Total Fat: 2 g, Sat. Fat: 0 g, Carbs: 27 g, Fiber: 4 g, Sugars: 5 g, Protein: 5 g, Sodium: 21 mg, Cholesterol: 0 mg

Grilled Eggplant

Serves 6. **Hands-on time:** *15 minutes*. **Total time:** *25 minutes*.

Eggplant is known as a meaty vegetable. We've treated it that way in this recipe by marinating it before grilling. You'll be surprised (and impressed!) with its flavor!

INGREDIENTS:

- 1 mint teabag
- ½ cup boiling water
- 1 eggplant
- 1 Tbsp lemon juice
- 1 tsp olive oil
- ½ tsp coarse sea salt
- ½ tsp black pepper

INSTRUCTIONS:

ONE: Place teabag in boiling water and steep for five minutes. Meanwhile, prepare eggplant. After removing ends, slice eggplant lengthwise into half-inch slices (six or seven for a medium eggplant). Place eggplant slices in a single layer in a large, shallow casserole dish.

TWO: After teabag has steeped, remove. Whisk lemon juice and olive oil into hot tea. Pour mixture over eggplant. Turn over slices to coat. Sprinkle salt and pepper evenly over slices. Marinate eggplant for 10 minutes, turning once.

THREE: Place eggplant onto medium-hot grate and grill, turning once, until flesh is tender (and gives slightly in the middle), about eight to ten minutes.

Nutrients per slice: Calories: 30, Total Fat: 1 g, Sat. Fat: 0 g, Carbs: 5.5 g, Fiber: 3 g, Sugars: 2 g, Protein: 1 g, Sodium: 162 mg, Cholesterol: 0 mg

Mock Sangria

*Serves approximately 15. **Hands-on time:** 10 minutes. **Total time:** 10 minutes.*

In Spain, no party is complete without a pitcher of sangria, a fruity medley made with a base of wine, perhaps with a dash of brandy or triple sec, and a variety of sliced fresh fruit. Our clean-eating version replaces the alcohol with freshly squeezed juices and sparkling grape juice for a fizzy, fruity drink that will jazz up any get-together.

INGREDIENTS:

- 3 to 4 lemons, cut into quarters
- 12 strawberries, sliced
- 3 to 4 small oranges, cut into thin quarters
- 6 oz orange-blossom honey syrup*
- 24 oz freshly squeezed orange juice
- 12 oz freshly squeezed lemon juice
- 12 oz white cranberry juice
- 2 cinnamon sticks
- Chilled sparkling white grape juice

INSTRUCTIONS:

ONE: Reserve half of fresh fruit for garnish. Place rest of ingredients (excluding sparkling grape juice) into a large glass container, cover and refrigerate overnight.

TWO: When ready to serve, pour mixture into an ice-filled pitcher to two-thirds full. Add one-third of fresh sliced fruit and top with sparkling grape juice. Stir gently to mix. Serve in ice-filled goblets garnished with additional fresh fruit.

HINT: Have fun and experiment with other seasonal fruits and juices; just make sure they are fresh!

*To make orange-blossom honey syrup, dissolve one part orange-blossom honey in an equal amount of hot water and allow to cool.

Nutrients per serving: *Calories: 83, Total Fat: 0 g, Sat. Fat: 0 g, Carbs: 22 g, Fiber: 1 g, Sugars: 18 g, Protein: 1 g, Sodium: 3 mg, Cholesterol: 0 mg*

NUTRITIONAL BONUS: With orange, lemon, grape and cranberry juices plus lemons, strawberries and oranges, it's no surprise this thirst quencher has almost a full day's requirement of vitamin C in one serving. If the fruit in this concoction doesn't give your guests a non-alcoholic energy buzz, the sweet scent of cinnamon definitely will!

Tropical Vanilla Fruit Salad

*Serves 8. **Hands-on time:** 15 minutes. **Total time:** 25 minutes.*

The refreshing flavors of fruit are the perfect ending to complement a barbecued meal.

INGREDIENTS:

- 1 pineapple, peeled, cored and cut into ½-inch slices
- 2 mangos, peeled, pitted and cut into ½-inch slices
- 2 large, slightly green bananas, halved lengthwise and then sliced in half
- 1 vanilla bean, halved lengthwise (or 1 tsp pure vanilla extract)
- 2 Tbsp lemon juice
- 2 Tbsp orange juice

INSTRUCTIONS:

ONE: Place fruit slices in a large, shallow bowl. Scrape vanilla bean (or pour vanilla extract) into a small bowl and stir with lemon and orange juices. Drizzle fruit with juice mixture and toss very gently to coat all pieces.

TWO: After scraping grate clean with a wire brush, dab one teaspoon of olive oil onto a paper towel held by tongs, and rub onto grate. Place fruit directly on grill over medium-high heat for about two to three minutes. Turn with a spatula or tongs and grill for two to three more minutes.

THREE: Place grilled fruit in alternating layers in a large glass bowl. Serve immediately.

Nutrients per ¾-cup serving: *Calories: 98, Total Fat: 0.5 g, Sat. Fat: 0 g, Carbs: 25 g, Fiber: 2 g, Sugars: 11 g, Protein: 1 g, Sodium: 1 mg, Cholesterol: 0 mg*

Tropical Vanilla Fruit Salad

Web Bonus!
Keep your burger classic with clean, home-made ketchup! Check out **cleaneatingmag.com/cleanketchup** for the recipe.

Give Your Burger an Instant Upgrade

No one likes a dry bun, but traditional condiments can be not-so-nutritious (think fatty dressings) or just plain boring (lettuce and tomato slices again?). The solution? New topping ideas that let you create dozens of deliciously clean variations on the classic burger.

1 Sliced Mango

INSTEAD OF: *tomatoes*

NUTRITION: 27 calories per quarter cup plus carotenoids, antioxidants that support immune function.

2 Roasted Zucchini Strips

INSTEAD OF: *pickles*

NUTRITION: a quarter of one large zucchini has 19 calories plus potassium and magnesium, both of which may help lower your blood pressure.

3 Radicchio

INSTEAD OF: *iceberg lettuce*

NUTRITION: two calories per leaf plus vitamin K, which helps your body absorb the calcium necessary for maintaining optimal bone health.

4 Nonfat Greek-Style Yogurt

INSTEAD OF: *mayonnaise*

NUTRITION: 30 calories per quarter cup plus five grams of protein, which keeps hunger in check by preventing rapid spikes in blood sugar.

5 Caramelized Onions

INSTEAD OF: *sliced onions*

NUTRITION: 41 calories per two tablespoons plus quercetin (also found largely in apples), an antioxidant with antihistamine and anti-inflammatory benefits.

6 Salsa

INSTEAD OF: *ketchup*

NUTRITION: four calories per tablespoon plus vitamin E, which works as an antioxidant to help keep atherosclerosis and asthma at bay.

7 Crumbled Goat Cheese

INSTEAD OF: *American cheese*

NUTRITION: 80 calories per ounce and up to 355 fewer grams of belly-bloating sodium than the same amount of low-fat American cheese.

8 Sautéed Mushrooms

INSTEAD OF: *Thousand Island dressing*

NUTRITION: 32 calories per two tablespoons plus niacin, which may help lower cholesterol and reduce your risk of osteoarthritis.

4 Weeks of Meal Plans & Shopping Lists

M TOTAL NUTRIENTS Calories: **1549**, Fat: **48 g**, Sat. Fat: **10 g**, Carbs: **185 g**, Fiber: **28 g**, Sugars: **78 g**, Protein: **103 g**, Sodium: **2028 mg**, Cholesterol: **114 mg**

BREAKFAST	SNACK 1	LUNCH	SNACK 2
Peach Melba Yogurt Smoothie (p. 157), 4 egg whites, 1 whole-wheat English muffin	1 apple with 1 handful unsalted almonds, ½ cup low-fat Greek yogurt	Roasted Red Pepper & Cucumber Tea Sandwiches on Pumpernickel (p.159); 1 celery stalk with 1 Tbsp natural peanut butter	½ cup 1% cottage cheese, 1 sliced nectarine, 8 whole-wheat crackers

T TOTAL NUTRIENTS Calories: **1578**, Fat: **43 g**, Sat. Fat: **19 g**, Carbs: **223 g**, Fiber: **45 g**, Sugars: **87 g**, Protein: **86 g**, Sodium: **2140 mg**, Cholesterol: **97 mg**

BREAKFAST	SNACK 1	LUNCH	SNACK 2
½ cup oatmeal, 1 chopped apple, ½ tsp cinnamon, 1 cup low-fat milk	½ cup raspberries, ½ oz Neufchâtel cheese	Caponata Sandwiches with Goat Cheese & Basil (p.84)	½ cup low-fat Greek yogurt, ¼ cup chickpeas, 1 nectarine

W TOTAL NUTRIENTS Calories: **1505**, Fat: **64 g**, Sat. Fat: **11 g**, Carbs: **157 g**, Fiber: **33 g**, Sugars: **29 g**, Protein: **107 g**, Sodium: **1988 mg**, Cholesterol: **91 mg**

BREAKFAST	SNACK 1	LUNCH	SNACK 2
Breakfast Wrap (4 scrambled egg whites, 2 oz low-fat Swiss cheese, 1 diced scallion, 2 Tbsp diced tomatoes in 1 whole-wheat tortilla); **½ cup red grapes**	1 slice whole-wheat toast; 1 Tbsp natural almond butter	**Tomato-Tuna Salad** (1 diced tomato, 1 cup shredded arugula, 1 Tbsp chopped red onion, 1 Tbsp chopped basil, ½ cup cooked chickpeas, 3 oz tuna, 1 tsp extra virgin olive oil, 1 tsp balsamic vinegar); **½ cup sliced strawberries; 3 Ryvita crackers**	8 carrot sticks, ¼ cup hummus, 4 whole-wheat crackers

T TOTAL NUTRIENTS Calories: **1668**, Fat: **61 g**, Sat. Fat: **12 g**, Carbs: **211 g**, Fiber: **38 g**, Sugars: **84 g**, Protein: **90 g**, Sodium: **2074 mg**, Cholesterol: **84 mg**

BREAKFAST	SNACK 1	LUNCH	SNACK 2
1 cup cubed cantaloupe, ¾ cup 1% cottage cheese, ⅛ teaspoon cinnamon, 1 cup Kashi granola	1 banana with 1 Tbsp natural peanut butter, 2 oz tuna	Curried Carrot Soup (p. 133); 1 handful unsalted almonds	1 cup edamame, 1 kiwi

F TOTAL NUTRIENTS Calories: **1583**, Fat: **45 g**, Sat. Fat: **11 g**, Carbs: **182 g**, Fiber: **26 g**, Sugars: **74 g**, Protein: **118 g**, Sodium: **2162 mg**, Cholesterol: **338 mg**

BREAKFAST	SNACK 1	LUNCH	SNACK 2
1 oz diced ham scrambled with 2 egg whites, 1 Tbsp Mexican cheese blend; 1 slice rye toast, 6 oz fresh squeezed orange juice	1 low-fat string cheese, 1 orange, 1 oz tuna	**Turkey Sandwich** (3 oz deli-fresh low-sodium turkey breast, 1 oz Jarlsberg Light cheese, ⅛ sliced avocado, 1 lettuce leaf, 1 slice tomato on 2 slices whole-wheat bread); **1 apple, 1 Tbsp natural almond butter**	½ cup low-fat plain yogurt, 1 cup sliced strawberries

S TOTAL NUTRIENTS Calories: **1672**, Fat: **53 g**, Sat. Fat: **7 g**, Carbs: **199 g**, Fiber: **42 g**, Sugars: **98 g**, Protein: **112 g**, Sodium: **1111 mg**, Cholesterol: **165 mg**

BREAKFAST	SNACK 1	LUNCH	SNACK 2
Strawberry Smoothies (½ cup strawberries, 1 scoop protein powder, ½ cup low-fat plain yogurt, ½ banana, ¼ cup fresh squeezed orange juice); **1 handful unsalted almonds**	4 dried apricots, ½ cup 1% cottage cheese, ½ cup Kashi granola	**Vegetarian Wrap** (4 oz sautéed firm tofu, ½ oz low-fat jalapeno cheese, ¼ cup low-sodium black beans, 2 Tbsp low-sodium salsa on 1 whole-wheat tortilla); **10 celery sticks**	¾ cup low-fat kefir, ½ cup sliced red grapes and 1 kiwi

S TOTAL NUTRIENTS Calories: **1517**, Fat: **60 g**, Sat. Fat: **8 g**, Carbs: **175 g**, Fiber: **37 g**, Sugars: **43 g**, Protein: **87 g**, Sodium: **720 mg**, Cholesterol: **117 mg**

BREAKFAST	SNACK 1	LUNCH	SNACK 2
½ cup oatmeal with ½ cup low-fat milk, ½ cup raspberries; 3 egg whites	3 oz smoked salmon; 4 whole-wheat crackers, ½ avocado	1 cup edamame, ½ cup brown rice, 2 plums	1 banana, 2 Tbsp natural almond butter

SHOPPING LIST

DINNER

4 oz baked chicken breast, 1 cup steamed cauliflower, 1 medium sweet potato with 1 Tbsp whole-grain mustard

DINNER

Sautéed Halibut with Artichoke Hearts, Cherry Tomatoes & Cannellini Beans (p. 57); Mixed Berry Crisp with Date Oat Streusel (p. 235)

DINNER

Chinese Five-Spice Flank Steak with Grilled Peppers (p. 61)

DINNER

Light & Healthy Pork "Fried" Rice (p. 46); Coconut Chai Chocolate Cake (p. 231) (take zest from 1 orange and reserve the orange for tomorrow's snack)

DINNER

Lemon Paprika Prawns with Zucchini & Couscous (p. 113); Easy Egg Custard with Fresh Peaches (p. 212)

DINNER

Easy & Elegant Salmon with Fennel & Carrots in Parchment (p. 110); 1 pear

DINNER

Spice Roasted Vegetables with Sage & Rosemary (p. 136); 4 oz baked chicken breast

Proteins & Dairy

- 1 (15-oz) can low-sodium black beans
- 1 (15-oz) can cannellini beans
- 1 lb beef flank steak
- 1 (16-oz) container low-fat (1%) cottage cheese
- 4 oz goat cheese
- ½ oz low-fat jalapeno cheese
- 1 oz Jarlsberg Light cheese
- 1 oz Mexican cheese blend
- 1 oz Neufchâtel cheese
- 1 pkg low-fat string cheese
- 2 oz low-fat Swiss cheese
- 8 oz boneless, skinless chicken breast
- 1 (15-oz) can chickpeas
- 1 (18-oz) pkg edamame
- 2 dozen eggs
- 4 (5-oz) halibut fillets
- 1 oz ham
- 1 (16-oz) container low-fat kefir
- 1 L low-fat milk
- ½ lb pork cutlets
- 1 lb large wild prawns, peeled, deveined and tails on
- 1 container protein powder
- 4 oz smoked salmon
- 4 (5-oz) wild salmon fillets
- 4 oz firm tofu
- 1 (6-oz) can tuna
- 3 oz low-sodium deli-fresh turkey breast
- 1 pint plain, low-fat yogurt
- 1 (16-oz) container low-fat Greek yogurt

Veggies/Fruits

- 3 apples
- 1 pkg frozen artichoke hearts
- 1 bunch arugula
- 1 avocado
- 1 small bunch bananas (3 or 4)
- 1 (700 g) pkg frozen mixed berries
- 1 head broccoli
- 1 bag carrots
- 1 cantaloupe
- 1 bunch cauliflower
- 1 bunch celery
- 1 English cucumber
- 1 eggplant
- 1 bulb fennel
- 1 bulb garlic
- 1 large bunch red grapes
- 2 kiwis
- 2 leeks
- 4 lemons
- 1 head Boston lettuce
- 2 nectarines
- 1 bunch green onion
- 1 red onion
- 1 orange
- 1 parsnip
- 3 peaches
- 1 pear
- 1 pkg frozen peas
- 3 sweet red peppers
- 1 yellow pepper
- 2 plums
- 1 pint raspberries
- 1 rutabaga
- 1 scallion
- 1 pint strawberries
- 2 medium sweet potatoes
- 1 pint cherry tomatoes
- 1 (15-oz) can diced tomatoes
- 2 ripe red tomatoes
- 2 baby zucchini

Whole Grains

- 1 small loaf rye bread
- 1 small loaf whole-wheat bread
- 1 pkg Ryvita crackers
- 1 box whole-wheat crackers
- 1 pkg whole-wheat couscous
- 1 pkg whole-wheat English muffins
- 1 pkg whole-grain flour
- 1 pkg whole-wheat flour
- 1 box Kashi granola
- 1 container 5-minute oatmeal
- 1 pkg whole oats
- 1 small loaf whole-grain pumpernickel rye bread
- 1 pkg brown rice
- 4 whole grain rolls
- 1 pkg whole-wheat tortillas

Nuts/Seeds/Oils

- 1 jar unsalted raw almonds
- 1 small jar natural almond butter
- 1 bottle virgin coconut oil
- 1 bottle extra-virgin olive oil
- Olive oil cooking spray
- 1 small jar natural peanut butter
- 1 bottle safflower oil

Extras

- 1 jar unsweetened applesauce
- 4 dried apricots
- 1 bottle Asian Fish sauce
- 1 box baking powder
- 1 box baking soda
- 24 fresh basil leaves
- 1 (35-oz) container low-sodium vegetable broth
- 1 jar capers
- 1 container cardamom
- 1 container cayenne pepper
- 1 bottle fresh chile sauce
- 1 container Chinese Five Spice powder
- 5 fresh cilantro leaves
- 1 container cinnamon
- 1 container cocoa powder
- 1 bottle coconut extract
- 1 small container low-fat coconut milk
- 1 small pkg toasted coconut
- 2 oz unsweetened flaked coconut
- 1 container cornstarch
- 1 container cumin
- 1 pkg dried currants
- 1 container curry powder
- 20 pitted dates
- 4 small sprigs fresh dill
- 1 container garlic powder
- 1 container fresh grated ginger
- 1 bottle organic honey
- 1 container hummus
- 1 small bottle lemon juice
- 1 small jar whole-grain mustard
- 1 container fresh ground nutmeg
- 1 container orange juice
- 1 container paprika
- 1 container ground black pepper
- 1 container red pepper flakes
- 1 bunch fresh rosemary
- 1 bunch fresh sage
- 1 jar low-sodium salsa
- 1 container sea salt
- 1 bottle low-sodium soy sauce
- 1 bottle vanilla extract
- 1 bottle balsamic vinegar
- 1 bottle red wine vinegar

week 2

M — TOTAL NUTRIENTS Calories: **1578**, Fat: **60 g**, Sat. Fat: **8 g**, Carbs: **198 g**, Fiber: **41 g**, Sugars: **59 g**, Protein: **92 g**, Sodium: **1156 mg**, Cholesterol: **73 mg**

BREAKFAST	SNACK 1	LUNCH	SNACK 2
1 whole-wheat English muffin with 2 Tbsp natural peanut butter, 1 banana	4 whole-wheat crackers, 1 oz low-fat cheddar cheese	**Tofu & Edamame Salad** (2 cups romaine lettuce, 5 oz sautéed firm tofu, ½ sliced red bell pepper, ½ cup steamed shelled edamame, 1 oz low-fat jalapeno cheese with 3 Tbsp red wine vinegar and 1 tsp extra-virgin olive oil)	1 apple, ½ cup chickpeas

T — TOTAL NUTRIENTS Calories: **1668**, Fat: **55 g**, Sat. Fat: **15 g**, Carbs: **216 g**, Fiber: **39 g**, Sugars: **45 g**, Protein: **107 g**, Sodium: **2449 mg**, Cholesterol: **229 mg**

BREAKFAST	SNACK 1	LUNCH	SNACK 2
4 egg whites scrambled with 1 slice diced Canadian bacon, 1 slice diced tomato, ¼ cup diced onion, ¼ cup diced green bell pepper; ½ cup low-fat milk	2 Tbsp hummus, 10 sugar snap peas, ½ avocado	**Sautéed Sole Sandwiches with Citrus Slaw** (p. 42)	1 pear, 1 oz Stilton cheese, 4 whole-wheat crackers

W — TOTAL NUTRIENTS Calories: **1557**, Fat: **49 g**, Sat. Fat: **10 g**, Carbs: **175 g**, Fiber: **37 g**, Sugars: **26 g**, Protein: **118 g**, Sodium: **1426 mg**, Cholesterol: **373 mg**

BREAKFAST	SNACK 1	LUNCH	SNACK 2
Breakfast burrito (1 whole-wheat tortilla stuffed with 4 scrambled egg whites, ½ oz shredded cheddar cheese, ½ cup each diced red bell pepper and green bell pepper); **6 oz fresh squeezed orange juice**	**Chocolate Smoothie** (blend 1 cup low-fat milk with ¼ cup chocolate protein powder, ½ cup frozen strawberries and 5 ice cubes); **1 handful unsalted almonds**	**French Tuna Salad with Green Beans, Potatoes & Capers** (p. 87)	½ grapefruit, 15 un-salted raw cashews

T — TOTAL NUTRIENTS Calories: **1659**, Fat: **64 g**, Sat. Fat: **19 g**, Carbs: **183 g**, Fiber: **39 g**, Sugars: **75 g**, Protein: **117 g**, Sodium: **2213 mg**, Cholesterol: **206 mg**

BREAKFAST	SNACK 1	LUNCH	SNACK 2
1 whole-wheat tortilla with 2 Tbsp natural peanut butter and 1 sliced banana	1 low-fat string cheese, ½ grapefruit	**Ham & Cheese Salad** (2 slices low-sodium uncured lean ham—save some for tomorrow's lunch; 1 oz Jarlsberg Light cheese, 2 cups assorted salad greens, ½ cup chopped tomatoes and ½ cup cooked white beans with 2 Tbsp balsamic vinegar, 1 tsp Dijon mustard and 1 tsp extra-virgin olive oil)	1 cup low-fat Greek yogurt with 1 tsp pure maple syrup and ½ cup blueberries

F — TOTAL NUTRIENTS Calories: **1526**, Fat: **54 g**, Sat. Fat: **13 g**, Carbs: **160 g**, Fiber: **25 g**, Sugars: **46 g**, Protein: **111 g**, Sodium: **2782 mg**, Cholesterol: **334 mg**

BREAKFAST	SNACK 1	LUNCH	SNACK 2
3 egg whites and 1 whole egg, scrambled, 1 cup sautéed baby spinach and 1 oz mozzarella on half of a whole-wheat English muffin; 1 cup low-fat milk	½ sliced cucumber, ½ red bell pepper, 1 handful unsalted almonds	2 oz low-sodium uncured ham, 2 oz sliced deli-fresh low-sodium turkey breast, 1 Boston lettuce leaf, 1 slice tomato, 1 slice avocado on 2 slices whole-grain quinoa bread; ¾ cup low-fat Greek yogurt, 1 cup frozen straw-berries (thawed)	1 cup cherry tomatoes, ½ cup chickpeas

S — TOTAL NUTRIENTS Calories: **1786**, Fat: **56.5 g**, Sat. Fat: **12 g**, Carbs: **219 g**, Fiber: **50 g**, Sugars: **61 g**, Protein: **118 g**, Sodium: **1728 mg**, Cholesterol: **103 mg**

BREAKFAST	SNACK 1	LUNCH	SNACK 2
½ cup 5-minute uncooked oats mixed with ¾ cup 1% cot-tage cheese and ½ cup sliced strawberries	1 handful unsalted almonds, 1 grapefruit	**Citrus Protein Salad** (2 cups romaine lettuce, 2 hardboiled egg whites, ½ cup chickpeas, 2 Tbsp unsalted sunflower seeds, 1 clementine with 2 Tbsp balsamic vinegar, 1 tsp Dijon mustard and ½ tsp extra-virgin olive oil); **1 pear**	2 low-fat string chees-es, 10 red grapes

S — TOTAL NUTRIENTS Calories: **1518**, Fat: **49 g**, Sat. Fat: **12 g**, Carbs: **160 g**, Fiber: **44 g**, Sugars: **35 g**, Protein: **110 g**, Sodium: **2387 mg**, Cholesterol: **303 mg**

BREAKFAST	SNACK 1	LUNCH	SNACK 2
Omelet made with 4 egg whites and one whole egg, ½ cup green bell pepper, ½ cup red bell pepper, ¼ cup onion and 1 oz shredded low-fat cheddar cheese	½ avocado, ½ cup cooked white beans and ½ cup diced tomato with 1½ Tbsp balsamic vinegar and ½ tsp extra-virgin olive oil	1 veggie burger patty with 1 oz part-skim mozzarella cheese, 1 Boston lettuce leaf, 1 slice tomato, 1 slice onion on 2 slices toasted bakery whole-wheat bread; ¼ cup chopped carrots, ½ cup chopped celery, ½ cup chopped cauliflower, 2 Tbsp red wine vinegar, 1 tsp extra-virgin olive oil	¼ cup hummus, 15 carrot sticks and 2 rye crispbreads

SHOPPING LIST

DINNER

Farro Risotto with Wild Morels, Asparagus & Truffle Oil (p. 134); **4 oz grilled chicken**

DINNER

½ cup brown basmati rice, 1 cup assorted stir fried vegetables (sautéed in 1 tsp extra-virgin olive oil), **3 oz seared tiger shrimp; sauce: 1 Tbsp balsamic vinegar, 2 tsp whole-grain mustard**

DINNER

4 oz grilled chicken breast, 1 small sweet potato (cut into ½-inch chunks, oven baked), **1 cup broccoli**

DINNER

Turkey Meatballs with Whole-Wheat Spaghetti, Spinach & Ricotta (p. 45)

DINNER

Chicken & Summer Vegetable Cacciatore with Polenta (p. 58)

DINNER

Roasted Eggplant & Kale Penne with Toasted Pine Nuts & Feta; 4 oz grilled chicken breast (grill 8 oz and save 4 oz for tomorrow's dinner)

DINNER

Fajita Salad (4 oz grilled chicken cut into strips, 1 cup romaine lettuce, ¼ cup sliced red onion and ¾ cup sliced green bell pepper sautéed in ½ tsp extra-virgin olive oil; ¼ cup chopped tomatoes, 1 Tbsp chopped scallions, ¼ cup low-sodium salsa with juice of 1 lime); **1 slice whole-wheat bread**

Proteins & Dairy

- ❍ 1 slice (2 oz) Canadian bacon
- ❍ 1 cup white beans
- ❍ 3 oz low-fat cheddar cheese
- ❍ 1 (16-oz) container 1% cottage cheese
- ❍ 2 oz low-fat feta cheese
- ❍ 1 oz low-fat jalapeno cheese
- ❍ 1 oz Jarlsberg Light cheese
- ❍ 2 oz part-skim mozzarella cheese
- ❍ 2 oz Parmigiano-Reggiano cheese
- ❍ 1 oz Stilton cheese
- ❍ 1 pkg low-fat string cheese
- ❍ 6 oz low-fat ricotta cheese
- ❍ 1 ½ lb boneless, skinless chicken breast
- ❍ 1 (15-oz) can chickpeas
- ❍ 1 pkg frozen edamame
- ❍ 2 dozen eggs
- ❍ 4 oz low-sodium, uncured ham
- ❍ 1 L low-fat milk
- ❍ 1 container chocolate protein powder
- ❍ 4 (5-oz) sole fillets
- ❍ 3 oz tiger shrimp
- ❍ 5 oz firm tofu
- ❍ 1 (6-oz) can white tuna
- ❍ 2 oz deli-fresh low-sodium turkey breast
- ❍ 1 lb extra-lean ground turkey
- ❍ 1 (16-oz) container low-fat Greek yogurt

Veggies/Fruits

- ❍ 1 apple
- ❍ 1 small bunch baby asparagus
- ❍ 2 avocadoes

- ❍ 1 small bunch bananas
- ❍ 1 cup fresh green beans
- ❍ 1 small container blueberries
- ❍ 1 pkg frozen broccoli
- ❍ 1 head green cabbage
- ❍ 1 bunch carrots
- ❍ 1 pkg frozen cauliflower
- ❍ 1 bunch celery
- ❍ 1 clementine
- ❍ 1 English cucumber
- ❍ 1 eggplant
- ❍ 1 bulb garlic
- ❍ 2 red grapefruit
- ❍ 1 small bunch red grapes
- ❍ 1 bunch kale
- ❍ 1 lemon
- ❍ 1 head Boston lettuce
- ❍ 1 head red leaf lettuce
- ❍ 2 heads romaine lettuce
- ❍ 1 lime
- ❍ 2 cups cremini mushrooms
- ❍ 1 cup morel mushrooms
- ❍ 2 red onions
- ❍ 1 navel orange
- ❍ 10 fresh sugar snap peas
- ❍ 2 pears
- ❍ 2 green bell peppers
- ❍ 4 red bell peppers
- ❍ 1 orange pepper
- ❍ 1 small bunch radishes
- ❍ 1 medium sweet potato
- ❍ 4 Yukon gold potatoes
- ❍ 1 bag salad greens
- ❍ 1 bunch scallions
- ❍ 2 shallots
- ❍ 5 cups baby spinach

- ❍ 1 small yellow squash
- ❍ 1 pint fresh strawberries
- ❍ 1 pkg frozen sliced strawberries
- ❍ 4 ripe red tomatoes
- ❍ 1 pint cherry tomatoes
- ❍ 1 pkg veggie burger patties
- ❍ 1 bag frozen stir-fry veggies
- ❍ 1 small zucchini

Whole Grains

- ❍ 1 pkg brown basmati rice
- ❍ 1 pkg farro
- ❍ 1 container 5-minute oats
- ❍ 1 small pkg rye crispbreads
- ❍ 1 container whole-grain breadcrumbs
- ❍ 1 small loaf whole-grain quinoa bread
- ❍ 4 whole-grain rolls
- ❍ 1 small loaf whole-wheat bread
- ❍ 1 box whole-wheat crackers
- ❍ 1 pkg whole-wheat English muffins
- ❍ 8 oz whole-wheat penne
- ❍ 8 oz whole-wheat spaghetti
- ❍ 1 pkg whole-wheat tortillas

Nuts/Seeds/Oils

- ❍ 1 small can unsalted almonds
- ❍ 1 small can unsalted raw cashews
- ❍ 1 bottle extra-virgin olive oil
- ❍ 1 small bottle truffle-infused olive oil
- ❍ 1 small jar natural peanut butter
- ❍ 2 Tbsp pine nuts
- ❍ 1 small pkg unsalted sunflower seeds

Extras

- ❍ 1 tube anchovy paste
- ❍ 1 bunch fresh basil
- ❍ 1 container low-sodium chicken broth
- ❍ 1 container low-sodium vegetable broth
- ❍ 1 small jar capers
- ❍ 1 small container celery seed
- ❍ 1 small jar Dijon mustard
- ❍ 1 sprig fresh dill
- ❍ 1 small bottle organic honey
- ❍ 1 container hummus
- ❍ 1 small jug orange juice
- ❍ 1 small bottle lemon juice
- ❍ 1 small jar whole-grain mustard
- ❍ 1 small jar pitted mixed olives
- ❍ 1 bunch fresh oregano
- ❍ 1 bunch Italian flat leaf parsley
- ❍ 1 can tomato paste
- ❍ 1 container freshly ground black pepper
- ❍ 1 container cayenne pepper
- ❍ 1 container crushed red pepper flakes
- ❍ 1 pkg polenta
- ❍ 1 jar low-sodium salsa
- ❍ 1 container sea salt
- ❍ 1 small bottle pure maple syrup
- ❍ 1 bunch fresh thyme
- ❍ 1 bottle balsamic vinegar
- ❍ 1 bottle red wine vinegar

M

TOTAL NUTRIENTS Calories: **1547**, Fat: **59 g**, Sat. Fat: **16 g**, Carbs: **168 g**, Fiber: **26 g**, Sugars: **67 g**, Protein: **100 g**, Sodium: **1165 mg**, Cholesterol: **117 mg**

BREAKFAST	SNACK 1	LUNCH	SNACK 2
Egg Sandwich (3 egg whites and 1 slice part-skim mozzarella on 1 whole-wheat English muffin); ½ grapefruit	1 oz raw, unsalted cashews	1 whole-wheat wrap with 2 Tbsp unsalted natural cashew butter and 1 small sliced banana; ¾ cup low-fat plain yogurt with ½ cup blueberries	¾ cup low-fat Greek yogurt, 1 Tbsp cocoa powder, 1 cup sliced strawberries

T

TOTAL NUTRIENTS Calories: **1559**, Fat: **48 g**, Sat. Fat: **10 g**, Carbs: **196 g**, Fiber: **29 g**, , Sugars: **72 g**, Protein: **101 g**, Sodium: **1183 mg**, Cholesterol: **227 mg**

BREAKFAST	SNACK 1	LUNCH	SNACK 2
3 Tbsp hummus on 2 slices toasted whole-wheat bread; ½ grapefruit	2 clementines, 6 oz low-fat Greek yogurt	Salmon Salad (5 oz chilled baked salmon leftovers, 1 chopped hardboiled egg white, 2 cups romaine lettuce, ¼ cup chopped red bell pepper, ¼ cup chopped celery, 1 Tbsp chopped red onion, 2 Tbsp balsamic vinegar, 1 tsp Dijon mustard, 1 tsp extra virgin olive oil); 1 apple	1 cup chopped broccoli with 2 Tbsp low-sodium salsa; ½ cup low-fat milk

W

TOTAL NUTRIENTS Calories: **1614**, Fat: **59 g**, Sat. Fat: **13 g**, Carbs: **214 g**, Fiber: **32 g**, Sugars: **83 g**, Protein: **78 g**, Sodium: **842 mg**, Cholesterol: **69 mg**

BREAKFAST	SNACK 1	LUNCH	SNACK 2
1 toasted whole-wheat wrap with 2 Tbsp natural peanut butter and 1 small sliced banana	Roasted Red Pepper & White Bean Hummus with Crudités (p. 160)	Tofu Salad (5 oz baked tofu, ¼ cup brown rice with ¼ cup unsalted sunflower seeds, 1 cup spinach, ½ cup chopped red bell pepper, 2 Tbsp shredded low-fat jalapeno cheese with 2 Tbsp balsamic vinegar and ½ tsp extra-virgin olive oil); 1 apple	½ cup dried apricots, halved, mixed with ½ cup Nature's Path Optimum Banana Almond Cereal

T

TOTAL NUTRIENTS Calories: **1848**, Fat: **61 g**, Sat. Fat: **13 g**, Carbs: **252 g**, Fiber: **40 g**, Sugars: **137 g**, Protein: **90 g**, Sodium: **1149 mg**, Cholesterol: **105 mg**

BREAKFAST	SNACK 1	LUNCH	SNACK 2
½ cup oatmeal, 1 cup low-fat milk, ½ cup dried apricots, halved, and 1 small sliced banana	2 clementines, 5 carrot sticks, 1 handful unsalted almonds	2 cups low-sodium tomato soup, 1 cup chopped apple with 1 oz walnuts	2 stalks celery with 2 Tbsp peanut butter and 1 oz raisins

F

TOTAL NUTRIENTS Calories: **1574**, Fat: **60 g**, Sat. Fat: **18 g**, Carbs: **182 g**, Fiber: **33 g**, Sugars: **42 g**, Protein: **103 g**, Sodium: **1440 mg**, Cholesterol: **345 mg**

BREAKFAST	SNACK 1	LUNCH	SNACK 2
½ cup low-fat ricotta cheese pureed with ¼ cup 1% cottage cheese and 1 tsp Sucanat; top with ½ cup fresh cherries and ½ tsp sesame seeds	1 cup low-fat milk (skim, rice, almond); 1 hardboiled egg; 8 whole-wheat crackers	4 oz cooked tilapia topped with 1 boiled potato, chopped, 1 cup cooked green beans, chopped, ¾ cup cooked artichoke hearts, chopped, 1 Tbsp chopped onion, 2 tsp red wine vinegar and 1 tsp extra-virgin olive oil	1 low-fat string cheese, 8 carrot sticks

S

TOTAL NUTRIENTS Calories: **1534**, Fat: **29 g**, Sat. Fat: **5 g**, Carbs: **219 g**, Fiber: **45 g**, Sugars: **70 g**, Protein: **111 g**, Sodium: **1105 mg**, Cholesterol: **183 mg**

BREAKFAST	SNACK 1	LUNCH	SNACK 2
1¼ cups Post Shredded Wheat Spoon Size Original cereal with ¾ cup low-fat milk; 1 orange	2½ Tbsp Spicy Black Bean Hummus (Puree ½ cup cooked black beans with 1 tsp fresh lime juice, ¼ tsp chili powder, and ½ tsp finely chopped cilantro – makes 5 Tbsp; save leftovers for lunch tomorrow); 5 whole-wheat crackers	Thai Ground Turkey Burgers (Broil or sauté 5 oz extra-lean ground turkey, formed into 3 patties, wrap in lettuce leaves and top with ¼ cup chopped mango, 2 tsp fresh lime juice, 2 tsp chopped almonds and 2 tsp chopped cilantro); 1 apple	10 grapes, 1 handful unsalted almonds

S

TOTAL NUTRIENTS Calories: **1528**, Fat: **24 g**, Sat. Fat: **7 g**, Carbs: **234 g**, Fiber: **36 g**, Sugars: **79 g**, Protein: **107 g**, Sodium: **878 mg**, Cholesterol: **71 mg**

BREAKFAST	SNACK 1	LUNCH	SNACK 2
Strawberry Chocolate Shake (blend 1 cup sliced strawberries, 1 cup low-fat milk and 1 oz chocolate protein powder); 1 banana	1 cup chopped cooked butternut squash, 1 Tbsp chopped walnuts, ½ tsp Sucanat and dash of cinnamon	5 whole-wheat crackers dipped in leftover Spicy Black Bean Hummus; 1 cup low-sodium lentil soup; 1 orange	Mini Yogurt Parfait (8 oz low-fat Greek yogurt with ½ sliced banana and ¾ cup Post Shredded Wheat Spoon Size Original cereal)

DINNER

5 oz baked salmon (cook 10 oz and save 5 oz for tomorrow's lunch); **10 spears steamed asparagus; 1 medium baked sweet potato**

DINNER

12 large broiled shrimp brushed with 2 tsp extra-virgin olive oil; 1 cup cauliflower sautéed in 1 tsp extra-virgin olive oil and 1 tsp diced garlic; 1 cup wild rice mixed with ½ cup steamed yellow corn

DINNER

Zucchini Pasta (Sauté 3 oz cubed chicken breast, 1 sliced zucchini, 1 diced onion, 1 minced clove garlic in 1 tsp olive oil; toss with 1 cup cooked whole-wheat elbow macaroni, ½ cup shredded basil and 2 tsp Parmesan)

DINNER

Steak Salad (Mix ½ cup each cooked red beans, frozen whole kernel corn, thawed, chopped tomatoes, chopped cucumber and sliced carrots with 4 oz cubed cooked steak, 1 tsp extra-virgin olive oil, 2 tsp red wine vinegar and 1 Tbsp organic sweet relish and 3 cups shredded lettuce)

DINNER

Roast 4 slices eggplant (6 oz) **brushed with 1 tsp olive oil at 450° for 10 minutes; Sauté 3 cups spinach, 1 Tbsp broken walnuts, 1 small diced tomato and 1 crushed clove garlic, and mix with 1 cup cooked whole-wheat spaghetti and 1 Tbsp Parmesan**

DINNER

4 oz broiled pork tenderloin, 1 baked sweet potato, 1 cup cooked spinach, 1 cup cooked sliced carrots

DINNER

4 oz broiled cod; 1 cup sliced summer squash or zucchini, steamed; 1 white potato, sliced and baked

SHOPPING LIST

Proteins & Dairy

- ❑ Black beans (dried or canned)
- ❑ 1 (15-oz) can cannellini beans
- ❑ Red beans (dried or canned)
- ❑ 1 (8-oz) container 1% cottage cheese
- ❑ 1 block low-fat jalapeno cheese
- ❑ 1 small block part-skim mozzarella cheese
- ❑ 1 container grated parmesan cheese
- ❑ 1 (8-oz) container low-fat ricotta cheese
- ❑ 1 pkg low-fat string cheese
- ❑ 3 oz boneless, skinless chicken breast
- ❑ 1 dozen eggs
- ❑ 4 oz cod fillet
- ❑ 2 (5-oz) salmon fillets
- ❑ 4 oz tilapia fillet
- ❑ 1 (16-oz) bag of lentils
- ❑ ½ gallon low-fat milk (skim or unsweetened soy, almond or rice milk)
- ❑ 4 oz pork tenderloin
- ❑ 1 container chocolate or vanilla protein powder
- ❑ 1 bag frozen tiger shrimp
- ❑ 4 oz steak
- ❑ 5 oz firm tofu
- ❑ 5 oz extra lean ground turkey
- ❑ 1 (16-oz) container of low-fat, plain Greek-style yogurt
- ❑ 1 (16-oz) container of low-fat, plain yogurt

Veggies/Fruits

- ❑ 4 apples
- ❑ 2 (3-oz) pkgs dried apricots
- ❑ artichoke hearts (frozen or canned)
- ❑ 1 bunch asparagus spears
- ❑ Assorted crudités

- ❑ 1 bunch bananas
- ❑ 1 small bag green beans
- ❑ 1 pint blueberries
- ❑ 1 bunch broccoli
- ❑ 1 bag of carrots
- ❑ 1 head cauliflower
- ❑ 1 head celery
- ❑ 1 handful fresh, pitted cherries
- ❑ 4 clementines
- ❑ 1 (16-oz) bag frozen, whole kernels corn
- ❑ 1 cucumber
- ❑ 1 small eggplant
- ❑ 1 bulb of garlic
- ❑ 1 grapefruit
- ❑ 1 bunch red grapes
- ❑ 1 head romaine lettuce
- ❑ 1 lemon
- ❑ 2 or 3 limes
- ❑ 1 mango
- ❑ 1 red onion
- ❑ 1 white onion
- ❑ 1 orange
- ❑ 2 red bell peppers
- ❑ 2 potatoes
- ❑ 2 (12-oz) bags fresh spinach
- ❑ 1 pint strawberries
- ❑ 1 butternut squash
- ❑ 2 sweet potatoes
- ❑ 2 tomatoes
- ❑ 2 zucchini

Whole Grains

- ❑ 1 loaf whole-wheat bread
- ❑ 1 box Shredded Wheat Spoon Size original cereal
- ❑ 1 box whole-wheat woven wheat crackers
- ❑ 1 pkg whole-wheat English muffins
- ❑ 1 container rolled oats
- ❑ 1 box whole-wheat elbow pasta
- ❑ 1 box long-grain brown rice or wild rice

- ❑ 1 box whole-wheat spaghetti
- ❑ 1 pkg whole-wheat tortillas (8-in. diameter)

Nuts/Seeds/Oils

- ❑ 1 (8-oz) bag unsalted almonds
- ❑ 1 jar raw, unsalted cashews
- ❑ 1 bottle extra-virgin olive oil
- ❑ 1 jar natural nut butter (peanut, cashew or almond)
- ❑ 1 bag unsalted sunflower seeds
- ❑ 1 bag unsalted walnut halves

Extras

- ❑ 1 bunch fresh basil
- ❑ 1 small jar chili powder
- ❑ 1 bunch cilantro
- ❑ 1 small jar ground cinnamon
- ❑ 1 container cumin
- ❑ 1 container hummus
- ❑ 1 small bottle Dijon mustard
- ❑ 1 container freshly ground black pepper
- ❑ 1 (4-oz) bag unsweetened raisins
- ❑ 1 jar organic sweet relish
- ❑ 1 jar low-sodium salsa
- ❑ 1 container sea salt
- ❑ 1 small bag sesame seeds
- ❑ 1 bag Sucanat
- ❑ 1 (32-oz) container low-sodium tomato soup
- ❑ 1 bottle balsamic vinegar
- ❑ 1 bottle red wine vinegar

M | TOTAL NUTRIENTS Calories: **1707**, Fat: **38 g**, Sat. Fat: **12 g**, Carbs: **249 g**, Fiber: **41 g**, Sugars: **101 g**, Protein: **101 g**, Sodium: **1669 mg**, Cholesterol: **99 mg**

BREAKFAST	SNACK 1	LUNCH	SNACK 2
½ cup oatmeal with 1 apple, chopped, ½ banana, ½ tsp cinnamon; 1 cup low-fat milk	1 cup chopped pineapple, 1 handful unsalted almonds	Veggie Burger (1 veggie patty with 1 oz goat cheese, 1 slice tomato, 1 slice red onion and 1 Boston lettuce leaf on a whole-wheat roll); 2 plums	¾ cup 1% cottage cheese with ½ cup raspberries

T | TOTAL NUTRIENTS Calories: **1798**, Fat: **61 g**, Sat. Fat: **14 g**, Carbs: **243 g**, Fiber: **35 g**, Sugars: **84 g**, Protein: **88 g**, Sodium: **1518 mg**, Cholesterol: **113 mg**

BREAKFAST	SNACK 1	LUNCH	SNACK 2
Peanut Butter Breakfast Wrap (2 Tbsp peanut butter, 1 tsp honey, ¼ tsp cinnamon, ½ banana, sliced, on 1 whole-wheat tortilla); 1 cup low-fat milk	1 cup pineapple with ¼ cup low-fat feta cheese	Asian Tofu Stir-Fry (¾ cup sliced carrots, 1½ cups shredded cabbage, 4 oz light tofu, 2 Tbsp sliced green onion, ½ tsp each chopped garlic and ginger in 1 tsp sesame seed oil; toss with 2 tsp low-sodium soy sauce, 5 shredded Thai basil leaves and ½ tsp crushed red pepper flakes; serve over 1½ cups cooked soba noodles)	1 apple, 1 Tbsp natural peanut butter, 4 multigrain flaxseed crackers

W | TOTAL NUTRIENTS Calories: **1597**, Fat: **63 g**, Sat. Fat: **16 g**, Carbs: **158 g**, Fiber: **31 g**, Sugars: **55 g**, Protein: **118 g**, Sodium: **1625 mg**, Cholesterol: **167 mg**

BREAKFAST	SNACK 1	LUNCH	SNACK 2
1 cup Peach Coconut Smoothie (Blend 1 cup sliced peaches, 1 oz vanilla protein powder, ½ cup light coconut milk, ½ cup low-fat milk and 4 ice cubes – freeze leftovers as pops); ½ cup oatmeal, 3 egg whites	¼ cup hummus on 8 multigrain flaxseed crackers; ½ cup grapes	Spinach Salad (3 cups spinach, ¼ cup chopped mango, ¼ cup sliced onion, 3 oz chopped roasted chicken, 1 tsp extra-virgin olive oil, 1 tsp orange juice, 2 tsp fresh lime juice)	1 Peach Coconut Smoothie Pop (leftovers from breakfast); ½ cup strawberries, 2 Tbsp natural almond butter

T | TOTAL NUTRIENTS Calories: **1710**, Fat: **45 g**, Sat. Fat: **13 g**, Carbs: **214 g**, Fiber: **26 g**, Sugars: **85 g**, Protein: **101 g**, Sodium: **1041 mg**, Cholesterol: **133 mg**

BREAKFAST	SNACK 1	LUNCH	SNACK 2
1 banana with 1½ Tbsp natural almond butter; 4 hardboiled egg whites	Make Ahead Watermelon Freeze (Purée 2 cups watermelon chunks with ½ tsp fresh lime juice; freeze in a small cup with stick to make freeze pop); 1 cup low-fat milk	2 cups torn Boston lettuce, 3 oz tuna, ¼ cup each chopped carrots, celery, cucumber, scallions and basil with 2 Tbsp red wine vinegar and 1 tsp extra-virgin olive oil; ½ cup brown basmati rice	1 cup blackberries, 2 oz goat cheese, 4 multigrain flaxseed crackers

F | TOTAL NUTRIENTS Calories: **1527**, Fat: **60 g**, Sat. Fat: **15 g**, Carbs: **163 g**, Fiber: **44 g**, Sugars: **63 g**, Protein: **88 g**, Sodium: **1438 mg**, Cholesterol: **364 mg**

BREAKFAST	SNACK 1	LUNCH	SNACK 2
1 hardboiled egg; 1 apple, 1 slice whole-grain bread, 2 Tbsp natural almond butter	1 pear, 1 oz goat cheese	3 oz grilled chicken, ½ cup spinach, ¼ cup each green and red bell pepper with 1 Tbsp red wine vinegar and ½ tsp fresh ground black pepper on 1 whole-wheat tortilla; 1 cup low-fat milk	2 Tbsp hummus, 10 carrot sticks, 4 multigrain flaxseed crackers

S | TOTAL NUTRIENTS Calories: **1844**, Fat: **68 g**, Sat. Fat: **18 g**, Carbs: **185 g**, Fiber: **30 g**, Sugars: **91 g**, Protein: **89 g**, Sodium: **1336 mg**, Cholesterol: **340 mg**

BREAKFAST	SNACK 1	LUNCH	SNACK 2
1 cup quinoa (make 1½ cups; save ½ cup for tomorrow's dinner) with 1 sliced banana; 1 cup low-fat milk	8 multigrain flaxseed crackers, 2 Tbsp natural almond butter, 1 apple	3 oz shredded or pulled lean pork, ¼ cup onions and ¼ cup green pepper with 1 Tbsp low-sugar barbeque sauce on 1 whole-wheat sandwich roll; ½ cup strawberries	2 oz goat cheese, ½ cup blackberries

S | TOTAL NUTRIENTS Calories: **1890**, Fat: **65 g**, Sat. Fat: **8 g**, Carbs: **239 g**, Fiber: **48 g**, Sugars: **70 g**, Protein: **101 g**, Sodium: **956 mg**, Cholesterol: **85 mg**

BREAKFAST	SNACK 1	LUNCH	SNACK 2
½ cup oatmeal, 1 chopped apple, ½ tsp cinnamon and ¼ cup low-fat milk; 3 egg whites	2 Tbsp natural almond butter, 1 whole-wheat English muffin	½ cup edamame, ¾ cup wild rice; ½ cup blueberries with ¾ cup low-fat plain yogurt	1 sliced banana with 1 Tbsp natural peanut butter wrapped in 1 whole-wheat tortilla; 1 handful unsalted almonds

DINNER

1 cup whole-wheat spaghetti with ½ cup low-sodium tomato sauce, ¼ cup fresh torn basil leaves, ½ cup cherry tomatoes, halved, and 1 oz shredded part-skim mozzarella; 3 oz grilled chicken breast cut into strips

DINNER

4 oz diced broiled chicken breast mixed with 1 cup wild rice blend, ½ cup sliced red or green grapes and 2 Tbsp chopped walnuts; 5 steamed asparagus spears (steam 10 and freeze 5 for later this week); ½ cup mango

DINNER

2 cups spring mix greens, 4 oz tuna, ¼ cup each cooked chickpeas, shredded carrots and chopped tomato and 5 cucumber slices with 2 Tbsp balsamic vinegar and 1 tsp extra-virgin olive oil; ½ cup blackberries

DINNER

4 oz grilled chicken breast, ½ sweet potato, 5 asparagus spears (leftover from Tuesday); 1 cup pineapple with ½ cup low-fat plain yogurt

DINNER

Turkey and Chickpea Salad (4 oz 7% lean cooked ground turkey crumbled in 2 cups romaine lettuce, ½ cup chopped tomatoes, ¾ cup chickpeas, 2 Tbsp low-fat jalapeno cheese, 2 Tbsp red wine vinegar and 1 tsp extra-virgin olive oil)

DINNER

Spinach Salad (2 cups spinach, 3 oz tuna, 1 chopped hard-boiled egg, ½ cup mandarin oranges and 1 oz chopped walnuts with 1 Tbsp balsamic vinegar and 1 tsp Dijon mustard); ¾ cup low-fat plain yogurt with 1 tsp honey

DINNER

3 oz grilled lean pork chop; 1 cup torn romaine lettuce and ½ cup chopped cucumbers with 1 Tbsp balsamic vinegar and ½ tsp extra-virgin olive oil; 1 cup cooked black beans; ½ cup cooked quinoa (leftover from Saturday)

SHOPPING LIST

Proteins & Dairy
- ○ 1 (15-oz) can black beans
- ○ 1 (8-oz) container 1% cottage cheese
- ○ 2 oz low-fat feta cheese
- ○ 1 oz low-fat jalapeno cheese
- ○ 2 oz shredded part-skim mozzarella cheese
- ○ 2 lbs boneless, skinless chicken breast
- ○ 1 (15-oz) can chickpeas
- ○ 1 pkg frozen edamame
- ○ 1 dozen eggs
- ○ 2 L low-fat milk
- ○ 7 oz lean pork
- ○ 1 small container vanilla protein powder
- ○ 1 pkg quinoa
- ○ 4 oz light tofu
- ○ 1 (6-oz) can white tuna
- ○ 4 oz 7% lean ground turkey
- ○ 1 (16-oz) container low-fat plain yogurt

Veggies/Fruits
- ○ 5 apples
- ○ 10 spears asparagus
- ○ 1 bunch bananas
- ○ 1 pint blackberries
- ○ 1 small container blueberries
- ○ 1 head cabbage
- ○ 1 bag carrots
- ○ 1 small bunch celery
- ○ 2 English cucumbers
- ○ 1 small bunch grapes
- ○ 1 head Boston lettuce
- ○ 1 head romaine lettuce
- ○ 1 mango
- ○ 1 red onion
- ○ 1 bunch green onions
- ○ 1 small can mandarin oranges (packed in water)
- ○ 1 peach
- ○ 1 pear
- ○ 1 green bell pepper
- ○ 1 red bell pepper
- ○ 1 pineapple
- ○ 2 plums
- ○ 1 (8-oz) container raspberries
- ○ 1 bunch scallions
- ○ 6 cups spinach
- ○ 1 pkg spring mix greens
- ○ 1 pint strawberries
- ○ 1 medium sweet potato
- ○ 1 red ripe tomato
- ○ 1 small container grape tomatoes
- ○ 1 watermelon half

Whole Grains
- ○ 1 small loaf whole-grain bread
- ○ 1 box multigrain flaxseed crackers
- ○ 1 pkg whole-wheat English muffins
- ○ 1 pkg soba noodles
- ○ 1 container 5-minute oats
- ○ 1 pkg wild rice
- ○ 2 whole-wheat rolls
- ○ 12 oz whole-wheat spaghetti
- ○ 1 pkg whole-wheat tortillas

Nuts/Seeds/Oils
- ○ 1 small can unsalted almonds
- ○ 1 jar natural almond butter
- ○ 1 jar natural peanut butter
- ○ 1 bottle extra-virgin olive oil
- ○ 1 small bottle sesame seed oil
- ○ 1 small can walnuts

Extras
- ○ 1 container cinnamon
- ○ 1 small bottle low-sugar barbeque sauce
- ○ 1 bunch fresh basil
- ○ 1 bunch fresh Thai basil
- ○ 1 small container light coconut milk
- ○ 1 clove garlic
- ○ 1 fresh ginger root
- ○ 1 small bottle honey
- ○ 1 container hummus
- ○ 1 small bottle fresh lime juice
- ○ 1 small container orange juice
- ○ 1 container fresh ground black pepper
- ○ 1 container red pepper flakes
- ○ 1 bottle low-sodium soy sauce
- ○ 1 (8-oz) can low-sodium tomato sauce
- ○ 1 pkg frozen veggie patties
- ○ 1 bottle balsamic vinegar
- ○ 1 bottle red wine vinegar

Cooking Terms

Al Dente
Cooked until firm but not crunchy. Usually used in reference to vegetables and pasta.

Bake
To cook in a dry heat chamber – usually an oven without direct exposure to the heat source.

Bain-marie
A container filled with hot water in which another container holding food is placed, to cook that food gently.

Baste
To pour liquid over food (normally meat) while it cooks, helping to retain moisture.

Beat
To stir vigorously with a spoon, fork or beater to incorporate air into the food, giving it a light texture.

Blanch
To place a food in boiling water briefly. This is often done to help remove skin (tomatoes or almonds for example), or to prepare vegetables for freezing.

Bouillon
A clear broth made from boiling meat and vegetables with seasonings and then straining.

Braise
To brown meat on all sides and then add a small amount of liquid and cook, covered. This method is used to tenderize tough meats.

Brown
To use dry heat to caramelize the outside of a food, normally a piece of meat. This gives a nice flavor and an appetizing color.

Broth
A thin soup generally made with stock, with meat and/or vegetables added. This word is sometimes incorrectly used instead of the word "stock."

Butterfly
To increase surface area and speed cooking, a thicker food item is split almost in two and folded out.

Caramelize
To use a high heat to cause a reaction between amino acids and natural sugars present in food, creating a rich taste and appearance.

Cheesecloth
Loosely woven cotton cloth that allows liquids but not solids to pass through.

Chop
Method of cutting a food item quickly into fairly small, uneven pieces.

Curry
A dish or, as curry powder, a spice mixture. As a dish, this is a stewed mixture of meat, lentils or vegetables along with spices. As a spice mixture, it commonly contains the following ingredients: turmeric, ground coriander, ground cumin, chile pepper and fenugreek.

Deglaze
To add a small amount of liquid to a pan in which a food item has been cooked in order to loosen the caramelized food from the bottom of the pan and make a sauce.

Degrease
To remove the fat that congeals at the top of a sauce or other liquid.

Dice
To chop into even cubes approximating the size of a single dice but often smaller.

Fish sauce
A condiment and cooking ingredient made from fermented fish, very common in Eastern Asian countries.

Fold
A gentle method of mixing a light substance in with a heavier substance that allows for the light texture to remain. To do this, you first place the lighter substance on top and then use a spatula to scrape down the side to the bottom and gently bring that section to the top in a folding motion, continuing this around the bowl.

Julienne
Cutting method that produces thin slices a couple of inches long.

Jus
The liquid released when cooking meats.

Marinate
To soak food in a liquid normally containing both seasoning and an acid that acts to tenderize the food. The acid is commonly vinegar, wine or yogurt.

Mince
To chop very finely.

Mousse
What is produced when whipping a great deal of air into a batter or other thick liquid.

Parboil
To cook partially in boiling water. Normally used as a timesaving action or to keep foods in a firm state but partially cooked for use in another recipe.

Parchment paper
A nonstick paper used for baking. Similar to wax paper but with a higher temperature tolerance.

Pare
To peel very thinly.

Poach
To cook a food item by submerging it in a simmering liquid.

Purée
To mash or mix a food until it becomes a smooth pulp. Normally achieved with a blender or food processor.

Reduce
To thicken a liquid by cooking until enough water evaporates that desired thickness is achieved.

Reduction
The thickened substance that results from reducing a liquid.

Roast
As with baking, to roast is to cook in a dry heat chamber such as an oven. Normally the term "bake" is used when the food fills the cooking container and the term "roast" is used when air circulates around the food within the container.

Roulade
A food item rolled around a stuffing. Eg. Christmas "log."

Roux
Oil or melted fat mixed with flour or cornstarch and heated; used as a starter and thickener for sauces.

Sauté
To cook quickly with a small amount of fat in a very hot pan.

Sear
Use a very high heat to brown meat quickly, resulting in caramelization, a pleasing color and texture.

Steam
To cook food via direct contact with steam but not the boiling liquid that produces that steam. This results in a moist food with nutrients fairly intact.

Stew
To first brown food (normally meat) and then cook in plenty of liquid over a long time. This cooking method normally produces a thick sauce, which is eaten as part of the stew.

Stir-fry
This is similar to sautéing, but the cooking surface area is usually larger and the stirring is more constant. Food is cut into small pieces with a relatively large surface area and cooked on very high heat with little fat, stirring to prevent sticking.

Stock
The resultant liquid after simmering food in water for long periods of time and then straining. Normally stock is made by simmering bones along with some herbs, spices and vegetables.

Sweat
Cooking food in a small amount of fat or oil over low heat, covered, until the food softens. Normally used to cook vegetables.

Whip
To beat in an exceptionally vigorous manner that directs plenty of air into the food, making it very light and fluffy.

Cooking Tools: Useful Pots and Pans

Saucepan

Likely what you think of as a "pot," the saucepan has a chamber for placing food, one handle and normally a tight-fitting lid.

Frying Pan/Skillet

This shallow pan is generally for quicker cooking. It has a larger flat surface that allows more food to touch the surface at once. This pan will have one long handle and may have a lid.

Omelet Pan

A specialized smaller frying pan with a more rounded bottom, allowing the cook to easily access the bottom with a spatula.

Sauté Pan

A larger pan with a large flat surface and higher sides, a sauté pan allows for cooking larger quantities of food as well as cooking food with more ingredients and liquid.

Casserole Dish

A casserole dish holds enough food for an entire meal, has a smaller handle at each side and is ovenproof.

Roasting Pan

Larger pan made to hold large pieces of meat or whole birds such as a turkey. The sides are fairly high, to give room for adding more items to the pan and making gravy.

Broiling Pan

A medium-depth pan used for broiling meats. Broiling is similar to grilling, but the heat comes from above in the oven rather than below on a grill. The pan has an insert with slots in it where the fat drips through when cooking.

Stockpot

A large pot made for cooking stock, so it has plenty of room for bones and water. This pot is also useful for making soup or large quantities of pasta, stew or chili.

Dutch Oven

A large, heavy, lidded pot with two handles. Similar to a casserole dish, but is used on a burner instead of in the oven. Great for cooking one-pot meals.

Griddle

Similar to a frying pan but completely flat with no sides. These are great for cooking food that is flipped, such as pancakes, tortillas and eggs.

Saucier

Specifically designed for making sauce, this pan is like a rounded frying pan with higher sides. The roundness of the bottom makes it easy to stir properly and the higher sides reduce spillage and allow for more volume.

Wok

A large metal bowl used over high heat. Because of its unique shape, a wok has an exceptionally large surface area, which works well for stir-frying.

Double Boiler

A double pot, wherein the bottom pot holds water to be heated and the top pot, which fits inside, holds the food being cooked. This is a gentle method of heating food, and is useful when a food item is easily burnt or scalded.

Pressure Cooker

A pressure cooker is a pot that seals shut, increasing both the pressure and temperature inside. This means foods cook much faster, using less energy and retaining more nutrients. Because it's hotter, this method is also superior for killing any microbes in the food.

Springform Pan

Two-piece baking pan made up of a flat, round base and a side piece with a latching mechanism. Once the item within is cooked and cooled, the latch is opened. This allows for removal of the food item without disturbing the sides, especially when the food item cannot be dumped out of the pan without destroying it. Cheesecake is usually made in this pan.

Cooking Tools:
A Trio of Knives

You could have blocks filled with different knives, but you really need only three. Spend your money on quality versions of these knives before purchasing others.

Your knives should be made from one piece of metal, and that metal should extend right to the end of the handle. Most chefs prefer forged steel to stamped steel, and carbon steel as opposed to stainless steel. The knife should feel balanced in your hand and should have a bit of weight but not be too heavy.

Paring knife – 3½-5 inch

Serrated knife – 8-10 inch

Chef's knife – 8-10 inch

Conversion Table

Liquid or Volume Measure (approximate)

1 teaspoon		⅓ tablespoon	5 ml
1 tablespoon	½ fluid ounce	3 teaspoons	15 ml, 15cc
2 tablespoons	1 fluid ounce	⅛ cup, 6 teaspoons	30 ml, 30cc
¼ cup	2 fluid ounces	4 tablespoons	60 ml
⅓ cup	2⅔ fluid ounces	5 tablespoons & 1 teaspoon	80 ml
½ cup	4 fluid ounces	8 tablespoons	120 ml
⅔ cup	5⅓ fluid ounces	10 tablespoons & 2 teaspoons	160 ml
¾ cup	6 fluid ounces	12 tablespoons	177 ml
⅞ cup	7 fluid ounces	14 tablespoons	207 ml
1 cup	8 fluid ounces/½ pint	16 tablespoons	240 ml
2 cups	16 fluid ounces/1 pint	32 tablespoons	480 ml
4 cups	32 fluid ounces	1 quart	950 ml
1 pint	16 fluid ounces	32 tablespoons	480 ml
2 pints	32 fluid ounces	1 quart	946 ml, 0.946 liters
8 pints	1 gallon/128 fluid ounces	4 quarts	3785 ml, 3.78 liters
4 quarts	1 gallon/128 fluid ounces	1 gallon	3785 ml, 3.78 liters
1 liter	1.057 quarts		1000 ml
128 fluid ounces	1 gallon	4 quarts	3785 ml, 3.78 liters

Dry or Weight Measurement (approximate)

1 ounce		30 grams
2 ounces		55 grams
3 ounces		85 grams
4 ounces	¼ pound	125 grams
8 ounces	½ pound	240 grams
12 ounces	¾ pound	375 grams
16 ounces	1 pound	454 grams
32 ounces	2 pounds	907 grams
1 kilogram	2.2 pounds/35.2 ounces	1000 grams

Credits

Contributors:

Tony Abou-Ganim, Ryan Andrews, Robin Asbell, Heather Bainbridge RD, John Berardi, Jeannette Bessinger, Jonny Bowden PHD CNS, Paula Bowman, Paula Brown, Kierstin Buchner, Diana Burrell, Chris Cander, Claudia M. Caruna, Lisa Cherkasky, Teresa Cochran, Sandy Cordeiro, Jennifer Danter, Tara Mataraza Desmond, Christine Gable, Aliza Green, Peggy Hall, Julie O'Hara, Tiffany Haugen, Ricki Heller PHD RHN, Jill Silverman Hough, Lisa Howard, Jeanette Hurt, Matthew Kadey MSC RD, Nancy Kennedy, Stacy Kennedy, Alison Lewis, Joanne Lusted, Linda Melone, Robin Miller, Adia Mollenkamp, Minh Nguyen, Tosca Reno, Amy Rosen, Bonnie Siegler, Kate Trainor, Diane Welland MS RD, Marianne Wren, Allison Young

All new recipes created by Kierstin Buchner

Photographers:

Bradshaw, Douglas: 92, 186-187, 240-241, 243-244, 247

Buceta, Paul: 8 (Alicia Rewega)

Chou, Peter: 36, 72, 105, 226

Duivenvoorden, Yvonne: 13-14, 17, 30, 33, 39, 55, 64-65, 78, 82, 85, 101, 103, 106, 120, 142-143, 145-146, 149, 153, 166-167, 169-170, 176, 184, 188-189, 191-192, 195-196, 199-200, 203, 205, 209, 219-220, 229, 233

Fotolia: 163 (oats)

Griffith, Donna: 8 (Sautéed Halibut, Easy Egg Custard with Peaches), 25, 43-44, 47, 56, 59-60, 67-68, 70, 74, 80, 86, 89, 111-112, 116-117, 127, 132, 135-136, 157-158, 161, 213-214, 230, 234

iStock: 2, 28, 62-63, 77, 90, 115, 138-141, 162-163, 165, 207-208, 236-239, 250-251, 261-264, 266

James, Greg: 272

Manovlich, Michael: 18, 223-224

Pond, Edward: 8 (Cajun Catfish Po'boy) 10-11, 22, 29, 34, 40, 48, 51-52, 76, 91, 95-98, 100, 104, 108-109, 119, 123-124, 131, 150, 154, 172-173, 175, 179-180, 183, 215, 222, 249

Pudge, Jodi: 21, 26, 37, 71, 73, 81, 128, 210-211

Trauttmansdorff, Andreas: 216

Tsakos, Joanne: 27, 31, 41, 137, 155, 206

Cover Photography by Andreas Trauttmansdorff

Back Cover Photography: Douglas Bradshaw (Ultimate Turkey Burgers), Peter Chou (Carrot Cake with Cream Cheese Honey Drizzle, Grilled Stone Fruit with Pears & Balsamic Pan Sauce), Donna Griffith (Light & Healthy Pork-with "Fried Rice", Salmon Melts, Whole-Wheat Oricchiette, Chicken Almondine), Edward Pond (One-Skillet Lamb Chops)

Food Stylists:

Lasha Andrushko, Ashley Denton, Ruth Gangbar, Adele Hagan, Nancy Midwicki, Chantal Pyaette, Lucie Richard, Claire Stubbs, Sugar Tart, Marianne Wren, Nicole Young, Julie Zambonelli

Prop Stylists:

Martine Blackhurst, Laura Branson, Catherine Doherty, Lynda Felton, Ryan Jennings, Madeleine Johari, Jay Junnila, Andrea McCrindle, Carolyn Souch, Janet Walkinshaw, Genevieve Wiseman

Models:

Rachel Corradetti, Erin Fuentes, Jamie Goden, Brandon Hughes, Kyla Hughes, Sharon Hughes, Sherry Hughes, Jennifer MacKenzie, Neil Smith, Samantha Israel

Hair & Make-up:

Laima Krasaukas, Valeria Nova

Index

THE BEST OF CLEAN EATING

We hope you enjoyed the meals in this book as much as we enjoyed compiling them for you.

From the *Clean Eating* family to yours,

Bon Appétit!

For more healthy and delicious recipes for you and your family visit **cleaneatingmag.com**